With a Little Help from my Friends

Planning Corruption in Ireland

Paul Cullen

Gill & Macmillan

Gill & Macmillan Ltd
Hume Avenue, Park West, Dublin 12
with associated companies throughout the world
www.gillmacmillan.ie
© Paul Cullen 2002
0 7171 3431 8
Index compiled by Helen Litton
Design and print origination by Carole Lynch
Printed by The Guernsey Press, Guernsey

This book is typeset in Goudy 10.5 on 13.5pt.

*The paper used in this book comes from the wood pulp of
managed forests. For every tree felled, at least one tree
is planted, thereby renewing natural resources.*

A CIP catalogue record for this book is available
from the British Library.

3 5 4 2

All photographs have been supplied by *The Irish Times*,
unless where otherwise specified.

Contents

'A certain class of dishonesty, dishonesty magnificent in its proportions, and climbing into high places, has become at the same time so rampant and so splendid that men and women will be taught to feel that dishonesty, if it become splendid, will cease to be abominable.'

— Anthony Trollope[1]

Preface

This is a book about greed. It tells the story of men who abused their positions of privilege and responsibility in the scramble for wealth. Who betrayed the founding principles of their parties and of the State. Who perverted the systems of local administration and planning for their own benefit, and for the benefit of their friends. And who conspired with others to keep the rest of us in a state of blissful ignorance.

It is also a book about denial. And denials — by the limousine-load. People who saw no wrong in their wrongful actions. People who knew what they were doing was wrong, but couldn't find the words to admit it. People who hid behind lawyers and accountants and spin-doctors and bad memories rather than tell the truth.

Finally, this book is about the struggle for the truth. This has taken many forms over the years. Journalists, politicians, lawyers and residents' groups have at different times taken the lead. They have all had to struggle against denial, incredulity, lack of cooperation, blatant lies and even sinister threats. This book is dedicated to all those who struggled to trace the origins of corruption's stink.

Like a good movie, the story-line is complex, and filled with heroes and villains, major characters and bit-players. Yet the same characters and locations keep cropping up, the same golden circle of people in positions of influence.

The prising open of this can of worms is a story I've been privileged to cover daily in *The Irish Times*. The Flood tribunal and other inquiries have confirmed many of the worst suspicions about our society. They have provided unexpected entertainment, as well as serving as an important public forum for dispensing justice. There have been bizarre and unexpected turns — the arrest of George Redmond, the evidence of Frank Dunlop, the fire at Liam Lawlor's house. But the tribunals have also cost huge amounts of money and have taken a long time, so long that many of the people under investigation have bowed out of positions of power.

Charles Haughey casts a long shadow over many of the matters covered, but he is not a central figure in this narrative. His deeds and misdeeds are adequately described elsewhere. Haughey's contribution was to foster a culture of 'low standards in high places' which was perfected by those who followed in his wake.

There is no happy ending to the story recounted in these pages, and no simplistic victory of good over evil. The Flood tribunal still has a long way to go. Corruption — an invisible crime — is notoriously difficult to prove. It is undoubtedly a feature of present-day business and political life. Arguably, the tribunal's focus on earlier events has deflected attention from current cases. Certainly, the sums of money at stake today are larger than ever.

Some would say, in response to the controversies of recent years, that 'they're all the same'. This kind of cynicism is understandable, given the number of scandals we've had. But 'they' are emphatically not 'all the same'. Everyone has a choice. Some people have blown the whistle on the events they witnessed; others have helped to cover them up. For every councillor who allowed his vote to be influenced by a brown envelope, there is another councillor who spurned all crooked approaches. For every politician who bunged money in an offshore account, there is another politician who has fought unstintingly for ethical standards in public life.

I have covered the Flood tribunal since 1997 for *The Irish Times*. I would like to thank my editors, the library and Paul Hayden of the picture desk for their help in putting together this book. Thanks are also due to my colleagues in other media who have 'done time' in Dublin Castle. A special appreciation is due to those who rang me over the years with nuggets of information — you know who you are. Thanks too to Noel and Jacinta for their suggestions. This book would not have come about without the encouragement of my editor at Gill & Macmillan, Fergal Tobin, and his staff. My mother Mary imparted to me a sense of right and wrong, which underpins this book.

Finally, I dedicate this book to Deirdre who was a constant source of encouragement and support throughout the year it took shape.

Paul Cullen
April, 2002

Introduction

'Property has its duties as well as its rights.'
— Thomas Drummond, Under-Secretary for Ireland during the
1830s. The words appear on the plinth of a statue of Drummond in
the elegant Rotunda of Dublin's City Hall — barely a stone's throw
from the offices of the Flood and Moriarty tribunals.

The small man with the smart glasses and the double-breasted
suit and the honeyed words was in a spot of bother. 'Could
I ... Mr Hanratty, begging your indulgence, could I leave the
stand?' he whispered to the lawyer from the witness box at the Flood
tribunal.

Frank Dunlop had just imploded. The man who once boasted he
had 'balls of iron and a spine of steel' was now a shivering wreck. The
man who had always projected an aura of supreme confidence and
invulnerability was escorted to a waiting Mercedes in evident physical discomfort. A man who had only ever known success in his career
had just blown away everything he had worked so hard to acquire.

The public gallery and the rows of media could only hold their
breath, knowing that what they were witnessing was a tragedy for
one man but a triumph for the rest of society. It was shortly before
3 p.m. on 19 April 2000 — Spy Wednesday — and Dunlop had just
revealed the biggest bribery plot in the history of the State.

Who could have thought that Dunlop, the king of the spin-
doctors, the 'Deep Throat' behind so many media headlines, would be
the man to break under questioning at the tribunal? Other, weaker
mortals had come to Dublin Castle, delivered their prepared lines or
lies, and escaped unscathed.

Dunlop, the former government press secretary turned lobbyist
for developers, came to the tribunal that month with the same game-
plan. Sure, he told tribunal lawyer Pat Hanratty at first: I got money
from developers, but it was all just 'personal income'. 'If you are
suggesting to me that any monies out of my account were used for

illicit or improper purposes, the answer is an emphatic no,' Dunlop exclaimed early on in his testimony.

But, over three days, the lies and contradictions started to mount. The sums didn't add up. Dunlop came up with a revised version of the monies he spent. He was caught out again. The tribunal turned up a hitherto secret account. Gently, but with undeniable menace, the tribunal chairman Mr Justice Flood advised the witness to 'reflect' on his evidence.

The former Fianna Fáil press secretary reflected, and announced the next day that, yes, a councillor had sought money in return for his vote on a rezoning motion. He wrote the name of the councillor on a blank piece of paper. It was a politician. A dead politician. A dead Fine Gael politician.

The chairman asked Dunlop to try harder. The threat of imprisonment was dangled in front of the witness.

On the third day, the former seminarian was a changed man. Sure, he parried for a while. Like so many before him, he used the mantra of 'political donations' to explain the payments he made to politicians. But his heart wasn't in it, and soon all the sordid details started tumbling out. Name by name, he listed fifteen Dublin county councillors to whom he had paid a total of over £100,000. The final list included 'Mr Big', who got £40,000 stuffed into a plastic bag, 'Mr Insatiable', who got £2,000 and kept coming back for more, and many others.

Each fresh detail was a nail in the coffin of Dunlop's career. More importantly, his evidence was confirmation of the worst rumours about corruption in Irish planning. After years of investigation by the media, the gardaí and the tribunal, someone on the inside had finally come clean. Dunlop was One of Them and here he was, breaking the code of *omerta* that had kept the system of corruption hidden for a quarter of a century. Nothing would ever be the same again.

⋖≳⋗⋖≲⋗

For most of its history, the State has turned a blind eye to corruption. In the early decades of a newly-independent and determinedly Catholic country, it was regarded as something akin to illicit sex and hot summers — only to be found elsewhere. From the British we inherited high standards in much of our political, administrative and judicial systems. From the founding fathers of the State came a fiery idealism, allied to a seemingly puritanical pursuit of ascetic living and balanced budgets. Both Fine Gael and Fianna Fáil espoused patriotism and the common good over personal gain when they came to power in the 1920s and 1930s.

It helped that the country was so poor, and the opportunities for graft correspondingly limited. The Catholic Church, too, played its part in the promotion of a 'we're all in this together' national ethic.

Yet the seeds of corruption were there. There was no rezoning of land in those days, of course, but local government was always a problem area. Appointments to the local government service were in the gift of county councillors, some of whom learned to love a bribe. The county councils soon became a 'by-word for corruption' in their appointments, as historian Professor Joe Lee has written.[1] According to former taoiseach Garret FitzGerald, £1,000 — equivalent to £35,000 today — could secure a dispensary doctor post.[2]

Widespread jobbery forced Cumann na nGaedheal to set up the Local Appointments Commission in the mid-1920s. 'The idea that assessors boards might evaluate candidates on their professional merits, rather than on their foresight in being born with the right connections, or at least in cultivating the right connections, imposed intolerable strains on many an imagination,' Lee remarks.[3]

But the problem persisted. There were repeated allegations of corruption involving local authorities in the 1930s and the 1940s. Some councillors took bribes in return for their votes in Senate elections. A former chairman of Dublin county council, John A. Corr, was charged with bribery after the 1944 election. Corr was sentenced to three months' imprisonment for what the District Justice called 'an unusually serious offence which in my opinion has been aggravated by perjury'.[4] Éamon de Valera conceded to the *Irish Independent* in 1945 that 'some senators have been elected through corrupt practices, through bribery'.[5]

Corruption wasn't confined to local government. There was the scandal of the Irish Hospitals Sweepstake, for example, which raised money for the Irish health services by selling lottery tickets abroad. In the 1940s, selling tickets for foreign lotteries was illegal, so from the start the business involved subterfuge, backhanders and bribes on a massive scale. Back in Ireland, large fees, salaries and expenses were deducted from the proceeds that made it back from North America. The owners of the Sweep, including a former government minister, amassed a fortune estimated at £100 million from the venture.

Corruption continued to be a major issue in post-War politics, with a new party, Clann na Poblachta, claiming to represent a 'new political morality'. The first judicial tribunals set up to investigate the issue also date from this period. One was established to investigate allegations about a Fianna Fáil parliamentary secretary, Dr Francis Conor Ward. Despite being cleared of most of the allegations, Ward resigned after the tribunal found that he had not paid tax on payments he received from a bacon factory he owned.

The Locke's Distillery scandal of 1947 also led to a tribunal of inquiry. Allegations of corruption were levelled at de Valera and other Fianna Fáil ministers in connection with the proposed sale of the distillery in Kilbeggan. The foreign buyers were exposed as charlatans, but only after they had been invited for tea with the President, Seán T. O'Kelly. The tribunal report, published after forty-one days of evidence in 1947, dismissed the allegations but was regarded by some as the first tribunal whitewash.

It is hard now to credit the widespread belief in patronage that existed for much of the State's history. There was no embarrassment about supporting a policy of 'jobs for the boys'. Fine Gael TD Oliver Flanagan summed up a common view in 1965 by describing himself as 'a great believer in putting a friend into a good job'. His ambition was to fill 'every post I can, subject to qualifications and ability, with my own friends and political supporters'.[6] For those without connections, there was always the emigrant boat. Even today, senior appointments in many areas — the judicial and legal systems, the gardaí, State boards and so on — are heavily influenced by party political considerations.

Things changed utterly towards the end of the 1950s as Ireland embarked on its first major period of industrial expansion. There were houses and factories to build, and new government posts to fill. Local government had been run down because of the suspicion of corruption, so central government had immense powers. The influence of those with their hands on the levers of power was enormous.

Into this promising new era stepped a new breed of ambitious politicians and businessmen. The 'men in the mohair suits' wanted the best for the country, and the best for themselves. Counting Charles Haughey as their most prominent member, these young Turks cut a swathe through Irish public life. They were brash and arrogant, impatient with regulations and the requirements of petty laws. During the 1960s boom, unhealthily close links were forged between Fianna Fáil and the business community. The Taca fundraising machine created the first modern 'golden circles', as businessmen queued up to rub shoulders with the elite for £100 a plate, equivalent to a month's wages in those days. George Colley talked pointedly about 'low standards' in 'high places' in the party.

Meanwhile, the 1963 Planning Act created a new area of decision-making involving potentially vast sums of money. The simple act of designating a piece of land for housing instead of agriculture could greatly increase its value. It didn't matter that there were no roads or sewers to the land, or that there was plenty of building land else-where. The designation of land would be decided at periodic reviews but, crucially, county councillors were given the power to override the decisions taken by their officials.

Many of those involved in redeveloping Dublin during this period believed they were killing two birds with one stone. Not only were they profitably replacing old buildings with high-income office blocks, but by demolishing rows of once-elegant Georgian houses, they were erasing hated vestiges of British rule from the Irish landscape. Remarkably, they seldom had difficulty in finding State tenants to rent out space in their concrete monoliths, however ugly they were.

Dublin's city centre was the first battleground of this struggle between the old and the new, between conservation and redevelop-ment. But there were skirmishes elsewhere, too. Dublin was growing fast — its population was relatively stable, but the amount of land the city occupied expanded each year. Developers led the way to the suburbs and the citizens, many of them in search of the rural idylls they had left behind to find jobs in the city, followed.

Town planning was weak or non-existent. The senior official in the county, we were to learn only many years later, was on the make. Services and infrastructure — sewerage, roads, shops and churches — simply weren't in place. But this juggernaut was unstoppable —

the profits to be made from development were too great. Historic houses were burned, farmers driven off their land and councillors bribed in the great rush to turn the muck of country fields into lucrative bricks and mortar.

❖

This is the background to the events described in these pages, and investigated by the Flood tribunal since 1997. Planning has been the focus of controversy for the past thirty years, with good reason. This book traces the stories of some of the main characters involved in this controversy. Chapter 1 deals with the rise of Ray Burke, who features in so many of the matters under investigation by the tribunal. Brennan and McGowan, the builders who created Burke by bank-rolling his career, also appear in this chapter, and in Chapter 3, which tells the strange life and times of their friend, George Redmond. Chapter 2 tells the story of James Gogarty, retired builder and tribunal whistle-blower, and his nemesis, Joseph Murphy senior.

Chapter 4 describes the lengthy battle to discover the truth behind the lies, obfuscations and failed investigations of earlier years. This finally culminated in the setting up of the Flood tribunal, and its roller-coaster progress is recorded in Chapter 5. Liam Lawlor, that other ubiquitous figure in controversies, is dealt with in Chapter 6, which pays particular attention to the Fianna Fáil deputy's dealings with the likes of James Kennedy, Frank Dunlop, Larry Goodman and others.

When the tribunal discovered a further payment of £35,000 to Ray Burke in the summer of 1989, it had no choice but to investigate further. The result was the Century Radio affair (Chapter 7), a case history in the back-scratching ways of businessmen and their politician friends. Chapter 8 shows how the stories spun by Burke and Brennan and McGowan finally unravelled, as the tribunal went on the money trail and found massive undisclosed payments to the politician. Tom Gilmartin, Frank Dunlop, the controversy surrounding the rezoning of Quarryvale and the resulting fallout are dealt with in Chapters 9 and 10. Finally, Chapter 11 looks at what we've learned, whether the tribunal has been worth it and what needs to be done to avoid the same thing happening again. Estimates of the present-day value (in Punts and Euro) of the principal sums mentioned in the book are supplied in an appendix.

Some might say this story should not be written until the Flood tribunal has finished its work. I don't agree. Firstly, the tribunal has completed its investigations into the matters for which it was originally set up. Nothing more will be learned about the payments by James Gogarty to Ray Burke or George Redmond. The tribunal has also finished its inquiries into Burke's involvement with Century Radio.

Second, the tribunal has many more years to run. Should the matters it is investigating be written about while they are still fresh and have relevance to contemporary political life, or should they be left to some distant day in the future? Some would prefer the latter option, but I disagree. Finally, the work of the tribunal — or some equivalent body — will probably never be done. It is clear that the taint of corruption is a recurring problem in our society. A permanent problem needs a permanent solution, in the form of constant monitoring and investigation.

1

With a Little Help from my Friends

'Burke has one quality which is essential in politics — he can sense danger before it appears over the horizon.'

— P.J. Mara on Ray Burke, 1992

A good rumour goes a long way. In 1974, Ray Burke became the first modern-day politician to be snared in the media's investigations into planning controversies. A quarter of a century later, Burke was fighting for his reputation at a tribunal set up specially to examine payments he received.

In the intervening period, the man known half-jokingly as 'Rambo' enjoyed a soaring career as a poll-topper and government minister without ever managing to douse completely the allegations swirling about him. His eventual resignation in 1997 came as the result of an accumulation of scandals and controversies over the twenty-three preceding years.

In spite of his prominence — or, arguably, because of it — Burke remained an enigmatic character throughout his career. What friendships he had were forged in his early years, and he was close to very few of his political colleagues, even in Fianna Fáil. He could be charming and gregarious in company, his toughness leavened by a dry wit, but there was always a certain distance about him. As one journalist recalls, 'he was very "hail fellow, well met" but he wouldn't get that pally with you'. Perhaps the distancing effect operated from both sides, for few of those who met Burke were unaware of the rumours he carried as baggage for his entire political life.

No-one denied his ability or the energy with which he attacked his various Cabinet briefs. Yet neither could anyone tie down his political beliefs. They veered from one side of the Fianna Fáil leadership struggle to another, from conservatism to liberalism, and from republicanism to soft nationalism, depending on circumstances and the fashions of the day. In the 1970s, for example, he was an ardent supporter of plans to build a nuclear power station in Ireland; in the 1980s, he metamorphosed into a strident campaigner against the Sellafield nuclear plant in Britain.

In summary, Burke was an ambitious, populist politician of some ability. His loyalties lay with himself, his family and his family friends, his supporters and local party organisation, and his constituents, in that order. He created his political machine with the support of the 'Mayo Mafia' inherited from his father and felt little need to confide in circles beyond north Dublin.

Where Burke differed from others of his ilk was in his attitude to business, particularly his own business. He became a councillor and estate agent within months of each other in 1967, at the tender age of 24. Thereafter, until he was promoted to ministerial rank a decade later, he intermeshed his political and business careers with scant concern for possible conflicts of interest. As a senior politician, he collected colossal sums of money, given in cash or paid to offshore accounts, and passed on next to nothing to party headquarters. Right to the end of his political life, he was using the same bank account for his personal and political expenses. As he said himself: 'My life was seamless. I was a politician from the time I got up in the morning until I went to bed at night'.

The persistent allegations about Burke's closeness to developers put him permanently on the defensive. He developed a savage but effective debating style, and was used by the party as a political Rottweiler in media interviews. Physically large, he took to the role of bully with ease. He ruled his bailiwick in Swords with an iron fist, tolerating no dissent and exerting total control over his cowering colleagues on the council.

Burke's power was founded on fear, but once that power was removed his support melted away. On the day he resigned in October 1997, Bertie Ahern told the Dáil 'an honourable man' had been 'hounded' from office. But no tears were shed and Burke and his achievements were quickly forgotten.

⋘∙⋙

Raphael Patrick Dermot Burke (the full name would be of importance later in his life) was born in Swords in September 1943, just six months before his father Paddy was elected to the Dáil for the first time. Between them, father and son would hold the Dublin north seat for Fianna Fáil for fifty-three years.

Ray grew up in the family home attached to Portrane hospital, where Paddy Burke had worked as a nurse. Later, as his father grew more successful, the family moved to Santry, from where Ray took the bus each day to O'Connell's Christian Brothers school in the city centre.

Paddy Burke was undoubtedly the biggest influence on the young Ray. When Ray was elected to the Council, Paddy was there to show him the ropes. When Paddy suffered a stroke on the night of the Dublin bombings, Ray was ready to step into his shoes in Leinster House a short time after. He named his estate agency, P.J. Burke (Sales) Ltd, in his honour, although his father had no involvement in the firm.

'The Bishop' Burke had hailed from Kilmeenagh, near Westport, 'from a humble background in the West of Ireland' — as Ray Burke would tell the Dáil many years later. He played a minor role in the War of Independence before moving to Dublin in the 1920s. A year after the founding of Fianna Fáil in 1926, he set up the party's first cumann in Portrane, north county Dublin. He continued to represent the party in that area for almost fifty years until ill-health forced his retirement in 1973. An assured clientelist politician, he earned his nickname by being a profligate attender of constituents' funerals. Whenever anyone from north Dublin was being buried, 'The Bishop' Burke was sure to turn up to comfort the bereaved and buy drinks for the thirsty. Ray learned politics at his father's feet, attending his first cumann meeting at the age of 11 and pounding the constituency beat in his teenage years.

'The Bishop' was fodder for the backbenches, not vaunted for his political sophistication but well-regarded by those who knew him. On one occasion shortly before his retirement, he rose to speak out of turn in the Dáil. It was shortly after the Arms Trial, and Charles Haughey had been exiled to the backbenches, from where he observed the goings-on with an angry glare. As Burke began his intervention, Haughey hissed from the row behind him: 'Sit down, you old fool'.

'The Bishop' sat down. 'I thought Ray Burke would never forgive Haughey for what he did to his father,' a journalist who witnessed the exchange recalls. 'But in a few years, Burke was running around after Haughey like all the rest, with his tongue hanging out.'

'The Bishop' attracted the same whiff of sulphur that was to settle permanently on his son. A rumour blossomed that he had acquired land cheaply from a patient in the mental hospital where he worked in Portrane. Nothing was ever proven, but the gossip continued to rankle with Ray decades after his father's death.

When Ray Burke was growing up, north county Dublin was still an area of small villages and country fields. Market gardeners supplied food to the big city a few miles to the south; Dubliners came on their holidays to the beaches by the coast. But the booming sixties changed all this, and the area became a magnet for builders looking for sites on which to build bright suburban homes. The young Ray, ambitious and well-connected, took out an auctioneer's licence and went into the estate agency business. He also set himself up as a travel agent.

Paddy Burke had never forgotten his early friends from county Mayo, many of whom had also moved to Dublin. Now Ray simply inherited these contacts. Men like the young builders Tom Brennan and Joe McGowan had roots in the same part of the West as Burke's family and provided him with a ready-made social circle. Later, he would draw on the same reservoir to provide party workers or nominees to State boards; as late as 1989, Burke was still appointing people whom he knew through his father.

Ray Burke made an immediate impression on Dublin County Council and it was soon clear he was destined to succeed his father in the Dáil. But the attention he received wasn't always favourable. The fact that he was an enthusiastic rezoner of land didn't make him unusual. He wasn't even unique in acting as an estate agent while serving on the Council at the same time — John Boland of Fine Gael shared that distinction. What marked Burke out from most of his colleagues was his dual role in development; very often, the houses he was engaged to sell had been built on land which he had pushed to have rezoned. On top of this, the young councillor's social ties with the biggest beneficiaries of rezoning, his friends Brennan and McGowan, set tongues wagging.

Like Burke, Tom Brennan and Joe McGowan were in their twenties, highly ambitious and deeply attached to their Mayo roots. Brennan, a quiet-spoken daily communicant, tended to the nuts and bolts of the business, leaving the more exuberant McGowan to do most of the talking. The two men shared Burke's passion for Fianna Fáil, though they weren't above helping out politicians in other parties if it suited. Brennan had campaigned for Fianna Fáil since 1965, and later organised teams of canvassers for Burke and Brian Lenihan during election campaigns.

Brennan spent seven years working in construction in the US before returning home. In 1965, he formed a partnership with McGowan, who had just completed the Leaving Certificate. They started in a small way building on a few sites they bought in Foxrock, but business boomed as the two men acquired the knack of putting up houses fast and cheap and selling them even faster. As well as building their own houses, they licensed sites for other builders to develop. Both men were on their sites at 8 a.m. each morning and knew the name of every worker. They dealt ruthlessly with sub-contractors and trade unions. 'If you were strong, you got what you wanted. If you weren't, you didn't,' remembers one union representative who dealt with the pair frequently.

Brennan and McGowan's technique was to acquire options on agricultural land, which the planners never intended for development, and then push hard to have it rezoned. New companies were formed for each new venture, creating a labyrinthine company structure that kept the owners out of the prying eyes of residents' groups or journalists. The pair seemed to possess the Midas touch, seemingly always correctly anticipating the future direction of urban growth. It helped that the county councillors rode roughshod over the advice of the planners by turning fertile, low-value agricultural land into gold. At this time, land in north county Dublin that is worth tens of millions of pounds today could be bought for a few hundred pounds an acre. Once it was rezoned for housing, its value multiplied by a factor of ten or more.

Big wasn't beautiful in the case of Brennan and McGowan's handiwork. At one point, they were finishing twenty houses a week — and it showed. As *Hibernia* magazine noted in 1978: 'Their housing schemes in Lucan, Rathfarnham, Tallaght, Castleknock, Swords and so on have often changed shape on the drawing board and on the ground without warning. Their planning applications for retention of existing houses have almost been as frequent as those for the construction of houses from scratch'. Many individual houses also gave rise to complaint, with warped doors, split window frames, cracks in gable walls, and roof trusses below specifications.

By the mid-1970s, largely thanks to a massive rezoning at Kilnamanagh, near Tallaght, Brennan and McGowan were well on the way to becoming the largest housebuilding firm in Ireland. Burke was also going places. He was a leading figure on Dublin County Council, a newly-elected member of the Dáil and his estate agency was flourishing. Burke was on £40 commission for every new house he sold on behalf of the two builders.[1]

One of the most persistent rumours about Burke concerns the house in Swords in which he lived most of his adult life. In 1974, not long after he was elected to Dáil Éireann, he moved into Briargate, an imposing pile on the Malahide Road. The house had been built by Oak Park Developments, a company part-owned by Tom Brennan, and it was said locally that Brennan and McGowan had given their friend the house for nothing.

Over twenty years later, Burke himself raised the matter obliquely during his Dáil speech of September 1997. At this time, he was fighting for his political life under a welter of allegations from James Gogarty. Towards the end of his speech, he raised the matter of the allegations about his father. He said of Paddy Burke that he 'still met people the length and breadth of the country who knew and admired him, and respected and had great affection for him'. Then he referred to a newspaper article printed a short time before. This claimed that the land Burke's house was built on was originally acquired by his father, who bought it from an inmate of the mental hospital at Portrane.

His voice quivering with emotion, Burke said this was a 'complete and utter lie'. He explained that his father had worked as a nurse in Portrane until the mid-1950s. Burke brought with him to the Dáil the Land Registry documentation for his house in Swords. This showed that 'far from being bought from a hospital patient under his care, the house and site was transferred to me and I bought it in a normal commercial transaction from Oak Park Developments. The house was built in the normal commercial manner'. The transaction, he pointed out, had been investigated by gardaí in 1974.

Some twenty-seven years after it was completed, this deal came back to haunt Burke at the Flood tribunal. The records showed this was no 'normal commercial transaction'. Tribunal lawyers found no evidence that money changed hands when the politician acquired the land near Swords and then had a large bungalow built on the site.

At the time, Brennan and McGowan were building large numbers of houses around Dublin. In most cases, Burke's estate agency handled the sales and Sheerin Wynne solicitors carried out the conveyancing. In March 1972, Oak Park paid £7,000 for a two-acre site in Swords. The vendor, according to Land Registry documents, was Joseph Coleman, who was described as a ward of court.[2] In the 1970s, Coleman was an inmate of St Ita's hospital in Portrane, where P.J. Burke had once worked; he died later in St Brendan's psychiatric hospital. Shortly after Oak Park bought the site, it agreed to sell part of it to Burke. The company passed on the conveyancing work to Esmonde Reilly, a young solicitor with Sheerin Wynne. In what he describes as 'a very abnormal transaction', Reilly says no money was paid as Burke acquired the site.[3] When the signed contracts were returned, no deposit cheque was enclosed and Reilly was told not to expect the balance due at closing.

Burke responded to this revelation at the tribunal in typical fashion, by accusing Reilly of trying to 'vilify' him and pointing out that Reilly was the son-in-law of the former Labour minister for local government, James Tully. Reilly responded that if he had wanted to vilify Burke, 'the easiest thing in the world would have been to tell James Tully'. However, he hadn't done this.

Then Oak Park built the house, Briargate, on the site. The architect for the job was John P. Keenan, who worked for Brennan and McGowan and whom Burke subsequently appointed to An Bord Pleanála. Oak Park says Burke paid £15,000 directly to the company for the site and house, but no evidence has emerged, then or since, to support this claim. The managing director of the company, Jack Foley, described the deal as 'a once-off for a man more or less employed by us'. Foley maintains the £15,000 was paid by a building society in three instalments of £5,000; Burke, in contrast, insists the money came from a different financial institution in a single payment. Oak Park's records, and those of the two financial institutions, show nothing to support either claim. Burke also says that, in addition to the £15,000 for the house, he waived commissions on house sales to a value of £7,500 to pay for the site. Again, no documentation has been found to support this claim. 'There is such a thing as a word of honour and that's it,' he told the tribunal.

For some reason, Burke did not register title to Briargate until 1980, when he needed it for security for a loan. Many years later, the house was to achieve notoriety as the venue for James Gogarty's payment to Burke in 1989. In 1994, twenty years after he had acquired the land, Burke's name was finally entered on Land Registry documents when these were updated. The effect of this change was to add almost a quarter acre to his holding. Briargate remained Burke's home until 2000, when he sold the house, its tree-lined entrance drive and surrounding land to the developer of a shopping centre for an estimated £3 million.

By 1974, Burke's behaviour on the Council had begun to attract media scrutiny. In June that year, investigative journalist Joe McAnthony reproduced documents in the *Sunday Independent* showing a £15,000 payment to Burke from Dublin Airport Industrial Estates, a company owned by Brennan and McGowan, under the heading 'Planning'. The money represented his share of the proceeds when land at Mountgorry, near Swords, was sold. Brennan and McGowan had an option on the land, which had been the subject of a number of rezoning motions in 1971. Each of the motions was seconded by P.J. Burke and supported by his son, Ray. In spite of the opposition of planners, and the fact that it lay in the flight path of the airport, the land was successfully rezoned.

The article created a stir. Burke claimed in his defence that the sale of the land had not gone through. He denied any conflict of interest between his roles as estate agent and public representative. He declared that it was not his practice to speak on matters in which he had a commercial interest. At the time, there was no legal requirement on politicians to declare their commercial interests. McGowan told the tribunal the £15,000 figure represented a percentage of the sale price, due to Burke for negotiating the sale of the property.

However, when told the figure represented exactly 3.71 per cent of the sale price, he agreed this wasn't the normal type of percentage charged by estate agents.[4] Hugh Owens, whose accountancy firm prepared the document, said it was a 'typing error'. The entry should have referred to Burke as 'estate agent' to the company, he said.

On the day after McAnthony's article appeared, the document in the Companies Office on which it was based was destroyed. Michael O'Hanrahan, a solicitor with Binchys, which acted for Brennan and McGowan, looked up the reference to Burke and 'Planning' on the file for Dublin Airport Industrial Estates. He raised the matter with the registrar. 'I agreed with her that that document shouldn't be on the file and I took it away with her permission on the same day,' he told the tribunal.

O'Hanrahan brought the document to his offices and tore it up. Before destroying it, he made a copy, something he did not mention to gardaí who interviewed him about the allegations.[5] As far as Burke was concerned, the document was not properly lodged in the Companies Office. It had not been properly stamped and was there 'in error'. McAnthony's article led to a Garda investigation later that year. According to the Garda report, a 'thorough and painstaking' investigation had not disclosed evidence to warrant any prosecutions.

In 1982, the *Magill Book of Irish Politics* reported that the Garda Fraud Squad interviewed Burke more than twenty times over the newspaper allegation. 'While the presumption must be that there was no basis for a criminal charge arising out of the affair as the DPP did not institute any prosecution, the ethical aspects of the case were never explored,' it commented.

If Burke was concerned about this allegation, he didn't let it show. Shortly after the *Magill* book appeared, he stuck his head around the political correspondents' room in Leinster House. 'Did ye hear,' he said, 'I'm the most interviewed deputy in the House'. 'That's great, Ray,' said a journalist. 'Yeah, by the fuckin' guards,' Burke retorted.

Burke's house in Swords was being built just as the waves of his first scandal were breaking over the young politician's head. Esmonde Reilly, the solicitor who handled the sale of the site, knew that no money had changed hands in the transaction. Now, several weeks after the *Sunday Independent* article, he received an unexpected call about the matter. Reilly says it came from Oliver Conlon, a solicitor who acted on behalf of Burke.

He says Conlon told him to 'bury or lose' the file on the transaction. 'It was the most extraordinary phone call I have ever received in thirty-two years of practice,' Reilly recalled when breaking his silence before the tribunal in May 2001. He placed the file in a sealed envelope and stored it in a filing cabinet 'lest I be contacted by a Garda investigation'. He never was contacted. Conlon, who was later involved in setting up an offshore company for Burke, denies the allegation made by his fellow solicitor. He says he doesn't know Reilly and has never spoken to him. Reilly did not report his information 'to any living soul' until he received a phone-call from the tribunal almost three decades later. 'This information has been in my head for the past twenty-seven years. I hoped it would never have to come out. I chose not to get involved,' he told the tribunal.

Burke married in November 1972, and took his bride Ann on honeymoon to Florida and Mexico. In those days, there were strict regulations controlling the export of money, but Burke got around these by telling the bank he was going on a business trip. He got the £1,000 spending money he wanted after claiming he would be viewing properties with 'Palm Beach Investment Property Inc.'.

Meanwhile, his political career progressed. He topped the poll on his first outing in a general election in 1973, with 10,652 votes. The newly elected 30-year-old was modest in victory, putting his success down to his father's popularity: 'I got in on his name, from now I have to do it on my own.'[6]

Brennan and McGowan played an important role in his victory. They bankrolled his election campaign, and provided teams of canvassers and a fleet of vehicles to transport voters to the polling booths. But this was nothing to the help they would offer in the years to come. The young TD needed money to finance his new lifestyle and burgeoning political career and so the two builders took it upon themselves to act as his chief backers and fundraisers. Between 1972 and 1984, they claimed to have raised about £150,000 on behalf of 'Mr Burke and Fianna Fáil' — although Fianna Fáil never saw any of the money. McGowan told the tribunal in April 2000 the funds were raised at annual dinners organised around major horse-racing meetings in Ireland and Britain.[7] He painted a picture of glittering social events at fine hotels in Cheltenham or Royal Ascot. 'On occasions the drink was flowing like a river,' he waxed, as donors queued up to help the cause. The annual target was £10,000, but Brennan and McGowan could be counted on to make up any shortfall. In good years, up to £20,000 would be raised. On one such occasion, 'one participant said: "put me down for any sum you think reasonable"!' When the fundraising efforts ceased in 1984, they had £50,000 in the kitty.

McGowan said the funds were handled by a treasurer from Britain, Ernest Ottewell, whom he described as 'an imposing and authoritative figure' and 'a passionate supporter of Fianna Fáil'. No receipts were issued or asked for. The mysterious Ottewell ranks as one of the more bizarre characters to emerge during the tribunal's investigations. According to McGowan, he was a man of 'deep honour' who held many trusts for his family, which he left 'very well off' when he died in the late 1990s. He was also, McGowan said, 'one of the greatest authorities on clocks and porcelain' in the world.

Not everyone would agree with this portrait of the businessman. In the 1970s, Ottewell shuttled back and forth between England and Ireland, buying antiques cheaply in one country and selling them for high prices in the other. On one occasion, it was said, he bought a silver plate in Ireland for £2,000 and sold it in Britain for more than £100,000. He claimed to be illiterate, once accusing a judge of being 'anti-somatic' though it was not certain that he was Jewish. 'He acted whatever part was necessary for his business. He had an Irish passport under the name O'Toole. He had the Star of David on his swimming pool to push his Jewish claims. And when dealing with Arabs, he dressed up in Arab robes. He created characters to suit the moment,' a source told the *Sunday Business Post* in April 2000. To parade his Britishness, he regularly wore knickerbockers; while in Ireland, he became joint master of the Galway Blazers.

His other career was as a property speculator. He would buy a site, obtain planning permission for a development and sell it on. As often as not, he ended up in the courts when his plans went awry. In the late 1970s, a string of court judgements was registered against him and his companies, including a tax demand for £103,000. Ottewell is believed to have left Ireland permanently shortly afterwards.

This was the man McGowan claimed was the treasurer of the fundraising efforts for Burke. But as one property developer commented: 'I would not have put him in as treasurer of anything. Whenever he did a deal, his associates would all end up fighting, because he used to tell them all different stories'.

Burke's vote-collecting abilities did not go unnoticed by the Fianna Fáil hierarchy, and he was made a junior minister when Jack Lynch led the party back to power in 1977. Confident of his future in politics, Burke says he gave up the auctioneering business, although Brennan and McGowan continued to make payments to P.J. Burke (Sales) Ltd until 1982. In fact, between 1975 and 1982, the builders paid Burke's company £1,000 a month. The total was £85,000, allegedly the commission due for selling 1,700 houses.

In October 1980, Charles Haughey appointed him Minister for the Environment, in spite of the fact that Burke had supported George Colley in a leadership struggle shortly before. The government fell in June 1981 but Burke was re-appointed in a later administration in March 1982. By now, there were numerous stories about the populist politician with the quick temper. When he was Minister for the Environment during the Dublin West by-election in June 1982, Burke arranged for the planting of young trees in a new housing estate in the constituency. After Fianna Fáil lost the vote, he ordered the local authority to dig them up again to show what he thought of the voters' unfaithfulness.

Frustratingly for Burke, this second spell in Cabinet was even shorter than the first, and he returned to the opposition benches in December 1982. With the Rainbow coalition firmly in power, Burke redirected his energies to local politics, and spent two years as chairman of Dublin County Council from July 1985. His tenure was marked by a firm Fianna Fáil whip imposed by Burke's north Dublin henchman Pat Dunne, and even Burke later admitted that he had been 'something of a bully' as chairman.

One of the most serious allegations levelled against Burke dates from this period. Unusually, it was made by one of his own party colleagues in north Dublin. Jim Geraghty is an amusement arcade owner from Rush, Co Dublin who served on the council for the Balbriggan area between 1985 and 1991. One day in 1986, he says he was in Burke's office discussing a planning matter when a well-dressed man in his thirties came into the office and deposited a sports bag on the table. Burke dismissed Geraghty, who walked down the corridor.[8]

However, Geraghty realised he had forgotten his briefcase and returned to Burke's office to retrieve it. He entered the office, and saw that the bag was open. It was full of money, probably in £20 notes, Geraghty told the tribunal. The unidentified man referred to a figure of 'Sixty', which Geraghty understood to mean £60,000, before being sent from the room by Burke. Geraghty says Burke explained the scene by saying it was a development levy. 'They won't like it upstairs,' Geraghty recalled him as saying, in reference to the money being in cash.

A few months later, Geraghty was again in Burke's office when someone came in with a black plastic bag. The man asked Burke if he wanted to 'check' that, but Burke said he didn't. Geraghty told the tribunal he thought the bag could have contained money or it 'could be anything'. A short time after the first incident, Geraghty told one of his Fianna Fáil colleagues about the large sums of money he had seen in Burke's office. A week later, Burke called him into his office to 'berate' him for discussing the matter with someone else, Geraghty claims. 'If I ever hear another word about it again, you will never stand on a Fianna Fáil ticket again. I will see that you're never elected again,' Burke is alleged to have said.

At the tribunal, Burke was scornful in his dismissal of Geraghty's allegations, declaring that 'it simply never happened.[9] Geraghty was a 'rejected, failed, one-term politician who blames everybody for his failure except himself'. Geraghty blamed Burke for his non-selection as a candidate in the 1987 general election. By the time he chose to make the allegation publicly, the party colleague in which he said he confided was dead. The allegation, therefore, comes down to a straightforward clash of testimony between the two men. It was interesting, though, that the tribunal felt Geraghty's evidence was of sufficient importance to have it heard in public.

Burke's political success was built on a well-oiled constituency machine. He mastered the art of parish-pump politics and reaped the reward by topping the poll repeatedly — nine times in general elections and three times in local elections. His confidantes exercised total control over the Fianna Fáil organisation in north Dublin and took care of routine business while the TD rose through the ministerial ranks. Burke greased his political machine with liberal injections of cash. He ran tabs for his supporters to buy drinks in local pubs and generously supported charitable causes in the area.

In June 1981, just a day before Fianna Fáil went out of office, he made three appointments to An Bord Pleanála, including John P. Keenan, the principal architect at Brennan and McGowan, who had designed his home in Swords. But he failed to appoint an official from his own department, leaving the board without a senior civil servant for the first time.

The following year, again on his last day as minister, he appointed Tony Lambert, a former salesman, to the appeals board. Lambert had been working in Burke's office on constituency matters. The other appointee, Patrick Malone, had served as Fianna Fáil director of elections in Laois/Offaly. Once again, no senior civil servant was appointed. Burke argued that the new members would help clear a backlog of appeals. In a Dáil debate on the matter two years later, Burke said he found it 'nauseating' that doubts were being cast on the decency of the members he had appointed. 'I stand over every appointment I made because they are decent and honourable men capable of carrying out their tasks,' he said.

At the time, there was an anomaly in planning law, which allowed property-owners to claim the full development value of their land if planning permission was refused other than for specified 'non-compensatable reasons'. It was as a result of this anomaly in the law that the second Burke-appointed appeals board became embroiled in controversy. A decision to refuse planning permission for a scheme in Fortunestown, Tallaght, exposed the county council to a £2 million claim from a company involving Tom Brennan. Another set of developers lodged an even bigger claim after planning permission was refused for an apartment complex in Killiney, although the eventual payout here was £150,000.

For the builders, it was a 'win-win' situation: a refusal to grant planning permission could prove as profitable as a positive outcome. The biggest winners in this controversy were Brennan and

McGowan, after one of their companies, Grange Developments, picked up the largest compensation award in the history of the State in 1989. Ironically, the cheque for £1.9 million was signed by the assistant Dublin city and county manager, George Redmond, just before his retirement. Grange claimed the compensation after being refused permission by An Bord Pleanála to build houses on land at Mountgorry, near Swords. By a further irony, some of this land had been rezoned years earlier with the help of Ray Burke. It was only after the Grange case that the authorities closed the loophole in the 1963 Planning Act.

By the early 1980s, Brennan and McGowan were the biggest housebuilders in Ireland. In 1983, their combined assets were conservatively valued at £11 million. Both men had moved out to the country to live the lives of squires on their respective stud farms. Their wealth was safely stored in offshore trust funds in the Channel Islands and Liechtenstein. Teams of lawyers and accountants were employed to maximise their privacy and minimise their tax bills. This was also the period of their greatest generosity to Burke, who received three massive offshore payments from the builders between 1982 and 1984.

Meanwhile back in the city, council officials battled with Brennan and McGowan's staff over unfinished housing estates and other breaches of the housing code. Two months after the payout to Grange, the two builders told the High Court they had insufficient funds to complete a road through one of their estates in Tallaght. The court gave them twelve weeks to complete the job.

After a series of legal disputes with business partners and advisers in the mid-1980s, the pair scaled down their housebuilding activities, though they continued to speculate lucratively in land. McGowan sold his stud farm at Hollywood Rath for £1.5 million and moved to England, though he retained his ties with Ireland. But the two builders continued to meet Burke, just like in the old days. One of Brennan's surviving diaries shows he met Burke seven times in a short period in 1985. They could count on the politician's support in their frequent battles with authority. In 1989, for example, Burke, as Minister for Industry and Commerce, made representations to the Revenue Commissioners on behalf of a Brennan and McGowan subsidiary, Bardun Estates, which had tax difficulties at the time. This followed extensive negotiations between the company's accountants and the Revenue, which refused to budge on its tax demand. Burke's intervention drew a written response from the chairman of the Revenue, who rejected the Minister's arguments for a lower settlement. On this occasion, Bardun settled for £2.2 million. In the 1980s, Oak Park Developments, the firm that built Burke's house, also made a large settlement, for £1.4 million, again after protracted argument with the Revenue.

⋘⋙

In his early days Burke had shown independence from Charles Haughey, but he later became one of the staunchest Haughey loyalists. Twice Burke opposed Haughey in Fianna Fáil's interminable leadership battles, and twice he fought his way back into the inner cabal. It is clear that Burke set aside any misgivings he had about Haughey, and any anger he had about the way Haughey had treated his father, in the name of personal advancement. The price Haughey extracted for this forbearance is not known, but on one occasion 'Rambo' was seen reduced to tears after a bruising session with the Fianna Fáil leader.

In 1987 the party returned to power, and Burke was made Minister for Energy and Communications. This gave him power over two crucial areas of public policy; the granting of oil exploration licences and the ending of RTÉ's broadcasting monopoly.

Within months of his appointment, Burke abolished royalty payments and State participation in oil finds, to the delight of the industry. In broadcasting, his long-standing antipathy towards RTÉ and its journalists was never far from the surface, notwithstanding the fact that his brother Seán worked as a cameraman in the station. For years, Burke had been telling anyone who would listen how he was 'going to get those arrogant fuckers' in RTÉ. It came as no surprise, therefore, when he announced plans to set up a network of commercial radio stations in competition with the State broadcaster. In 1988, Burke established the Independent Radio and Television Commission, which awarded the first licence, for a national commercial radio station, to Century Radio the following year. A decade later, it emerged that Burke had received £35,000 from Century's co-founder Oliver Barry; Charles Haughey's son-in-law John Mulhern was also unmasked as a secret investor in the station.

Uniquely for any minister, Burke took the Communications portfolio with him through three changes of department — from Energy, to Industry and Commerce, and then to Justice — and only relinquished it in 1991. His tenure at the Department of Justice surprised those who wrongly believed Burke was a dyed-in-the-wool Fianna Fáil traditionalist; in fact, he was a non-ideological populist happy to blow with the wind so long as he remained in power. As with his other ministerial portfolios, Burke approached the job with energy and a determination to get things done. Liberals found themselves praising the legislative changes he introduced in the areas of family law, rape and homosexuality. Burke got his first taste of giving evidence to an inquiry in Dublin Castle when he was called as a witness before the Beef tribunal in 1992, but came out of the experience relatively unscathed.

He actively plotted against Albert Reynolds when the latter took over the party leadership, and was dropped from the front bench as a result. But Burke was still in his forties and his long-term future looked bright. In the assessment of the Government press secretary, P.J. Mara, Burke had 'terrific political antennae, and an enormous, natural intelligence. He always had the ability to reduce every political situation to its bare essentials'. Mara predicted that his friend 'has a considerable future ahead of him because he is young enough to recover, once the political climate settles down'.

This prediction came true when, on Fianna Fáil's return to power in a coalition government in 1997, Bertie Ahern brought him out of the political wilderness. Burke was appointed Minister for Foreign Affairs and, it seemed, all his troubles were behind him.

In fact, they were only beginning.

2
Grumpy Old Men

'I came here to the tribunal to get the truth, warts and all, and if I did wrong I am ready to take my place in the queue to pay for it.'
— James Gogarty at the Flood tribunal, January 1999

Corruption is, in the words of one investigating Garda, 'a furtive crime'. Both the giver and receiver of money have a shared interest in keeping quiet. They deal in cash and verbal agreements, so no paper trail is left. This is one of the reasons why the rumours about wrongdoing in Irish planning over recent decades have remained just that — rumours. Even those later stricken with guilt pangs were inhibited by fears of loss of status and money, and possible imprisonment. They wrestled with their conscience, and lost.

But what if someone is too old to care about his advancement or status in society, or the sanction of imprisonment? What if he is driven by a burning resentment about his treatment at the hands of former colleagues? What if this person has a powerful memory and has carefully preserved the evidence of his wrongdoing going back over years?

Such a man is James Gogarty, an unlikely candidate for public attention at any time. At an age when most of his colleagues were already dead and buried, Gogarty burst into the limelight with his dramatic appearances at the tribunal in 1999. Suffering from a bad heart, arthritis, diabetes, deafness, kidney stones, blackouts, an overactive thyroid and stress, the 81-year-old was an unusual whistleblower save in one respect — he nursed a deep and bitter grudge. For all his frailties he ended up revelling in the attention, running rings around the lawyers and developing a cult following all of his own.

The background to the Gogarty story is at least as interesting as his evidence. Those early tribunal hearings shed light on his bizarre and feudal relationship to his former boss, Joseph Murphy senior. Even older than Gogarty, Murphy was a reclusive millionaire who once ruled his business empire like a dictator. But ill-health and heavy drinking had loosened his grip on power, and it was often hard to know who was in control, the servant or his master. Money, intrigue, jealousy, violence — all the elements of a Shakespearean drama are contained in this play within a play.

❦

James Martin Gogarty was born in Kells, County Meath, in May 1917, just three months after his long-term employer turned adversary, Joseph Murphy senior. He attended the local school up to the Inter Cert before finding work as a bricklayer and plasterer. In 1939, he joined An Taca Garda, a reserve force set up at the outbreak of World War II. Three years later, he transferred to the Garda Síochána and also began to study engineering in UCD. It was to take him seventeen years of broken study to obtain his degree; at one stage, he was pounding the beat as a Garda until 2 a.m., then rising early to attend lectures the following morning.

He left the gardaí in 1947 and got involved in building houses around Dublin. Economically, it wasn't a good time to start in business, but Gogarty made a decent living working with other country builders who were carving out the new housing estates of suburban Dublin. His first venture into business ended in disagreement with a partner in 1951 and he went to the High Court twice to seek the recovery of a £2,000 debt.[1]

Towards the end of the 1950s, he went to work with a prominent architectural firm, Higginbottom and Stafford, where he became chief engineer and stayed for ten years. During this period, he met the builders Batt O'Shea and Tom Shanahan. O'Shea was a friend of Joseph Murphy senior (and of George Redmond) and had a partnership in which Murphy bought the land and O'Shea and Shanahan did the housebuilding. In 1968, at the age of 51, Gogarty began working for Murphy, a man who shared his humble origins and Garda background. Murphy had bought a Dublin structural engineering company, George Milner and Sons, 'by accident' and he wanted Gogarty to run it. Shortly after, it changed its name to

Joseph Murphy Structural Engineering, or JMSE, with Gogarty as managing director.

Gogarty was one of the old school — thrifty and hardworking, but tough and censorious. JMSE's managing director in the 1990s, Frank Reynolds, remembers him as the epitome of the loyal company servant, the chairman who would take sandwiches to work rather than spend unnecessarily at the company's expense. 'He called me Frankie. I called him "Mr G",' Reynolds recalls.[2] Reynolds gave his boss rain gear and rubber boots to go on fishing trips. Gogarty would respond by unburdening his worries about 'Senior' and the direction of the company. Those who remember Gogarty this far back pay tribute to his intelligence, but say he was extremely difficult to work with. 'Talk to Gogarty! You might as well talk to a jackass,' was Batt O'Shea's verdict.[3]

Gogarty ran the Irish end of Murphy's empire with an iron hand. His dictatorial bent could be seen in the way he dealt with industrial relations problems at Moneypoint in County Clare, where JMSE had a £10 million contract to build an electricity generating station. When a strike broke out in 1981, the 64-year-old managing director intervened personally, giving as good as he got as he crossed the picket line. One former employee of the company claims Gogarty and Murphy paid him £1,200 to intimidate striking workers.[4] One of the strikers told gardaí he received a letter containing four bullets, and four men received mass cards at their homes.

During the tribunal, Flood decided not to dredge up these murky episodes from the company's past, but damaging details were deliberately leaked in the middle of his cross-examination under sensational headlines. But while Gogarty was not questioned about the dispute, his affidavit does refer to these incidents. It states that Murphy senior referred to one worker as someone who would be useful in dealing with other workers and would help 'sort out the Dubs' on the workforce. Gogarty says this person, whom gardaí allegedly told him was a 'maverick IRA man', sought protection money from the company. The dispute took its toll on Gogarty's health and he resigned as managing director in 1982.

But who was Joseph Murphy senior, the enigmatic millionaire who achieved unwanted notoriety in his ninth decade? The riddle starts shortly after his birth, for Joseph Murphy was actually christened John. In the 1930s, his elder brother Joe moved to England and, for his own reasons, took the name of John. So when Joseph Murphy followed his brother into emigration he was forced to switch his own name. The arrangement wasn't as unusual then as it seems today but it probably explains his lifelong desire for privacy.

Murphy was also fabulously rich, and had been so for decades. Wesley Boyd, a journalist who knew Murphy in the 1960s, says he was probably the last of the Irish emigrant labourers to find gold in the streets of London. In July 2000, the two Murphy brothers were separately listed among the ten biggest Irish builders in the UK. These ten Irish companies accounted for ten per cent of the £10 billion in revenues generated by the construction and civil engineering industry in Britain, according to the trade magazine *Construction News*.[5] Joe Murphy was so wealthy that he ran his Irish interests, which included over 1,000 acres of land in north Dublin, almost as an after-thought.

Murphy's other notable characteristic was his obsessive desire for secrecy. No photograph of him appeared in an Irish newspaper until he gave evidence to the tribunal near his home in Guernsey in autumn 1999. From behind the high walls of his mansion he controlled his interests via an army of proxies, notably his son, Joseph junior. A team of advisers worked to maintain his privacy and his reputation, though few dealt with him directly. Because of these multiple layers of secrecy, it was difficult to ascertain how much control Murphy exercised over his minions, and how much knowledge he had of their activities, particularly as he got older and more infirm. When he finally gave evidence, his legal team ensured that no journalist or member of the public would be allowed to share the same room as the octogenarian millionaire. Murphy's doctors had argued that merely being in the presence of the press could prove fatal for him.

Most of what we know about the remarkable life of Joseph Murphy comes via Gogarty and Liam Conroy, two men he employed and later came to hate. Neither offers an objective portrait of the reclusive millionaire, but their details tally in many respects.

Murphy was born in Caherciveen, County Kerry, in February 1917. He attended the local national school at Knockeen, as did Batt O'Shea, another builder who was to remain a life-long friend. After working locally as a general labourer and fisherman he moved to Dublin in 1939. Like Gogarty, he joined the police force and spent the Emergency in An Taca Garda. In 1945, he decided to follow his brother John into emigration in England. John, who already had his own pipe and cable-laying business, employed his younger brother as a manager. Their timing was perfect; Britain was picking itself up again after the war and a massive reconstruction programme was getting under way. One of the brothers' first jobs was the removal of shipping barriers in the English Channel between Dover and Calais.

In the late 1950s, they split and Joseph Murphy set up his own cable-laying business. The company prospered; there wasn't a great deal of competition and the supply of cheap, hard-working Irish labour was limitless. As an employer, Murphy had a reputation for toughness, but he paid well. These were the halcyon days of Irish builders in Britain, and Murphy was one of their leading lights. He was a frequent visitor to the Irish Club in London's Eaton Square where the successful emigrants of Ireland's western shores would gather for stout, sandwiches and long conversations into the night. These were also the days before financial advisers, offshore tax havens and labyrinthine family trusts, according to Wesley Boyd, then a reporter in London. 'They could have dined in Claridges and bought the finest champagne without causing a ripple in their bank accounts, but they were most comfortable in their own company,' he observed.

Murphy's first wife died in 1962 and he packed off his children Angela and Joseph junior (then only three months old) to live with relations near Arigna in County Roscommon.[6] Senior married his second wife Úna, a sister of his first wife, in 1968, the same year he purchased a mews house by the Grand Canal in Dublin.

By the late 1960s, Murphy was a multi-millionaire. Conroy and Gogarty say he was making so much money he delimited his companies. His financial adviser, Edgar Wadley, advised him to place his interest in the company into a trust. An Isle of Man trust, Armoy, was set up to control his UK interests. Subsequently, his Irish interests were vested in a second trust, Ashdale. In 1969, Murphy was advised to invest in a newly established bank in the Isle of Man, the International Finance and Trust Corporation (IFTC). A further trust was set up and Joseph Murphy and his brother John invested £6 million each in the late 1960s.

Around 1970, Murphy became non-resident in the UK. He tried living in Bermuda, the Bahamas and Ireland before settling in Guernsey in 1976. Meanwhile, Úna Murphy and the children moved to Carrick-on-Shannon in 1973, where their father came to visit each month. Home in Guernsey was a large gabled house, surrounded by a high wall, in a leafy quarter of St Peter Port, near the governor's house. Locals fondly remember Úna, who died in 1991, but say her husband was rarely seen in the town, aside from regular attendance at the local Catholic church.

Murphy would drop in to JMSE headquarters in Santry, near Dublin airport, on his regular trips between the Channel Islands and Roscommon. His Irish business interests, though they accounted for only a small proportion of his turnover, were an odd mix of activities. At one point, he owned over 1,000 acres of land in north Dublin, acquired in stages for its long-term investment value, but according to JMSE's managing director, Frank Reynolds, Murphy didn't even know where the lands were.[7] Murphy also owned the Gaiety Theatre in Dublin, which he refurbished in the 1980s.

In addition, he was active in housebuilding, though his involvement was not public knowledge. It came about through his friendship with Batt O'Shea, who was to introduce him to Gogarty. O'Shea had purchased a plot of land in Swords with his business partner Tom Shanahan, but had no money to develop it. In 1965, Murphy gave the two men a cheque for £40,000 in return for a one-third stake. While his stake was a minority one, and the company operated under the name of O'Shea and Shanahan, it was clear that Murphy took all the decisions that mattered. O'Shea and Shanahan also owned the Harp Bar in Swords, which would become a regular haunt of Ray Burke. O'Shea would have a drink there with Burke, but there isn't any evidence that Burke and Murphy met in the pub, or anywhere else.

O'Shea was made a director of many of the Irish companies in the Murphy group and generally acted as Murphy's man in Ireland until Gogarty came along. However, Murphy never relied on just one person for information from Ireland; for example, all the time Gogarty regarded himself as the 'loyal servant' of the expatriate millionaire, JMSE's financial controller Roger Copsey was also functioning as Murphy's 'eyes and ears' in Ireland.

Despite his vast wealth and long years in Britain, Murphy remained hugely attached to Ireland. He maintained the house in Dublin and visited frequently. He scorned the attractions of the English upper classes, preferring the company of rough-hewn Irish builders in his own mould. O'Shea later recalled the frequent culture clashes between Murphy and the suave, bespoke English advisers who did his bidding. At one meeting, Murphy walked out of a meeting after an accountant complained that 'the tall men' couldn't stop talking. 'You pick like a canary and shite like an elephant,' Murphy exclaimed as he left the room.[8] 'Joe, but you're a culchie still,' was O'Shea's observation on the row. Later, the two Kerrymen fell out, though O'Shea says they would still meet to get 'half jarred' during Murphy's less frequent trips to Dublin.[9]

When the oil crisis blew up in the 1970s, the IFTC bank ran into trouble. 'Joe was in trouble right up to his neck and he started drinking and going into very serious nervous problems and at this time he was associating with Liam Conroy,' Gogarty told the tribunal.[10] A businessman with his fingers in various pies, Conroy had befriended the ageing millionaire and soon became his right-hand man.

In 1981, IFTC went into liquidation, putting at risk Murphy's investment. Conroy assumed control of the rescue operation. He says he discovered that substantial funds belonging to Murphy in Swiss banks had been moved without the millionaire's knowledge. Solicitors acting on Murphy's behalf chased up funds in Switzerland which had been credited to a wrong account. Eventually, with the help of professional indemnity insurance, Murphy recovered almost 80 per cent of his investment. Ironically, several of those who advised Murphy during the IFTC fiasco would re-emerge by his side during later struggles.

In 1982, James Gogarty turned 65. If he had retired then, as most people do, the Flood tribunal would doubtless never have happened. Joseph Murphy would have lived out his last days quietly in Guernsey and Ray Burke might even have had an illustrious end to his political career.

However, Gogarty didn't retire. He stepped down as managing director of JMSE in May 1982, but stayed on as an executive chairman and remained as a director of various Murphy companies.

Although not tending to day-to-day matters, he continued to attend board meetings at a time when Murphy was growing old and infirm and increasingly distant from his business empire. Joseph Murphy junior, then in his early twenties and still at college, was too young to assume his father's mantle.

So, twenty years after he started working for Murphy, Gogarty was still in harness to the man he referred to simply as 'Senior', working twelve-hour-days at an age when most other men were thinking of retirement. He spent two years in his late sixties working on the Sellafield contract in Britain, living in a hotel and commuting home at weekends. Murphy would contact him at any time of the night or morning; once he even rang him on Christmas Day and summoned him to Guernsey the following day.

In all probability, Gogarty was more comfortable in the macho environment of work than at home, where his wife Anna ruled the roost. Work had been his life, he didn't play golf or frequent pubs, and suburban domesticity held few attractions. His oft-stated reason for hanging on was to secure a decent pension; he had seven children and was married to a 'fine girl' twenty years his junior who would have to be provided for when he was gone. Murphy promised him a pension lump sum of £500,000, but as this failed to materialise, his concern grew.[11]

Brendan Devine, an accountant to JMSE in the 1970s and 1980s, was well placed to observe the relationship between Murphy and Gogarty. According to Devine, who had good relations with Gogarty for much of this time, the two men were very close.[12] It wasn't Gogarty's practice to take action without first obtaining the assent of Murphy from Guernsey. Murphy's style was to direct policy and management by phone from Guernsey, or from his home in Dublin on his visits to Ireland. 'Mr Murphy didn't often convey his wishes by letters,' Devine says.

While Gogarty was away in England, dramatic changes were sweeping through Murphy's business empire. Within a few years, Liam Conroy had won the complete trust of 'Senior', who appointed him chief executive of his British and Irish companies. Little enough is known about Conroy, considering the prominent role he played in the Dublin business world at this time. Those who worked with him

— he died in July 1998, aged 62 — have sharply divergent memories; some remember an affable, efficient businessman with an eye for a new opportunity and a good line in storytelling. Others, especially those in JMSE, say Conroy misrepresented his past, his exploits and his experience, and lived off the wealth created by others.

Conroy studied science at UCD and worked for the sugar company in Tuam before establishing himself in business in Dublin. He was approaching his fifties when he married in 1985, and had no children. By then, he had a wide range of business interests, which included directorships of a merchant bank and the largest agricultural brokers in Ireland. George Redmond, who knew Conroy from Fitzwilliam Tennis Club as well as from business dealings, remembered him as 'urbane, suave' and said he and Gogarty were like 'chalk and cheese'.

According to Murphy, however, Conroy was a 'con-man' given to flights of fancy. Conroy had told him he was Cambridge-educated, an architect and a pilot who had flown all over the world, but Murphy later discovered that none of this was true. 'He suffered from imagination, that fella. He imagined things to happen. He imagined that he was taking a plane-load of money one time from Saudi Arabia, he was a pilot, to Switzerland, a plane-load of dollars. He had all that sort of fantasy about huge sums of money that he was carting from one part of the world to the other which was all lies. He had a 200ft yacht down in South America which he sailed every three months and he had a brother who was building a lot of skyscrapers in New York.'

'He had $100 million worth of machinery ruined one year by an early frost that damaged the machines. This man was totally bananas with his tales,' Murphy claims.[13] In the words of Murphy's lawyer, Conroy was 'a fantasist' and 'a Walter Mitty character' who invented qualifications and talents at the drop of a hat. He even claimed that he raced Formula 2 and shared a flat with the driver, Gilles Villeneuve.

In the 1970s, Conroy teamed up with Jack Manahan, an established Dublin architect with a small practice, to form Conroy Manahan. Conroy essentially acted as the commercial half of the partnership, touting for new business while Manahan did the professional work. However, he also used the firm to support a lavish lifestyle, as Manahan's son Tony was to find out to his horror. In 1993, Tony Manahan checked the books and found that Conroy had been steadily stripping the firm of its assets. Substantial bills for the

Shelbourne Hotel, credit cards, club memberships, musical equipment and a set of encyclopaedias were all paid from business funds.[14] Over six years, Conroy drew £135,000 from the business, while Jack Manahan, who founded the firm and did most of the work, drew only £42,000. When business slumped, Manahan was left with serious debts and had to sell the family home. While his son was seeking compensation from Conroy, Manahan was living on social welfare and the bank was chasing him to clear an outstanding overdraft.

By this stage, Manahan was old and unwell but Conroy had moved on to bigger things. As Batt O'Shea recalled, "Twas him [Conroy] that was chasing me around, buying me drink and all that caper. He knew I was buying land for Joe Murphy and he wanted to get in with Murphy'.[15] Conroy became acquainted with Joe Murphy senior after Conroy Manahan carried out work for the millionaire on a housing development scheme in 1978. The two men became friendly and Conroy helped to rescue Murphy's investments in the Isle of Man. He later claimed that he wasn't paid for this work.

By this stage, Murphy had passed retirement age and was in poor health, so he urged Conroy to become more closely involved with his companies. In 1982, Conroy became a non-executive director of JMSE. By 1983, he was chief executive of both the British and Irish companies in the group and he soon assumed full responsibility for the ageing millionaire's business and private affairs. His annual salary was £52,000 plus benefits. Conroy had responsibility for the UK operations, while Gogarty minded the smaller Irish end of the business. The two men did not get on; Conroy described Gogarty as 'extremely irascible and litigious' and 'virtually impossible to work with'. Gogarty was fit for 'small-type work but incapable of delegating'.[16]

The new boss was highly critical of the business empire he now ran. Murphy's companies in the UK were 'totally bereft' of management. Their managing director in Britain was 'virtually illiterate' and all the staff were 'blindly loyal' to Murphy but incapable of change, Conroy said. Conroy busied himself across the range of Murphy's business interests. He revamped a cable company and claimed to have developed an office block in Guernsey at a profit of £5 million. He rewarded himself with a steady flow of offshore payments, which were channelled through Pro-Eng, a shelf company based in Guernsey. Invoices were written for services in specific areas, such as advice given in 'bunker welding techniques', yet Conroy had no technical qualifications.[17] Conroy also paid his housekeeper small amounts, from £40 to £60 a week, out of a secret fund realised from the sale of scrap steel. This was the only evidence found of the 'slush fund' alleged by Gogarty.

Murphy also owned the Gaiety Theatre. Conroy's seat on the board of the theatre gave him an entrée to the leading figures in business and entertainment in Dublin, which he used to good effect. Friends and guests such as George Redmond were treated to free seats in the box for big performances. Conroy developed other interests in entertainment, most notably in radio. In 1988, he chaired a consortium set up to apply for one of the new commercial radio licences in Dublin. The bid by Capital Radio Productions was successful and it went on air in July 1989. The station has prospered since and is known today as FM104.

Within the Murphy empire, trouble was brewing. As early as 1985, Gogarty had begun to complain about Conroy's growing control.[18] He claimed stock and contracts were being overvalued in the books, and an auditor was called in. Although the auditor's report expressed satisfaction with accounting practices, Gogarty dismissed it and commissioned another report from English consultants. This found that there were serious questions to be asked about the accounting system. Conroy's relationship with Murphy remained good until October 1987. He blamed the deterioration that followed on Gogarty, who was accused of relaying a stream of allegations about the management of the company to his boss in Guernsey. As a result, Conroy says, Murphy constantly interfered with his instructions to staff and undermined his authority.

By 1988, things had really gone downhill. Gogarty was arguing, with some justification as it turned out, that Conroy was trying to take over the trusts set up for Murphy and his family. Murphy's trustees reached a conclusion; either Gogarty would have to go, or Conroy and his management team would go. After some consideration, Murphy decided that Conroy would stay and Gogarty, his lieutenant of twenty years, would be 'asked' to resign.

Conroy formally requested Gogarty's resignation in mid-1988. Murphy at first supported the call, but then seemed to change his mind. His *volte face* is explained by an extraordinary letter Gogarty sent him on 10 May, which warned Murphy that his businesses were being conducted in such a 'careless, negligent and reckless manner as to indicate that in a very short time the entire organisation will come crashing down'. It would be 'very difficult to prove that fraud had not taken place'. Gogarty warned that Murphy's trusts in the Channel Islands would collapse along with the organisation. 'As your loyal servant and colleague, and taking into account both my age and your age, I strongly and completely believe that together we can not only rescue the situation but can return the organisation to profitability once again.'[19] This would be 'challenging' and 'exciting' and the two men could aim to take the 'entire organisation' on to the stock market within two years.

Given what was to happen over the succeeding years, this letter must rank as either the most naïve or the most duplicitous message ever sent. Besides, Gogarty and Murphy were now both 71 years old and in poor health, and hardly in a good position to float a multinational enterprise on the stock exchange. Nonetheless, Gogarty's advice prevailed, and the two septuagenarians began a campaign to wrest control back from Conroy and his associates. Gogarty claims 'Senior' promised him a good pension deal once the problem had been dealt with.

Conroy called an extraordinary board meeting for 8 June, with the purpose of forcing Gogarty out. However, Murphy constituted a rival meeting at 6 a.m. on the same day, at which he ousted Conroy by appointing a new board. Locks were changed at the company's premises and the old management team was banned from entering. Conroy went to the High Court to seek redress. A further board meeting was held on 14 June to consider Conroy's suspension. Edgar Wadley, an accountant who had been involved in the IFTC fiasco, re-emerged at Murphy's side, much to Conroy's surprise. Two days later, Conroy accepted defeat and resigned.

One of those drafted in to help oust Conroy was Joseph Murphy junior, then only 26 years of age. Murphy junior had been educated in Ireland, in Carrick-on-Shannon and then as a boarder at St Gerard's in Bray. Describing himself accurately as 'not the studious type,' he repeated the Leaving Certificate and dropped out of UCD after a few desultory years studying economics and politics.[20] While a student, he spent his summers driving a truck for JMSE in Santry. After college, he worked as a labourer in London before resolving to make his way in his father's world 'from the ground floor up'. While the newcomer Conroy ran the company, the boss's son was the foreman of a work-gang in London.

Murphy junior's leisurely career plans were quickly overturned when the crisis erupted. He played an active role in the boardroom putsch which thrust him into the limelight alongside his father for the first time. Before long, he was the chairman of the Irish companies, and the seeds of future conflict with Gogarty were being sown.

Conroy's influence on Murphy and his companies persisted. He began a wrongful dismissal case against his former employer in the Isle of Man. For its part, the company began proceedings to have a sub-trust established by Conroy declared invalid. The affidavit Conroy filed for this litigation in March 1989 (two months before the payment to Burke) accuses Murphy of 'everything under the sun', as Gogarty put it to the tribunal. A piece of precisely-aimed character assassination, it paints a deeply unflattering portrait of Murphy by accusing him of tax evasion, breaches of exchange controls and heavy drinking.

The document stimulated Murphy's wrath considerably. As his legal adviser, Christopher Oakley, told the tribunal, Murphy senior didn't want a settlement, 'he wanted revenge'. Murphy gave a copy of the document to Gogarty and asked him to help Oakley prepare a counter-affidavit. The battle raged through the courts of the Isle of Man and other jurisdictions for a few years before a settlement was reached in August 1990 and Conroy received a payment of £625,000, considerably less than he originally sought. He was also required to promise never to divulge the contents of the affidavit and to return all the company documents in his possession.

There the story might have ended, were it not for Gogarty and the Flood tribunal. Murphy's lawyers fought tooth and nail to prevent the disclosure of the Conroy affidavit at the tribunal, claiming it was 'peppered with lies'. Any mention of the document provoked an angry response; when I published an article about the affidavit in April 1999, Murphy's legal team claimed it was a contempt of court, and demanded I be cross-examined.[21] After some legal debate, Flood refused this request. When the chairman ruled that the Conroy affidavit should be disclosed in public, Murphys fought the decision in the High Court and then the Supreme Court, but without success. Its contents were eventually disclosed at the tribunal in September 1999.

Aside from the insulting personal details it contains, the affidavit is particularly damaging to the company's case at the tribunal because it shows that Conroy and Gogarty, despite their mutual antipathy, were 'singing off the same hymn sheet'. The fact that the document contains harsh criticism of Gogarty adds to its credibility.

The affidavit claims that Murphy demanded total secrecy about his affairs, so Conroy could not use secretarial services or commit anything to writing.[22] The reason cited was Murphy's 'potential tax problems.' 'Mr Murphy informed me that he had evaded UK tax and exchange controls in the early 1970s and had deposited large sums of money in Switzerland in the name of two Liberian registered companies, Bremen Inc and Hammer and Springer Inc,' Conroy writes. 'He had also evaded Guernsey tax by having bank accounts in Éire in his name and UK accommodation addresses.' He also claims Murphy regularly breached Irish exchange control laws by exporting monies from the Republic without authorisation. Conroy says Murphy was concerned that the Revenue would become aware of his activities and seek to take action against him and the trusts.

The disputed Conroy affidavit is crucial to an understanding of Murphy's actions. For Gogarty, the affidavit is the first link in a chain of events that leads ultimately to Ray Burke's front sitting-room. Gogarty claims that because of the affidavit and the litigation with Conroy, Murphy 'wanted to dispose of all the lands [in Ireland] and remove the assets outside the jurisdiction because of the implication in the affidavit that if the Revenue was after him they would take the trust off him'. This potential tax exposure far exceeded the value of the lands, he argued. Murphy would later dismiss this line of thinking, describing Gogarty's claim as 'hogwash'.[23] And while it would explain why Murphy hurriedly offloaded the bank of land in north Dublin he had built up over decades, it does not enlighten us as to why £30,000 of company money ended up in Burke's bank account in 1989. Gogarty's version is that 'Senior' responded to the affidavit by ordering the sale of the 700 or so acres, and he insisted on a private treaty sale in preference to a public auction. Gogarty entrusted the job to an auctioneer friend, Fred Duffy of Duffy Mangan Butler.

Now that Conroy was out of the way, Gogarty believed his pension would be sorted out. A lifetime of striking hard bargains stood him well, and in May 1989 he offered to settle for a lump sum of £300,000 — an amount he said was equivalent to 'a lousy £18,000 a year' for his wife and family. What galled him was that Conroy had offered him £24,000 a year but he had refused this on Murphy's advice.

But Gogarty also demanded to be retained as a consultant for five years on his £23,500 salary, with car and phone expenses, as well as £70,000 in unpaid bonuses and other compensations. Finally, he wanted the right to earn commission on his last big job: the negotiations with the ESB over the final amount due to JMSE for its work in building the Moneypoint generating plant. Solicitors for Gogarty and his employers agreed that he would be paid half the remaining money due. A threshold was applied; the commission would 'only be paid in respect of any net offer in excess of that already offered by the ESB'.

At first, Gogarty wanted half of everything over £40,000, which was the ESB's original offer to JMSE. Eventually, he settled for a threshold of £130,000. He claims he worked hard to push up the amount due to the company and eventually secured agreement for the ESB to pay a final settlement of £700,000 including VAT. He said 'Senior' only expected another £10,000 and was delighted. However, JMSE claims Gogarty already knew he could get £700,000 from the ESB at the time he fixed the lower threshold with his employers. If this were the case, then he wouldn't have been entitled to any commission. Gogarty says the company's accusation of deception is 'a damned lie'.[24]

At this point, the three issues — the ESB commission, Gogarty's pension and the Conroy proceedings — become inextricably intertwined. Agreement was reached on Gogarty's pension in October 1989, but there were conditions attached. First, the deal was subject to the agreement of Joseph Murphy senior. Then, lawyers for Murphys drew up a counter-affidavit in the Conroy case and told Gogarty that if he didn't sign, his pension would not be settled. But Gogarty refused to sign. He withheld his signature from the company accounts, saying they were inaccurate. He also threatened legal action.

Gogarty had one further trick up his sleeve. On 10 October, a week after the deal on his pension, the board of the ESB agreed to pay JMSE £700,000 in final settlement of the Moneypoint contract. Gogarty's share of this was £215,000. But instead of allowing the payment to come into JMSE's offices in Santry in the normal way, Gogarty had the £700,000 cheque sent to the offices of his solicitor, Gerard Sheedy. On 31 October, Sheedy revealed to the company that he was in possession of the cheque. An enraged JMSE claimed the action was illegal. But the stroke worked. Three days later, Murphy finally approved Gogarty's pension settlement.

Sheedy held on to the cheque, suggesting that the company calculate the amount it was due after Gogarty's pension lump sum was deducted. JMSE accused Gogarty of misappropriating its money and complained unsuccessfully to the Law Society. The dispute rumbled on until 1990, when a settlement was reached.

⋘⋙

While all this bickering was going on within the Murphy group, something extraordinary was happening in the Ireland of the late 1980s. After years in the doldrums, the economy started to pick up. It would take some years yet for the Celtic Tiger to reach maturity, but the first signs of better times ahead were visible to those on the lookout. And no-one was better attuned to the laws of supply and demand than the builders who plied their trade around the fringes of Dublin. Emigration was dropping and people were returning to Ireland, they noticed. The demand for housing was rising and, with it, the demand for land on which to build houses.

For decades, Murphys had owned the largest private bank of undeveloped land in north Dublin. But Joseph Murphy ran his property like an absentee landlord, allowing buildings to go to rack and ruin and making little attempt to exploit the land's development potential. However, others were keenly aware of the possibilities offered by Murphy's holdings at the fringe of the expanding city. One of those who sensed an opportunity was Michael Bailey, a brash young builder who was active on sites near Murphy's properties in north Dublin.

Bailey belonged to a new generation of rough-hewn, hard-dealing builders fleeing hardship in the West of Ireland. One of eight children from a smallholding near Ballintubber, County Roscommon, his time at school was brief and unhappy. The story goes that on one occasion, a teacher decided to give him a lesson in discipline. The teacher rolled up a copy of the *Roscommon Herald* and put it down the back of Bailey's belt to act as a tail. The 12-year-old was ordered down on all fours and told to crawl through the five classrooms in the school. The teacher followed, slapping his backside with a cane and calling him an ass.

Not surprisingly, Bailey left school aged 15 and trained as a bricklayer. He moved up to Dublin and went into business in a small way, building a few houses in Dublin, where his younger brother Tom soon joined him. 'We had a good bank manager. Up to 1990, it was a long hard struggle. We bought sites at the right time. It was a case of luck rather than good management,' Tom Bailey modestly told *Business and Finance* magazine in 1996.

Their company, Bovale Developments, quickly grew into one of the largest housebuilding firms around Dublin. It specialised in mid-sized suburban semi-detached houses in the suburbs, especially around Swords. Michael Bailey later claimed credit for 'turning around' the fortunes of Swords by building large numbers of four-bedroomed houses in the area. Unlike Brennan and McGowan, Bovale enjoyed a good reputation with local authorities and homebuyers, and some of its schemes won awards. By 1996, the firm was building 100-150 houses a year, had a turnover of £10 million a year and a landbank of over 500 acres. But, Tom Bailey insisted: 'we are not high falutin' in our lifestyle'.

A tall, broad-shouldered man with a distinctive heavy moustache, Michael Bailey already had a name for exuberant public celebrations on the racecourse. In 1987, he stole the limelight at Cheltenham by breaking into the security around the winners' enclosure, where he grabbed the British Queen Mother by the arm and planted a kiss on her cheek. Bailey had just won £50,000 on the 13/2 favourite, *The Thinker*.

When he appeared before the tribunal, Bailey laid on modesty and family virtues with a brickie's trowel. He described himself as a 'reasonably successful businessman. I'm doing my best to rear my kids and look after my family. I don't like to be described as a remarkably successful businessman'.[25] 'I didn't spend ten or twelve years getting a degree trying to catch people up,' he told an uppity barrister at one stage. 'You're not going to make a fool of me, which I thought you were going to do.'

Bailey's statement to the tribunal describes him as 'a long-standing supporter of the Fianna Fáil party, for which I make no apology'. However, when questioned about this, he showed considerable reticence. 'I'm a businessman. I may be a Fianna Fáil man last week and a different man this week,' he told tribunal lawyers.[26] Nonetheless, most though not all of the thirty politicians who got money from Bovale between 1989 and 1997 are in Fianna Fáil. The total amount of donations was £26,000, with over £14,000 paid in 1997 alone.

Gogarty first had dealings with Bailey over a piece of land in Swords in 1988. He agreed to sell the Forest Road site to Bailey but there was a dispute in JMSE over the price. Gogarty says he felt sorry that Bailey ended up paying £1.45 million, which was £200,000 more than they had originally agreed.

By early 1989, Murphy had resolved to sell all his lands in north Dublin. Gogarty says this was because of the threat posed by the litigation with Liam Conroy. 'Mr Murphy is anxious to realise an early disposal of these properties and to this end he accepts that you may deem it necessary to discount some or all of the development element you have included in your valuations,' Gogarty wrote to the auctioneers in June 1989.

On this evidence, it was a fire sale. Murphy was preparing to sell his crock of gold for next to nothing. However, Murphy says he only made the decision to sell after being 'haunted' by Gogarty for months. 'Every time he phoned or I phoned … he'd say these lands are a nuisance to you, getting a few quid per acre, [you'd be] better off putting it in the bank,' Murphy told the tribunal.

By spring 1989, Bailey had emerged as the main party interested in buying the lands. He came up with two business proposals, which are summarised in the famous letter he sent to Gogarty on 8 June 1989. The first proposal was for the outright sale of the lands. The second was for shared equity, which would give Bovale a 50 per cent share in return for 'procuring' the necessary planning permission. Bailey says that he dealt only with Gogarty and never met Joseph Murphy senior.[27] The role he envisaged for himself under the shared equity proposal was to lobby community councils and local representatives for the rezoning of the land.[28] For this work, he would acquire 50 per cent ownership.

However, Bovale's accounts for that year showed profits of just £56,000 and reserves of £10,000. On this evidence — the accounts were later shown to be unreliable — the company could hardly afford its ambitious proposals for a joint venture on the lands. Unless, that is, the lands could be rezoned. At this point, Bailey's suggested purchase price was £2.868 million but with rezoning the lands would be worth much more. At £30,000 an acre, their overall value would rise to £21 million, the figure suggested later by the tribunal. With planning permission, and based on the price paid for the Forest Road land, their value would be even greater, at £47 million.[29] Under these (hypothetical) circumstances, Bailey's 50 per cent stake would be worth anywhere between £10.5 million and £23.5 million — not a bad return for schmoozing a few residents' groups and county councillors.

⋘⟐⋙

It was against this background that the payment to Ray Burke, the central event in the tribunal's first years of investigations, came to be made. Although the ten-minute meeting in Burke's house in Swords has been forensically scrutinised from every angle, there is little agreement among the participants on what happened, when it happened and, most important of all, why it happened.

Gogarty's version of events was the first in the field, and the most detailed. In May/June 1989, Gogarty claims he and a number of JMSE executives attended a series of meetings with Michael Bailey about Bovale's proposals. As part of his shared equity or '50/50' proposal, Bailey undertook to spend £2,000 per acre to get the necessary permissions to develop the land. Money would have to be paid to county councillors. Bailey then went into detail about how he would achieve his aims, Gogarty claims: 'There was five or six councillors that could organise or maximise the votes of Dublin County Council and that he [Bailey] was also in a position to cross the political divide; they were the words he says, "political divide", and that he could rely on close liaison with people in the county council, including Mr [George] Redmond.'[30]

After he received the letter, Gogarty says he attended a meeting of JMSE executives, at which he was told to go along with Bailey to a meeting in Burke's house. He claims Joseph Murphy junior said it had been agreed that the Murphy group and Bailey would each give Burke £40,000. The Murphy contribution — £30,000 in cash and a cheque for £10,000 — was counted at this meeting.

A few days later, Gogarty travelled with Bailey and Murphy junior to the meeting in Burke's house in Swords. On the way, in one of the more naïve interventions in Irish history, he asked whether they would get a receipt for the large amount of money they were handing over. 'Will we, fuck!' Bailey is said to have responded.

Burke, then Minister for Industry, Commerce and Communications and in the middle of an election campaign, was 'formally dressed, short of being in a dress suit' when he received the three gentlemen that evening, according to Gogarty. The minister ushered his visitors into a side-room off the hall and went to get some tea and biscuits. On his return, Gogarty placed an envelope on the table. He claims Bailey placed a second envelope on the table.

Gogarty says he expressed concern about the payment being made for an 'open-ended commitment'. Burke said Murphy and Bailey were 'well aware of how he had honoured his commitments in the past'. 'That's all right, Jim, leave it with me and Ray,' Bailey is supposed to have said. There was some small talk, and Burke looked at his watch. It was time to go. The visitors stood up, shook hands and wished the politician luck. Gogarty never saw the envelopes, or Burke, again.

Gogarty says his envelope was stuffed with £50 and £100 notes — £30,000 in all — and a £10,000 cheque made out to cash. Although he hadn't counted it, he was satisfied it contained £40,000. He assumed there was £40,000 in Bailey's envelope also, but didn't know for sure. 'There could be feathers in it for all I know,' he quipped at the tribunal.[31]

Virtually every detail of Gogarty's story is contested. Murphy junior says he wasn't at the Burke meeting, or any of the other meetings mentioned by Gogarty. He took no part in the negotiations with Bailey on the sale of the lands. Murphy senior says he didn't know Burke, and didn't sanction any payment to him. JMSE says the amount involved was £30,000, not £40,000. The company's account-ant, Tim O'Keeffe, collected £20,000 in cash from the AIB in Talbot Street, to which he was accompanied by the managing director,

Frank Reynolds. A cheque for £10,000 was written to make up the balance of the payment.

Bailey denies the allegation that he could, or would, bribe councillors or anyone else. His version is that Gogarty rang him early in June 1989 to say that Joseph Murphy senior wanted to make a contribution to Fianna Fáil.[32] Bailey ventured that Ray Burke was 'the man in the area' (in fact, JMSE was not located in Burke's constituency). He offered to make the introduction. Bailey rang Burke, set up an appointment and made it clear he was bringing someone from JMSE along. This conflicts with the account given by Burke, who said he was 'surprised' when Gogarty turned up at his door.

During the meeting, which took place mid-morning (Gogarty put the time at about 5 p.m.), Gogarty took two 'reasonably bulky' envelopes out of a folder and gave them to Burke. Bailey says they were each the size of two '9 in. by 2 in. blocks.' The builder could see the envelopes contained substantial bundles of cash. 'I said to myself, "is that real money"?' Despite his surprise at the amount of the donation, he displayed no curiosity with Gogarty on the return journey. 'I said was he happy with that, and he said he was.'

Burke remembers least about the meeting, but he was in the middle of a busy election campaign (not to mention his other fundraising exploits over these weeks). Michael Bailey rang him the day before the meeting, saying he wanted to make a political contribution. However, it turned out that Bailey brought Gogarty to the house the following morning. Burke was dressed up because he was due to appear on television later that day. He did not know Gogarty. The three men 'discussed very briefly the political campaigns' and Gogarty then handed him two 'reasonably sized' envelopes. Burke denies Gogarty's claim that refreshments were served. It was 'not his habit to furnish tea,' his lawyers told the tribunal.[33] No favour was asked for or given during the meeting.

One of the mysteries of this affair is the variation in the price of the Murphy lands. In March 1989, these were valued at £3.002 million, but they were ultimately sold for much less. Gogarty's explanation is that the threat of the Conroy affidavit, which dates from the same month, forced Murphy senior to offload his Irish land interests in a hurry. As noted, Gogarty told the auctioneers in a letter of instructions

in June 1989 that Murphy was anxious for a quick sale and was prepared to discount the development potential of the lands to achieve
this. However, this doesn't explain why the lands were sold for £2.3
million when Michael Bailey made an earlier offer of £2.868 million
in June 1989.[34]

Negotiations between Gogarty and Bailey on the sale continued
in the second half of 1989. One of Gogarty's handwritten notes from
this period refers to Bailey and the auctioneer Fred Duffy and a
purchase price of £2.4 million and adds: 'Duffy, would he give me
10,000K commission?'

Gogarty's explanation for this remark is that Duffy suggested sharing the sale commission with him. 'I said there was no necessity for
that. I didn't want that kind of thing,' he says.[35] Had he ever taken
money from Duffy? 'Never in my life,' he told the tribunal. However,
JMSE claims Gogarty sought a backhander from the auctioneer
when he was on the point of completing the deal with Bailey,[36] and
had never explained why the land was sold for the lower price of £2.3
million. Duffy can't enlighten us on these matters, as he died just as
the tribunal was starting.

Bailey eventually contracted to buy the north Dublin lands for
£2.3 million in December 1989. The closing date was set for April
1990, but after a fire broke out in a house on one of the lots the
matter became a subject of dispute and the deal took several years to
complete. This didn't stop Michael Bailey coming back to JMSE with
a dramatic new offer in July 1990. At a meeting with Gogarty, Murphy
junior, Reynolds and other JMSE executives, Bailey suggested that
Murphys buy back a half-share in the development of the lands for £8
million. Within six months, the value of the lands had jumped from
£2.3 million to £16 million. The lands hadn't even been rezoned.

Bailey's later explanation was that there had been an 'unbeliev-
able pickup' in the demand for property over the nine months that
intervened.[37] But he also claimed that the offer wasn't serious; it was
just 'an outrageous suggestion'. 'I threw out the figure of £8 million
to see if I would catch a sprat. If I did, well and good, he may turn
into a fish.' But Murphy junior's reaction was one of shock and Bailey
caught no fish on this occasion.

A month or so later, Michael Bailey met Gogarty at the Skylon
Hotel in north Dublin. Their accounts of this meeting, which cut

directly to the heart of this affair, are in direct conflict. Gogarty says Bailey tried to buy his silence on the Burke payment; Bailey claims that Gogarty demanded a finder's fee for the deal on the lands.

What is not disputed is that Bailey gave Gogarty a cheque for £50,000. 'He didn't want to get involved in court cases and he didn't want anything dragged in about Ray Burke or himself, because they would never get another bit of planning permission if anything surfaced,' Gogarty told the tribunal in January 1999.[38] 'He said that I should forget the whole thing and enjoy myself. When we stood up to leave he took a small envelope out of his pocket and put it into my breast pocket and he said "I'll be in touch with you later on".'

Gogarty said he opened the envelope when he went home and found it contained the £50,000 cheque, dated 30 September 1990. He says he put it in a biscuit tin with other papers and only found it when he was moving house over five years later.

Bailey has given three conflicting explanations of this episode. When first asked about the cheque in August 1997, by Frank Connolly of *the Sunday Business Post*, he said it was given in return for Gogarty's 'assistance' in his efforts to buy a JMSE-owned house on Baggot Street. However, Bailey hadn't purchased the house, let alone made a meaningful bid for it. In addition, the dates didn't match; the house was sold in October 1989, yet the cheque was dated almost a year later. When Connolly discovered this, he went back to Bailey, who then explained he had post-dated the cheque. Two years later, Bailey admitted he had lied to the journalist.[39]

In his evidence to the tribunal, Bailey came up with yet another explanation. The cheque was part of a backhander for arranging the sale of the north Dublin lands. The total sum sought by Gogarty was £150,000, he claimed. With interest, the total payment came to £162,500. Bailey says he paid £50,000 in cash and provided two £50,000 cheques as security until the rest of the cash was delivered. The balance was paid in small amounts over the following six years.

There are no records, receipts or acknowledgement to support this version of events. Bailey, on this own account, happily agreed to pay the money even before the land sale was even completed. He was also happy to rely on Gogarty's record of how much money had been paid. 'One day I gave him £1,000 and he came back to me on the phone and told me I was £20 short.'[40] It wasn't the most convincing of allegations.

In spite of his anger at the pension row, Murphy senior realised he still needed Gogarty to complete JMSE's largest contract, worth £20 million, at the Sizewell nuclear plant.[41] Murphy knew all about laying cables, but it was Gogarty who had the expertise in negotiating the terms in such large contracts. However, differences quickly emerged between Gogarty and JMSE's financial controller, Englishman Roger Copsey, over the terms of his consultancy agreement and his expenses. On 14 August 1989 — Copsey's 46th birthday — Murphy senior rang his financial controller to tell him he was fired.[42]

However, Gogarty's disputes with JMSE rumbled on. He agreed to settle his legal claims against the company in June 1990, but was soon back in dispute. Gogarty's working relationship with the company ended in October 1990 when Murphy banned him from incurring expenses without prior approval. In 1991, Gogarty sued for out-of-pocket expenses and the issuing of a P60 tax form for his ESB work. For reasons of 'tax efficiency', JMSE tried to have P60s issued to Gogarty from three companies for which he never worked. It told the Revenue that Gogarty worked for one of these companies for twenty years when, in fact, Gogarty had never worked for the company. It also told the Revenue that he had consented to waive the commission due for negotiating the ESB monies but Gogarty never agreed to this.[43]

Gogarty salted away his new-found riches in an offshore bank account. He transferred £80,000 from his trust fund in Guernsey to a bank in the Isle of Man in November 1989, and further lodgements followed over the succeeding years. He also kept a 'nest-egg' of £30,000 at home so his wife would have the money 'if anything happened to me'.[44] In November 1993, he declared £180,000 in Isle of Man bank accounts under the tax amnesty. It was, he admitted to the tribunal, a persistent tax fraud against the Revenue, but he expressed regret for what he had done.[45]

Gogarty and Murphy junior tried to sort out their differences at a meeting in the Berkeley Court hotel in February 1992, but the attempted *rapprochement* turned out badly. Murphy claims Gogarty banged the table and threatened to 'destroy' his companies unless he got an additional £400,000 on top of his pension settlement.[46]

There wasn't much on television on the night of Sunday, 19 June 1994, so James Gogarty retired to bed early. His wife was visiting relatives and the then 77-year-old was alone in the family home in Sutton. Sometime after 2 a.m., the phone rang. A man spoke, and Gogarty says he recognised him as Joseph Murphy junior.

Gogarty says what followed left him and his wife 'frightened out of their wits'.[47] 'I'm going out to your house and I'll break every fucking bone in your body and then I'll kick the fucking shite out of you and when I'm finished with you you won't have a roof over your head, and I'll put a stop to all your legal hassles,' Murphy is alleged to have said.

At the time, Gogarty was engaged in the latest round of his dispute with JMSE, this time over his demand for a correct P60 for consultancy fees. He won in the Circuit Court in March 1994, but the company appealed the judgement. In June, JMSE was ordered to pay Gogarty £618.70 and to issue the P60. Gogarty claims Murphy accused him of writing to the Revenue Commissioners about the case and bringing them in to JMSE. 'I said: "I did not, and I'll bet you £5 I didn't and what's more if you can produce a letter which I wrote to the Revenue, I'll eat it in your presence".' Murphy then called him 'a liar,' he claims.

The conversation continued in these terms until Gogarty hung up. He dialled 999 and spoke to the gardaí. 'I was very upset and felt weak at the time, fearful, while expecting the police. I took a drink of water and lay back on my bed to rest when the phone rang again. Thinking it was the police, I lifted the receiver and was shocked to hear him again.'

His wife Anna arrived home and listened in to part of the conversation. Murphy apologised for upsetting Anna but repeated the threats to her husband, according to Gogarty. At this stage, the gardaí arrived. They took a more benign view of the incident. Sergeant Bernard Sherry of Howth Garda station said that Murphy was 'under the influence' and was engaging in 'drink talk'. Sherry concluded that it would not be worthwhile bringing a case against Murphy because of the difficulty of proving the allegation and serving the summons (Murphy lived in London). He noted that Murphy had promised not to ring Gogarty again.[48] Murphy agrees that he phoned Gogarty very early one morning, for which he apologised. There was a heated discussion but he insists he did not threaten Gogarty.

Having promised the gardaí he would not ring Gogarty again he says he has kept his word.

For Gogarty, Murphy's late-night call fitted into a pattern of intimidation he had experienced. He outlined to his solicitor a series of unexplained events, including a 'shot' fired through the front window of his house in 1991, a series of nuisance phone-calls in 1992, and damage to his car and his wife's car in January 1994. There was less to the incidents than Gogarty saw; the gardaí who investigated the shot found 'two small holes' in the window, consistent with a marble or light ball-bearing fired from a catapult, and the other events were fairly commonplace. Following Murphy's call, Gogarty says he became a recluse. He and his family lived 'in fear and dread' because 'that blackguard' was out in the open and taunting him, he told the tribunal in 1999.

One person Gogarty did remain in touch with, however, was Michael Bailey. Gogarty had claimed he had no contact with the Baileys after their meeting in the Skylon Hotel in 1990, but when the tribunal checked the phone records it discovered a series of calls between the two for years after. Each side incorporated this fact into their version of events; the Baileys claimed Gogarty was 'pestering' them for money, while Gogarty's explanation was that the Baileys were 'hounding' him to stay quiet about the payment to Burke. Gogarty's explanation for his previous denial of any contact was that by 'contact' he meant face-to-face meetings.[49]

By 1995, the Murphys must have thought their experience of Gogarty was like a bad dream, slowly fading from memory. In fact their nightmare was just starting.

3
The Life and Times of JR

'*Lots of people do things for you in life and you never see them again.*'
— Michael Bailey explaining the generosity of George
Redmond in putting him in touch with James Gogarty.[1]

'*It was a sword of Damocles and in a way I buried it. I lived with that
sword over my head and it obviously has ruined my life.*'
— Redmond on the payments he received, tribunal evidence,
18 May 2000

Manx Airlines flight JE207 was on time but half-empty when it landed in Dublin Airport just after 7 p.m. on 19 February 1999. It was a busy Friday evening, so it didn't take long for the small, tanned pensioner carrying a grey holdall to be swallowed up in the disembarking crowds. George Redmond, a 74-year-old retired local authority official, was returning from a trip to the Isle of Man, having left his home in Deerpark, Castleknock, just before 7 a.m. that morning.

The peace of Redmond's quiet retirement was about to end in the most dramatic fashion. When he emerged into the arrivals lounge, the former official was met by a football squad of Garda officers. Detective Inspector Pat Byrne and eleven other officers from the Criminal Assets Bureau (CAB) were on hand to make the highest-profile arrest of the bureau's brief history. Within minutes, the story was all around Dublin. CAB, more used to pursuing drug barons, had made its first foray into the world of white-collar crime and its friends wanted the world to know.

Bureau detectives, who had shadowed Redmond's movements throughout the day, searched the pockets of his quilted grey anorak and found a series of sterling drafts which he had withdrawn from

Irish banks several weeks earlier but not cashed. There were also documents from a bank in the Isle of Man. They opened the holdall and found it stuffed with cash. Byrne took the bag and told Redmond he was being arrested. Redmond said nothing in reply, and was taken to Harcourt Terrace garda station. CAB detectives completed his night of ignominy by searching the retired official's house in Castleknock while he was being questioned.

The timing of the arrest was remarkable. Bureau sources told the newspapers they had only begun monitoring Redmond the previous weekend. Gardaí investigating the movement of money in and out of Irish banks claimed a 'confidential source' had tipped them off. This version of events did not impress the Flood tribunal, which had been on his tail for months. Redmond, who had turned up at the tribunal in the days leading up to his arrest, had just given its lawyers letters of authority to examine at least one Isle of Man account. Now there was talk that he would exercise his right to silence before the tribunal because of the pending criminal charges. Redmond was eventually released without charge after nineteen hours of questioning and deposited back to Castleknock in the back of a red Transit van.

In all, CAB officers seized £100,000 in punts, another £92,000 in sterling and cheques worth £95,000 made out to Redmond the previous summer by a Dublin stockbroking firm. The money had been moved offshore in 1996. A subsequent investigation uncovered twenty accounts opened in fourteen banks and building societies. Twelve days after his arrest, Redmond finally made a statement to the tribunal, admitting he got £25,000 from James Gogarty as a finder's fee on a land deal. For the first time in living memory, a senior public servant had confessed to receiving secret payments in connection with his work.

Redmond told friends later that his arrest came as a relief. At least it put paid to the long months of uncertainty, when he was being harried by the tribunal and his name was beginning to feature in the Sunday newspapers. At the start of February, he had turned up in the tribunal during Gogarty's evidence, personally protesting his innocence in bizarre fashion from the back of the hall. Only a week before he was arrested, Redmond had told *Ireland on Sunday* that he didn't have an offshore bank account; now he had been caught red-handed returning from the Isle of Man.[2]

The time for lies and obfuscation was over. Under the harsh strip-light of an interview room in Harcourt Terrace garda station, Redmond started to talk. Before long, the history of his bizarre and often sordid life of graft started to unfold.

⋖⋗∘⋖⋗

The year was 1948. Ireland was in an economic slump. People were emigrating in droves. But some people were getting ahead. George Redmond was a junior clerk in Dublin Corporation, a newly-promoted 24-year-old who was in the first years of his 'career for life' in the public service. Redmond's job was to look after the Council's corporate tenants. That year, he advised a businessman on the tax implications of a property he was renting from Dublin Corporation. The man expressed his gratitude by offering Redmond a voucher for a city centre hardware store. Redmond took it.[3]

So began four decades in the twilight zone of morality. At best, Redmond was over-helpful and too close to the developers and politicians with whom he hob-nobbed in the succeeding years; often, he was downright corrupt, taking money, favours, services, anything he could get his hands on, in return for advice, influence, access. He just termed it 'extra-mural activity'.

To this day, Redmond — 'J.R.' to his friends[4]— repeats the mantra that he was only offering 'advice' and that none of the gifts he received was ever solicited. But the scale of his activities tells a different story. His diary for 1988 — the only one to survive his retirement — is littered with dozens of meetings with developers, many held during office hours. Between 1979 and 1989 alone, £1.2 million passed through his many bank accounts. His salary at the time was £29,000 a year.

Like Charles Haughey, Redmond was a man of humble origins, who came through a tough childhood to prosper in his adult years. Like Haughey, he attended 'Joey's' Christian Brothers school in Marino (Haughey was in the year behind Redmond). The comparisons with Haughey end here; while the politician went on to revel in his riches, spending lavishly on the best food and wine, surrounding himself with the finest art in a grand period mansion, Redmond was a miser who never enjoyed his wealth. He spent a few years at O'Connell Schools on North Richmond Street, later to be Ray Burke's *alma mater*,[5] before joining Dublin Corporation in December 1941.

Not long after he cashed the hardware store voucher, Redmond mentioned to a client that a metal rocking horse had caught his eye in a store. The businessman invited him to charge the toy to his account. What started as a trickle became a flow. Redmond provided business people with tax advice and reaped the rewards. In the mid-1950s, he provided advice to someone who was trying to sell a 'decrepit' building in Temple Bar. Arising out of this, he was 'facilitated' with a trade-in on his old car,[6] and got a 'box of chocolates and a few pounds' every Christmas from the builder.

Redmond married in 1954 and got a site on the Howth Road, helpfully provided by the Corporation. He played badminton daily and, curiously, developed a profitable sideline in the trading of cigarette cards.

By 1965, Redmond was an assistant principal officer. He had extensive knowledge of property matters and was assuming responsibility for planning for the first time. Developers started dropping wads of notes in his pocket at Christmas-time. Car-dealers supplied him with new models. Builders were happy to carry out repairs at the Redmond home; later, he would pursue them to build extensions and carry out other improvements for no cost.

As the cycle turned from boom to bust and then boom again, Redmond's steady rise up through the ranks at Dublin Corporation continued. He was promoted at least ten times during his career, becoming assistant city and county manager in the late 1970s.

The swinging sixties were followed by Ireland's accession to the European Community in the early 1970s. The economy surged and Redmond's office was flooded with requests from property developers to rezone thousands of acres of land for housing. Paddy Tracey, a former colleague in the Corporation, urged Redmond to join him in the private sector. 'He was good-humoured, an extraordinary gambler. All the draughtsmen were doing private work, mainly houses, certainly Paddy was,' Redmond recalled to the gardaí. He declined Tracey's offer, but stayed friends, and Tracey brought him on golf outings to meet his new employers.

In the early 1970s, Tracey took his friend to Hollywood Rath in west Dublin to meet Matt Gallagher, one of the most successful developers of the period. Gallagher, along with his brothers James (who served as a Fianna Fáil TD) and Hubert, was typical of many developers of the post-War era. He was born west of the Shannon, in Tubbercurry, County Sligo, left school early, and made a fortune in the building trade in England. Then he came home to create a vast building and property empire through a combination of toil and business guile. By 1970, the Gallagher Group was the biggest housebuilder in Dublin. Matt was also a close friend and major benefactor of Charles Haughey. His son, Patrick Gallagher, gave Haughey £300,000 in 1979. The Gallagher Group built Redmond's second house in Castleknock in 1971 and later added a two-story extension.[7] He says Tracey gave him 'a good deal' on the house and was paid in cash. Redmond didn't need a mortgage.

Redmond told gardaí Tracey was Gallagher's 'bagman' but withdrew the description before the tribunal. He says he advised Gallagher on how to appeal when his planning applications were refused. He never solicited money but it came anyway. Redmond admits receiving £10,000 to £15,000 from Gallagher, or Tracey on his behalf, during the 1970s. Those were considerable sums; at the time, a university lecturer earned £2,000 a year, and £15,000 would buy a period house in Dublin 4. Holidays in Majorca were also paid for. Unsurprisingly, he 'idolised' Matt Gallagher, whom he described as a 'warm and affectionate man'.[8] Others remember Gallagher differently. He fought running battles with preservation groups trying to save Georgian Dublin from his wrecking ball. Then there was the way he dealt with unwanted tenants. 'The thing to do is to get two bags full of starving rats and let them loose in the attic. Your problems will be gone inside a week,' he once told a developer friend.[9]

Tracey also introduced Redmond to P.V. Doyle, another wealthy businessman with Fianna Fáil connections. Doyle owned a chain of hotels in Dublin, and in one of them, the Montrose, Redmond, Tracey and Doyle met up for a pre-Christmas drink one year. Doyle gave Redmond a few hundred pounds as a seasonal gift. Redmond says he never gave the hotelier any advice about planning. He described a second payment by Doyle as an attempt 'to ingratiate himself with me over his hotel development plans'. Another builder,

Batt O'Shea, who had difficulties with vandals on a site in Portmarnock, went to Redmond rather than the gardaí. Redmond helped ease the problem, and O'Shea threw him £200 'for golf balls'.[10]

These are the sort of pittances that Redmond can recall receiving. They amount to just a fraction of the overall sum of £1.2 million he says he got from businessmen and politicians. One of his main contacts was Pat Dunne, a henchman of Ray Burke's who was Fianna Fáil's chief whip on the County Council. Redmond told the gardaí he got £10,000 from Dunne in the mid-1980s after signing a compulsory purchase order on Buzzardstown House, a period property surrounded by farmland near Blanchardstown in west Dublin. Dublin County Council wanted the lands for use as local authority housing and paid the going rate, he said.

The owner of an electrical store in Portmarnock, Dunne lived above his shop and was not outwardly wealthy. It is believed that Dunne, who died several years ago, was acting on behalf of a property developer in the deal. Before the tribunal, however, Redmond changed his evidence and denied getting money from Dunne.[11] Asked why he lied to the gardaí, he said: 'I don't know what got into me'. The allegation was 'a balancing factor' to compensate for not having told the gardaí about another of his donors, he explained.

Of the few identified benefactors of George Redmond, Mayo-born builders Tom Brennan and Joe McGowan were the most generous. Brennan and Redmond met in the 1960s in connection with a building matter and were soon bosom pals. While McGowan ran with the horsey set, the more homespun Brennan became Redmond's regular golfing partner. Throughout the 1970s and 1980s, the two builders were also bankrolling Ray Burke.

By the mid-1970s, Brennan and McGowan were the largest firm of house-builders in Ireland, turning out more than 700 houses a year. However, their reputation for poor quality and unfinished work was already well established. The two builders were the targets of more litigation by Dublin County Council than any other developer, arising from breaches of the planning code on uncompleted housing estates.

Kilnamanagh, near Tallaght in west Dublin, was their first big project. It was supposed to be a 'landscaped garden suburb' of 1,600 houses, with plenty of open space and numerous other facilities.

When the scheme was announced in 1973, Brennan and McGowan promised: 'When you buy a home at Kilnamanagh, you get more than just a nice home. You buy a whole community — shops, super-markets, bank, pub, garage, schools, churches, a community club and 50 acres of open space'. Six years later, county councillors were call-ing for an inquiry into the 'mess' which had been created. Roads were unsurfaced, some of the houses were defective and the open space was littered with heaps of rubble. There was no sign — and wouldn't be for years — of the promised amenities.

There was nothing anyone could do about it. Attempts to compel the two builders to complete existing estates before they were granted new planning permissions came to naught. Operating through a maze of front companies, they continued to get permissions without any difficulty.

Brennan's generosity to his friend in the Corporation was enor-mous. Over twenty years, the builder says he paid Redmond £50,000 in a succession of small payments and seasonal 'gifts'. The money was the accumulation of a series of successful bets he had placed on Redmond's behalf, he explained to the tribunal. He'd place bets every two or three weeks. The amounts varied between £100 and £200. When he got a tip that a horse was 'well', he'd ring his friend: 'This horse has a chance — I'll put something on for you'.[12] Asked why Redmond didn't use his own money to place the bets, Brennan said it was 'no use' telling someone to back a horse four days before the race. The proper time to give the information was just before the horse left the ring, he explained to incredulous lawyers.

Redmond's estimate of the amount he got from Brennan was much higher, at about £250,000. There was no talk about horses and bets; rather, the money was a consultancy fee for giving opinions and advice about lands. 'He'd rather come to me than go to the Law Library,' Redmond said of his builder friend. For years, he would travel out to Brennan's stud farm in County Meath to collect a retainer of £300 or £400 each week.

Brennan and Redmond continued to play golf together until the mid-1980s. 'Then George had trouble with his knee and did not play as much,' said Brennan. But there was another reason for their estrangement, one that Brennan referred to delicately as 'the com-pensation issue'. At this time, Brennan and McGowan were suing

the County Council after one of their companies, Grange
Developments, was refused planning permission for a development at
Mountgorry, near Swords.[13] Redmond, as the *de facto* Dublin county
manager, was centrally involved in the Council's response to the
claim. In March 1989, Grange received the largest single payment in
Irish planning history when Redmond signed a cheque for £1.9
million. He claimed the Council faced bankruptcy unless it agreed to
pay. Brennan told the tribunal he never discussed Mountgorry with
Redmond. But their relationship 'cooled off dramatically' as a result
of the claim, he acknowledged.

⋐⋙∘⋘⋙

Before he became assistant city and county manager in the late
1970s, Redmond was in charge of planning for Dublin. If anything
moved in the land business in County Dublin, he knew about it. He
was deeply involved in day-to-day decisions on development control
and he knew all the big developers in the regions. He sat in on all
the Council meetings and parleyed with the local politicians.

He was the man to bring buyers and sellers together, to dispense
nuggets of planning information, to check the files in the Corporation.
He had the maps and he knew the future plans of the Council for
roads and sewerage. He had the say in decisions to grant planning
permission and the conditions to be attached. He had reserved
functions that allowed him to overrule the views of professional
colleagues. His input was crucial in determining the level of contribution a developer would make in return for roads, sewerage and
water supply being provided in new housing estates. He could decide
whether to order enforcement procedures on developers to make safe
a dangerous building or to complete housing estates.

Former colleagues remember a tyrannical boss, who was never
slow to point the finger of blame at others. Neither was Redmond
afraid to take on the councillors who disagreed with his view; he
frequently lectured the local representatives in the Council chamber
in O'Connell Street on their rights and responsibilities. If he had a
view of planning that extended beyond his self-interest, it was *laissez-
faire*. The developers — the same people who were beating down the
door of his office — knew best. In 1989, after the County Council

agreed to double the size of the Blanchardstown shopping centre at the behest of its developers, he explained this decision by saying: 'These fellows have done their sums and this is what they believe will work. Who are we to say it won't?'

Deeply insecure, Redmond never learned to enjoy his ill-gotten riches. Once the extra money went into his bank account it 'never came out,' he admitted.[14] Stories of his frugality abound. He was said to wear a coat at home to save on heating bills. Here was a man who brought his lunch to work every day in a sandwich-box, even when he rose to be the county's leading bureaucrat. He preferred to drive a twelve-year-old banger rather than buy a new car — unless, that is, one of his business contacts was willing to 'gift' him a new model. Rather than fork out money on the newspapers, he would read the front pages in the shop while his garage-owner friends filled his car with free petrol. He told gardaí he never spent more than £20 a week and described himself, not without pride, as an abstemious person.

Spanish holidays were his main, perhaps only indulgence. Redmond's all-year-round tan became a familiar sight at the meetings of Dublin County Council, in an era when winter holidays were rare. After one such holiday in the Canaries, he boasted that he had managed to live on £8 during the week.

Colleagues gleefully swapped stories and jokes about his stinginess. The story of Redmond haggling for a pair of shoes and then insisting on a free pair of laces did the rounds. When one official spotted a JCB digging on a street one day, he remarked to a friend: 'George must have lost a shilling'. The builder, Batt O'Shea, summed up Redmond to a tee. When asked to explain why he paid Redmond money in return for his help with a problem on one of his sites, O'Shea explained: 'I gave him £200 one time to buy golf balls. If his ball went into the rough, he'd spend the day looking for it. It was like 'twas gold to him'.[15]

Awash with cash and little inclined to spend it, he landed large sums on his children and grandchildren. When his son John married, Redmond gave him £42,500 to buy a house in Leeson Park, one of the finest streets in Dublin 4. By 1998, the tribunal has calculated, Redmond's gifts to his two sons totalled over £150,000 and a further £55,000 had been bestowed on grandchildren. There was also a holiday cottage in Wexford purchased in 1993 ('I didn't even like it,' he told the tribunal) and an apartment in Dublin he bought in 1995, with a total value of over £100,000. Redmond also purchased £210,000 in bonds for his two sons.

Outside work, his main pleasure was sport. He played tennis, badminton, squash and golf regularly and obsessively. He sorely missed this outlet when he was forced to give up most sport after suffering strokes in 1982 and 1991.

❧

Brennan and McGowan were Redmond's largest benefactors, but they weren't the only ones to give him money. The full list will probably never be known unless Redmond chooses to provide it, but details of a number of other payments have emerged in recent years. We know, for example, that Redmond got £10,000 as a 'personal thank-you' from Tom Roche senior of National Toll Roads (NTR) in 1997, allegedly paid for the official's help in advancing the West Link bridge project. Roche had already given Redmond £5,000 a few years earlier. The company denies any knowledge of the payment.

Roche was one of Ireland's leading businessmen, 'an entrepreneur with vision' in the words of an obituary printed in *The Irish Times* on his death in July 1999. He founded Roadstone Ltd and then masterminded the creation of Cement Roadstone Holdings (CRH), an amalgam of the largest and third-largest cement companies in the country. At the time, CRH's stranglehold on the cement market excited much comment, but Fianna Fáil in government was happy to live with it and Seán Lemass became its first chairman. Des Traynor, Charles Haughey's bagman, who smoothed the way for the new company, followed Roche as chairman and ended up using his office as an offshore bank; in 1987 eight of the fifteen members of the CRH board had connections to the Ansbacher bank in the Cayman Islands.

Roche then set up NTR, which secured the lucrative contracts to build and run the East Link and West Link bridges across the River Liffey. Redmond's palm was greased because he 'helped to hurry up progress in little bits of ways,' Roche explained. NTR needed to acquire a house owned by Redmond's friend, Jim Kennedy, at Strawberry Beds before the West Link toll bridge could proceed. The Council file on the property went missing, only to turn up years later when the Criminal Assets Bureau raided Redmond's house in February 1999. Roche also made substantial payments to the Fianna Fáil TD, Liam Lawlor, with whom Redmond was in frequent contact.

Garage owner Brendan Fassnidge paid Redmond £5,000 around the time the official intervened in a planning problem he was facing. Fassnidge needed access from his garage to the Lucan bypass at Palmerstown, although planning regulations prohibited such access to main roads for safety reasons. Redmond told his officials to seek £120,000 for the connecting strip of land, but Fassnidge offered only £5,000. A helpful county councillor took up the cudgels on behalf of Fassnidge and promised to raise the matter directly with Redmond. Employing the time-worn reasons put forward by politicians, he pleaded that Fassnidge was a local man and the area needed the filling station jobs.

Ultimately, Fassnidge paid £10,000 for the land. An envelope containing £5,000 slipped through Redmond's letter box shortly after. Redmond told the tribunal in May 2000 there was a shortage of petrol stations in the area. But even he had to admit this was 'an extraordinary transaction'. It emerged that Fassnidge didn't own the land on which his garage was situated; all he had was an option on the site, which he would then sell on with planning permission to one of the oil companies. Far from there being a shortage of filling stations in the area, official documents showed there were two other outlets within 600 metres of the site.

Another garage owner is alleged to have paid Redmond £10,000, again to secure access to a main road in west Dublin in the late 1980s. Redmond says he provided the businessman with information on the Council's plans for compulsory purchase orders and availed of free petrol at the garage, but denies receiving money. The garage owner has denied the claim.

Redmond also got £2,000 from Liam Conroy, chief executive of JMSE, 'as a throwaway gesture'[16] after he prepared a report for the company on the status of its lands in north Dublin in 1987. Again, Redmond didn't see the payment as inappropriate and said it had nothing to do with his official duties.

He has pointed the tribunal to other donors, some of whom had not been named at the time of writing. For example, he says he received £20,000 from one developer, later identified as Michael Bailey, in a number of cash payments, made in the vestibule of Dublin County Council offices and other venues in the 1980s. He didn't tie the payments to any particular piece of advice he gave. Bailey denies having paid any money to Redmond.

Another building firm, Dwyer Nolan Developments, denied an allegation that it gave £20,000 to Redmond. However, Eddie O'Dwyer told the *Irish Examiner* that his firm had carried out work on Redmond's home to the value of about £20,000.[17] Redmond told the tribunal he examined a file relating to one of the company's developments in Castleknock. 'I wanted to see what was involved,' he explained. According to O'Dwyer, Redmond continued to ask him to do further work. 'He was always suggesting something else to be done at the house.' Redmond also mentioned another landowner who sent him £5,000 each year over a three-year period, but claimed he never cashed the cheques.[18]

⋘◦⋙

June 1989 — the same month that Ray Burke and another Fianna Fáil minister, Pádraig Flynn, received their controversial donations — was pencilled in as Redmond's retirement date. In his last years in the job, Redmond worked hard to call in favours, tie up loose ends and extract promises of lucrative consultancy deals.

However, in February of that year, he got a terrible shock. Persistent reports of corruption in the planning system had forced the Government to order a Garda investigation. As the most senior official in the area, Redmond drew the attention of investigating detectives. Property developer Tom Gilmartin identified him to gardaí, without using his name, as a 'kingpin'. Two builders told gardaí that Redmond was rumoured to be 'heavily involved in bribery and illegal deals in connection with planning'. There was a further allegation that Redmond had been paid £100,000 in return for saving a developer over £500,000 for a connection to water and sewerage services across Council lands.

Redmond saw that his thin veneer of respectability was in danger of disintegrating. 'They scared the daylights out of me,' he told the gardaí in 1999.[19] For a time, he became a recluse, and kept his distance from his developer friends. After getting a tip-off from a Fianna Fáil councillor that he was under investigation, he cut what he later called the 'umbilical cord' with Tom Brennan. The danger passed, but Redmond kept his head down. Even when Paddy Tracey died in 1998, he was too afraid to attend the funeral.

Redmond's misdeeds might have gone unnoticed and unpunished if he hadn't suffered 'collateral damage' in James Gogarty's bitter war with Joseph Murphy senior. From 1995, the former JMSE chairman started drip-feeding his allegations about Ray Burke, Murphy and, almost incidentally, Redmond.

With each passing year, Redmond's state of panic mounted as the media's interest in 'a former leading planning official' grew. In the 1980s, he had survived Garda inquiries unscathed, but this time he was retired and powerless to influence events. He made a panicked visit to Gogarty's home in August 1997, two days after the *Sunday Business Post* had printed an extensive account of Gogarty's allegations. Gogarty was ill and wouldn't see him, so Redmond left a note. 'Jim, I would like to talk to you for a few minutes. Sorry you are unwell,' he wrote, but left without getting an audience. Gogarty kept the note.

Ironically, Redmond's dealings with Gogarty and the developer Michael Bailey date from the very end of his forty-seven-year career in the Corporation. In the late 1980s, while on a walk in the Phoenix Park, he ran into Bailey for the first time. The developer asked him if he knew of any building land for sale. True to form, Redmond rang Bailey in early 1988 with some information; James Gogarty of JMSE was selling land at Forest Road in Swords. He arranged for the three of them to meet in the Clontarf Castle hotel.

Asked why Redmond put himself out so much for a man he'd only met once before, Bailey said he couldn't explain it. 'Lots of people do things for you in life and you never see them again'. This was one favour he would live to regret.

Gogarty and Redmond knew each other through Batt O'Shea. Gogarty also knew Redmond through his company's ownership of the Gaiety Theatre, which Redmond would attend whenever JMSE threw him free tickets. Then in 1988, when JMSE had planning difficulties with land it owned at Forest Road in Swords, he approached Bailey to set up a meeting with Redmond. Bailey organised a meeting in Redmond's offices the following day, according to Gogarty.[20] Redmond's surviving diary for 1988 shows that he met Bailey and Gogarty regularly during this period.

Gogarty claims Redmond got a ten per cent 'cut' — somewhere between £12,000 and £15,000 — for the planning advice he provided on the Forest Road land. Murphys had planning permission to build 206 houses at Forest Road but had done nothing with it, and the permission was about to wither. It could always look for a new permission but this was likely to incur objections from residents, as well as new — and much higher — planning levies. Such levies are imposed on developers by local authorities to pay for the cost of road, sewerage and other essential services.

Redmond, Gogarty alleged, devised a stratagem for getting JMSE's existing permission extended with no additional levies. Under the deal, the company paid the old levy immediately, in return for which the Council agreed that no new levy would be imposed when a fresh planning application was lodged. According to Gogarty, Redmond even drafted the letter JMSE sent to achieve this aim in May 1988, a month before the planning permission was due to expire. The Council agreed to the proposal later that month and the company sent a cheque for £122,000 in June. The result was that Murphys succeeded in paying the levy at the minimal 1983 rate, in 1988. It promptly sold the land for over £1.3 million to Bailey, who inherited the benefit from the deal with the council when his company filed a new planning application.

Redmond says he had 'no hand, act or part' in the decision by the Council to accept the deal offered by Murphys. He claims Gogarty cut a secret deal with Bailey, and sold Forest Road for significantly less than the highest offer received. Redmond admits he received money from JMSE, but says it was paid as a 'finder's fee' for introducing Bailey to Gogarty. According to Redmond: 'I was doing Mr Gogarty a favour. There was nothing more than that'. One spring or summer evening in 1988 or 1989, he says he went to Clontarf Castle, where Gogarty handed him an envelope containing £25,000 with the words: 'This is for you, George'. But if, as the tribunal believes, Bailey and Gogarty already knew each other, this explanation falls apart.

Redmond also argued in response to Gogarty's allegations that he had no authority in the area of planning. 'I had limited powers and they did not include planning,' the 74-year-old declared from the back of the tribunal hall in February 1999. 'Gobbledegook!' retorted the 81-year-old witness, Gogarty. 'If he wanted to not be involved the man should have told me, "look, you should go to the planning department and the drainage department, the road department and the sewerage departments," and we wouldn't be here today.'[21]

Redmond claimed he actually saved the Council money on Forest Road but his former employers disagreed. Fingal County Council would later tell the tribunal that a fee of £302,060 to £342,860 would have been due on a new planning permission, depending on the method of calculation used.[22] Whatever happened, therefore, the tax-payer ended up paying £180,000 to £220,000 more than was necessary to develop the land.

Gogarty also alleges that his company offered Redmond a post-retirement consultancy. Liam Conroy, JMSE's former chief executive made the original offer, but after his departure in a boardroom coup in 1988, it could not be honoured. Redmond would need to be compensated. Gogarty claims Michael Bailey suggested a figure of £25,000 would suffice to pay off the official, but this was too much for the Murphys. Eventually, Gogarty claims, Redmond was paid £15,000 by Joseph Murphy junior over tea in Clontarf Castle in 1989. Murphy, Bailey and Redmond all deny Gogarty's claims.

Redmond also denied an allegation by Redmond that he 'stuck his neck out' on the demolition of a listed house, Turvey House. And then there were Gogarty's minor but colourful allegations which dovetailed with the popular image of Redmond as a grasping free-loader. For example, Gogarty claimed Redmond enjoyed a box at the Gaiety courtesy of JMSE. The official was also said to have asked Gogarty if he had any housepainters available to do a job in his house.

Redmond had one further dealing with Michael Bailey, just days before he retired in June 1989. On behalf of the Council, he bought a nine-acre parcel of land from Bailey to create a riverside park near Swords. Redmond boasted later how he 'browbeat' the developer into selling the land for £30,000. It was the final 'feather in my cap' at the end of a long career.

Unfortunately, the facts point to a rather different situation. Only two months before, the lands had been professionally valued at only £14,000. Swampy and uneven, they had little development potential, the valuer concluded. So anxious was Redmond to conclude the deal that he agreed to Bailey's offer on the same day the developer came to his office — a course of action that was unprecedented in the history of the Council. He consulted with no one, left no notes, sought no independent valuation and moved so fast he wasn't even sure how many acres were in the parcel of land.

After Redmond retired, Bailey claimed to council officials that the two men had agreed as part of the Swords deal to write off over £18,000 in levies he owed on another housing scheme. Redmond denies he made such an agreement, but he wasn't contacted at the time and the Council did waive the levy. After a further evaluation, it ended up paying £39,000. So, instead of getting the land for £14,000 the Council ended up spending £57,000. The 'feather' in Redmond's cap came with a far higher price than initially envisaged.

Once the Flood tribunal was set up in 1997, it was only a matter of time before Redmond came under its spotlight. At first, he played cat and mouse with the tribunal. Vainglorious to the last, he made great claims for his own importance in planning, asserting to know 'where the bodies are buried'. Yet when questioned on specifics he could remember little, claimed to have kept no accounts and was unable to dig up any records. He fended off the lawyers as long as possible, sometimes promising to cooperate but ultimately failing to provide much original information. The tribunal warned him he would have to pay his own and the tribunal's legal costs if he failed to cooperate.

Just before the tribunal's public hearings were due to start, Redmond went to the High Court to stop Gogarty's allegations being investigated in public. He lost, then appealed to the Supreme Court in January 1999. Again, he lost. The miserly official was left to contemplate horrendous legal bills, estimated at over £100,000, as Gogarty took the stand in the same month. On his arrest in February,

Redmond claimed the reason he withdrew cash from the Isle of Man was to clear his legal costs.

The net tightened. On 26 January, the tribunal ordered him to produce all his financial records for 1988 and 1989. In early February, there was intense speculation that Redmond might become a 'friendly witness' before the tribunal. On 10 February, he gave the tribunal a letter of consent allowing access to his accounts in the Isle of Man. However, talks between the tribunal and his lawyers were inconclusive, and on 19 February, the tribunal extended its order. It now wanted all his financial records back to 1970. This was the day Redmond boarded that fateful flight to the Isle of Man, which led to his arrest and later conviction on tax charges.

His bizarre, impulsive behaviour continued. On his release from jail, he showed up again at the tribunal. On meeting James Gogarty exiting from the hall one day, he called out: 'The two of us side by side, wouldn't that make a lovely picture, Jim?' The octogenarian witness nimbly sidestepped the younger man and made good his departure.[23]

Redmond filed a second statement, admitting for the first time that he got money from developers.[24] But he also contradicted his earlier denials of Gogarty's allegations. Having previously claimed there was no meeting at Clontarf Castle, he now said there were *two*. The only two contributors he identified at this stage were Gogarty and Liam Conroy.

The documents seized from Redmond's house on the night of his arrest then became the subject of a remarkable and still unexplained legal tussle between the tribunal and the Criminal Assets Bureau. CAB, a joint Garda/Revenue Commissioners operation set up in the wake of the Veronica Guerin murder in 1996, enjoyed far greater powers than the regular gardaí. The bureau spent its first few years snaring 'ordinary decent criminals' but the temptation to alter its profile and target white-collar crime was growing. Redmond, the Bureau's first white-collar 'catch', represented new ground and brought the promise of widespread publicity.

The two bodies fought a turf war all the way to the Supreme Court over two cardboard boxes containing Redmond's financial documentation. The tribunal argued that CAB was conducting 'a parallel criminal investigation' that would jeopardise its own inquiries. Mr Justice Flood described Redmond as the 'red apple in the basket'. 'The CAB came in, said "we like red apples" and took it away with them,' he remarked.[25] The tribunal eventually won the battle with CAB, but lost months of valuable time. The taxpayer, as ever, was left to foot the bill. Then, within hours of the court ruling in July 1999 that CAB should hand over Redmond's files, bureau detectives arrested Redmond. He even turned up at the Bridewell for his arrest by prior appointment with the detectives.

He was charged with failing to make tax returns over a ten-year period, hardly the most breathtaking of misdemeanours. The offence carries a theoretical maximum penalty of five years in jail and/or a fine of £10,000, but the reality is that no-one goes to jail for tax offences. Was it for this that CAB cut across the tribunal's investigation and engaged in so much time-consuming and costly litigation?

So why did CAB swoop on Redmond when it knew the tribunal was already investigating? After all, the gardaí had investigated Redmond in 1989 and 1997 without achieving much. The Bureau was not known to have any active interest in the former planning chief until the day of his arrest. In contrast, the tribunal had been on his case for months and had interviewed him several times. Redmond had begun to provide some information and on the very day of his arrest, the tribunal had issued an order for more documents to be provided.

The head of the bureau, Chief Superintendent Fachtna Murphy, later explained that that CAB had received information that had 'thrown a totally different light on the previous Garda investigation and the reasons why in respect of George Redmond there hadn't been a prosecution'. This tantalising reference has yet to be explained.

❦

Redmond finally made his long overdue appearance in the witness box in September 1999. At first, he exuded the old confidence, and it was as though the humiliations of the previous few months had never happened. There was more than a touch of Louis XIV to his self-image: 'I was the Council; I had the powers,' he declared.[26] Everything he did was on behalf of the Council. And like Louis XIV, he assembled vast tracts of land to create parks and gardens. During his time as assistant manager, Redmond noted with swelling pride, more than 4,500 acres of parkland was created in Ardgillan, Newbridge, Tymon and other areas of County Dublin.

But even if he wasn't providing the details at this stage, it was apparent that the former official had received a lot of money from 'entrepreneurs' over several decades. Pat Hanratty SC, for the tribunal, asked again and again if he had sources of income apart from his official salary. Redmond at first declined to answer the question, whereupon Flood reminded him that a failure to reply could land him two years in jail. Redmond paused for what seemed like an infinity, before acknowledging that, yes, he had got money.[27]

A seemingly contrite witness said he was sorry for what he had done. 'I deeply regret, in any circumstance, that I did what I did,' he said when asked about the fact that he took payments in return for advice.[28] It was clear he had broken the rules of conduct for local authority officials, which require the declaration of gifts or outside interests, and the avoidance of 'unjust enrichment' by officials drawing remuneration other than their salary. But how contrite was Redmond? When the tribunal asked him for permission to obtain his telephone records, he said he would first have to consult his solicitor. Then it was revealed that of all the diaries Redmond had given the tribunal, every single one was found to be blank.

By this time, a decade after his retirement, the 75-year-old former official cut a pathetic figure. Weakened by adversity, old age and a series of health scares, he clung to notions of his innocence and to old habits. On one occasion, he asked Flood for a longer lunch-break so he could travel from Dublin Castle to Castleknock where, presumably, his wife Maureen could fix him a lunch for free. Not surprisingly, the chairman rejected his request. Touched by reports of his plea, a local café-owner offered him a free lunch. But when Redmond turned up on succeeding days looking for a repeat deal, the story ended up in the newspapers, and he was made to look like a cheapskate.

In the witness box, Redmond's powers of recall continued to vary dramatically. He claimed no knowledge of massive contributions made to him by developers, yet the surviving records showed that he tracked his finances 'down to the last penny'. He doubled or halved the size of payments from builders at a stroke of recollection, yet he was able to correct tribunal lawyers over a mere £20 deposit he made in the mid-1980s. Under pressure, he remembered new donations he had neglected to mention to the gardaí in 1999, and retracted others he had related to CAB detectives in great detail. He had to be threatened with court proceedings before he produced to the tribunal details of his bank accounts.[29]

The seemingly modest official had an ability to conjure huge amounts of money out of almost nothing. For an ordinary bureaucrat on a modest annual salary — after-tax pay about £19,000 a year at its maximum — Redmond had a knack for investing that George Soros would be proud of. In 1988, for example, his investments were worth £660,000, or almost thirty-five times his yearly wage.[30] In the same year he lodged £171,000, after interests and inter-account lodgements were deducted, to his accounts, It was easily more than the £150,000 he earned in the decade spent as assistant Dublin city and county manager between 1980 and 1989.

With so much money sloshing around in his accounts, and Redmond providing little information on where it came from, tribunal lawyers had difficulty identifying the payments individually, let alone their source. From the witness box, Redmond asked for the tribunal's analysis of his accounts as an aide to his memory. It was pointed out that he had had this document for months beforehand. When he claimed to have made a full disclosure of his accounts, it was pointed out that he had declared just eight of the thirty-three accounts the tribunal eventually discovered.[31]

For much of his evidence, Redmond remained evasive and uncooperative. At one point, Mr Justice Flood accused him of 'selective amnesia' and of portraying himself as a gullible character. In a thinly disguised threat to impose costs, he was repeatedly asked to 'reflect' on his evidence and 'refurbish his memory'. Under sustained questioning, he finally admitted receiving about £350,000 in payments from various builders and other businessmen. But this was only a fraction of the amount he is believed to have received. The tribunal finally came to an estimate of £1,051,360 for the assets Redmond accumulated between 1971 and 1998. As Des O'Neill SC, for the tribunal, pointed out, in the 1980s alone he received the value of 'eight or nine houses'.

He finished his evidence in typical fashion, boasting, 'I put together two Phoenix Parks on my own' through land acquisition. He also admitted to 'conning' people out of hundreds of thousands of pounds by negotiating hard on behalf of the Council. However, the 'people' he had in mind were the same class of developers who paid him so much money, not the rest of us who had to listen to such guff.

The only prompt for his limited memory was a small pocket diary for 1988, the single record of a forty-year career to survive to this day. Found by the CAB when it raided his house in February 1999, the diary confounded many of the arguments he made in evidence. Redmond, in his evidence, called it 'a gift from the gods' and swore he didn't know of its existence. The diary lists contacts with nine separate politicians in this year, thereby contradicting Redmond's pretence that he 'rarely' met elected representatives. Fianna Fáil councillors Seán Walsh and Pat Dunne, both since deceased, feature strongly. There is evidence of eleven contacts with one developer, and ten with another. Both developers were major contributors.

Redmond's records revealed he hoarded £35,000 in cash in the bathroom of his home in 1984, £12,000 cash in the kitchen, and £8,000 in cheques. When DIRT tax was introduced, he opened an offshore account in the Isle of Man in 1986 with a lodgement of £105,000. As Mr Justice Flood noted, it showed Redmond knew his financial situation down 'to the last penny'. But as he admitted: 'I never did anything with it'.

Redmond put down his financial success to the fact that he was a 'heavy saver'. Interest rates were high at the time and his offshore savings more than doubled 'without doing anything'. As for records: 'I was a great discarder. I just tore things up'.

To disguise his wealth, he used a series of false or misleading names or addresses. He opened an account in the Ulster Bank at Dublin Airport — the same branch used by Ray Burke — in the name of Seoirse Ó Réamoinn, and another account elsewhere in the name of Seoirse MacRéamoinn. Unknown to them, he also used the addresses of a brother-in-law in Belfast, a sister-in-law in Northampton, England, and a cousin in Mijas, Spain. Many were registered under the Seoirse MacRéamoinn *alias*.

Right to the end of this saga, Redmond continued to live in a world of self-pity. In April 2000, he escaped a custodial sentence after pleading guilty to ten charges of failing to make tax returns. The Circuit Criminal Court imposed a fine of £7,500 after his counsel pleaded that the 75-year-old former official was 'effectively destitute' and in bad health. Only later did it emerge that Redmond, in spite of clear evidence that he had broken the rules of conduct for local authority officials, was still in receipt of a £30,000 annual pension. An appeal by the Director of Public Prosecutions against the leniency of this penalty was unsuccessful. The court later ordered the State to pay the costs of the appeal. His nightmare continued. In 2001, he appeared on corruption charges relating to two land deals in west Dublin.

Redmond's erstwhile pals, the developers he once loved to play golf or have lunch with, were well insulated from opprobrium or financial punishment, thanks to the vast fortunes they acquired through land speculation and rezoning. In contrast, the man from Artane had to sell his family home for £750,000 to meet the demands of the Revenue Commissioners. Under the settlement agreed with the Revenue, he paid a total of £782,000 in tax, interest and penalties.

Friends say Redmond is now a broken man, full of regret for his past behaviour. He rarely goes out and spends most of his time devouring books from the local library or tending to his garden. Yet contrition never came easily or fully. He still clings to the mantra that the advice he gave was unsolicited. Usually, he claims, it could have been obtained from the Council's planning department anyway. But if this were the case, the generosity of so many developers to Redmond is even harder to understand.

❦

If any single event symbolises the greed and neglect gnawing away at the fabric of Dublin, it is the destruction of Turvey House. In tribunal terms, Turvey and its demolition in controversial circumstances in 1987 was just another blind alley, with the truth buried under a welter of denials and conflicting statements. But there were in reality dozens of Turveys around Dublin, historic houses filled with human stories and priceless artefacts that were needlessly sacrificed to the wrecking ball and the avarice of developers.

Legend has it that when Sir Patrick Barnewall was granted lands at Turvey, near Donabate in north county Dublin, during the time of Henry VIII, he decided to build his family house on an area occupied by the convent of Grace Dieu. But when he went to dispossess the abbess, her nuns dropped to their knees and cursed his family, praying that it might 'never want an idiot or a lawsuit, and that the rightful owner should never see the smoke of its chimneys'.

Perhaps there was a curse on Turvey. The Barnewalls, one of Ireland's oldest Norman families, built their 56-room mansion in 1565 and survived there until they were forced to sell in 1918. The Counihan family bought it for £28,000, but fell on hard times and had to sell the property and its 155 acres in 1968.

Turvey saw the ups and downs of history over many centuries. Oliver Cromwell camped nearby. Soldiers returning from the Battle of the Boyne engraved their names on the east-facing drawing room window.[32] In 1933, the skeleton of a man in leg-irons was found in a small stream nearby; it is believed he was hanged for a murder committed in 1770. Primroses and wild violets lined the ditches on its perimeter each spring.

Turvey featured briefly at the Flood tribunal with James Gogarty's allegation that Redmond 'stuck his neck out' on the house. Gogarty said this was in 1989, when Redmond was looking for money from JMSE as compensation for not being taken on as a consultant after his retirement. However, Gogarty was unable to provide more information on the allegation and Redmond denied it.

Gogarty was the effective caretaker of Turvey after his employer, Joseph Murphy senior, bought the estate in 1968. However, JMSE had no interest in history or preservation; the purchase was a long-term investment of agricultural lands that would reach fruition when the estate house was gone and the lands were rezoned for housing. As Gogarty admitted to the tribunal — without conceding personal responsibility — the house was 'let go to rack and ruin'. The demise of Turvey is recorded faithfully in the dry, dusty files of Dublin County Council. By 1973, the house was 'being allowed to deteriorate,' a Council official noted. Fireplaces had been ripped out, the windows were gone and the door was permanently open. The Council told JMSE to board up the building and erect a notice to warn people to stay away. It spent £274 itself on boarding up the house and had to pursue the company in the courts for the money. Nothing then happened for twelve years.

It was February 1986 before the building came to the attention of the Council again. Turvey House was now 'beyond redemption,' senior executive architect Maurice O'Brien concluded after a visit. 'The upper floors are non-existent in places and totally beyond redemption in others. The roof is open to the elements generally.' Mr O'Brien estimated the cost of restoring the house at over £1 million. By contrast, it would cost £70,500 to demolish the house and its outhouses. Turvey House had 'no great architectural merit apart from its antiquity' and the department had 'no hesitation' in recommending its demolition, he concluded.

The conservationist and author Peter Pearson disagrees. 'In historical terms Turvey was a most unusual house; three storeys over basement, nine windows wide and with a magnificent cut stone doorcase which was topped by urns,' he says.[33] During the demolition piece of medieval stonework and carved door and window surrounds from the castle were found. Intact sixteenth-century carved stone fireplaces were unearthed. Pearson visited the derelict Turvey twice, and found it in need of 'stabilisation and repair, not demolition'.

The Council's planning officer said he was opposed to demolition — Turvey was one of only two buildings listed for preservation in County Dublin — but in July 1987 it was pulled down anyway. Gogarty arranged the operation, which was carried out at speed. However, its legality was dubious. Several days after the house was levelled, *The Irish Times* reported that Dublin County Council faced prosecution over the matter.[34] The Office of Public Works claimed the Council had 'illegally interfered' with the building and had failed to give the statutory two months' notice to the OPW of its intention to demolish.

Redmond was quoted as saying he was 'not aware' of the demolition or the fact that the building had been listed for preservation. Yet the Council file shows that officials were clearly aware of the house's listed status. The OPW considered it 'futile' to sue the demolition firm, however, as the order had been issued by the Council, itself a preservation authority under the National Monuments Act.

Redmond played a major part in the controversy that blew up after Turvey was demolished, but there is no evidence on the files that he was involved beforehand. Subsequently, he claimed the Council had contacted the OPW about the house two months before it was pulled down. The OPW said it had no record of this contact, said to be by telephone. The Council claimed it was told, incorrectly, that the building was not listed.

So why did the Council officials not spot the information about the listed status of Turvey that was obvious from their own files? Why did they not consult their boss before knocking down one of only two listed buildings in the Council area? And why did the Council order the demolition of the house in three days, having done virtually nothing for fourteen years?

According to Pearson, hundreds of fine historical buildings, mostly dating from the eighteenth century and often in need of repair, were wiped out in Dublin during the 1970s and 1980s. The Dangerous Buildings Act allowed developers to get rid of a 'difficult' — that is, costly — historical building easily. If vandals got in, smashed the roof and floors and allowed some masonry to tumble from the parapets, a dangerous buildings notice could be issued ordering the demolition of the structure.

In February 1999, just after Redmond's arrest, Progressive Democrat politician Michael McDowell summed up the anger of right-thinking people at the destruction of this priceless heritage. The evidence of how Gogarty presided over Turvey's destruction, 'aided and abetted' by Dublin County Council in the reign of George Redmond, 'makes me sick,' he wrote. 'Did the patron of the arts down the road at Abbeville [Charles Haughey's mansion] not know about Turvey and its destruction? Did the house-proud prince of North Dublin not care about the muck savages who were wrecking the heritage of his beloved hinterland? Truly, he did the State some service. The lot of them should be brought on a tumbrel to the site of Turvey House, tied to a stake and burned on a pyre. Of freshly repatriated cash.'[35]

Turvey estate was turned into a golf course and apartments, with the clubhouse built near the site of the house. It was placed on the market again in October 2000.

As *de facto* county manager, Redmond had reason to know most of
Dublin's councillors and TDs. He was also familiar with many of the
developers in the county. However, one name crops up more regularly than any other in relation to George Redmond during the
1980s. James Kennedy, a publicity-shy publican and businessman,
collaborated on a number of land deals that have yet to be fully
explained. According to one former Fine Gael county councillor, Jim
Fay, Kennedy claimed to act as Redmond's 'bagman' in these deals.[36]
Yet in spite of intense media interest, Kennedy, who is tax-resident
in the Isle of Man, has managed to remain a mysterious figure.

Kennedy started his career as a small farmer in Abbeyleix, County
Laois. In the early 1970s, his farm was compulsorily purchased and
the money provided the seed capital for his first foray into business
in Dublin. He bought The Laurels pub in Clondalkin for £200,000 in
1976 and local politicians and planners soon frequented the adjoining meeting rooms. Kennedy was a Fianna Fáil supporter and
supported the party's representatives in the area. Mary Harney, for
example, held constituency clinics at the pub and says she received
a total of £1,000 to £1,500 in election funding from Kennedy in the
early 1980s. A spokesman says the Tánaiste hadn't seen or heard of
Kennedy since she left Fianna Fáil.

Kennedy dabbled profitably in auctioneering and property
development. In 1989, a cattle dealer told a Garda investigation that
George Redmond had refused to buy thirty-two acres of his land for
the County Council. Yet when Kennedy was employed as auctioneer,
there was a change of heart. Kennedy charged twice the usual fee for
arranging the successful sale.

Kennedy bought an amusement arcade in Westmoreland Street
in Dublin's city centre and used it as his business base. Redmond says
he loaned Kennedy £110,000 in 1980 to invest in another arcade in
Clondalkin.[37] The planning official purchased his weekly shopping
on Kennedy's account at a local cash and carry.[38]

In 1986, Kennedy sold The Laurels for £700,000 and concentrated
on housebuilding. However, two of his property companies went into
receivership and a development at Cooldrinagh, in Lucan, was left
unfinished. Three years later, the gardaí heard allegations that
Redmond had arranged the sewage capacity for the development,
but nothing ever came of these rumours. Liam Lawlor, a business

associate of Kennedy's, says his only involvement in the matter was to lobby on behalf of local residents to have the estate completed.

In an incident that gardaí believe was linked to his problems with Cooldrinagh, Kennedy was the victim of a gun attack in 1992. A gang of men broke into his house in Weston Park in Lucan during the night. Kennedy was able to close a steel door at the top of his stairs to prevent the raiders reaching him. Shots were fired but he was unhurt.[39]

In the early 1970s, Kennedy built a house for himself near the River Liffey, at Strawberry Beds in West Dublin. The house, Oaklands, had no planning permission, which meant it was virtually worthless in resale terms. It was also affected by the plans of National Toll Roads to build the Westlink bridge nearby.

Given its illegal planning status, the County Council could have ordered the demolition of the house. Equally, NTR could have bought it — in fact, this was the original plan. Yet neither of these things happened. When Kennedy sought retention of Oaklands in 1986, the Council agreed, thereby greatly increasing its value. Even though officials could not find the planning file and the house was required for demolition to make way for the West Link, the Council offered to pay £136,000 for a property that had no planning permission.

The Democratic Left TD, Pat Rabbitte, raised the matter in the Dáil in 1990.[40] It 'seems extraordinary that one is expected to believe that there was no insider knowledge in that case,' he remarked. Later, Rabbitte said he had experienced considerable difficulties in getting answers about the transaction. One question he had tabled 'mysteriously disappeared' from the County Council's agenda on two occasions. As noted earlier, the Council's file on Oaklands turned up in Redmond's house when gardaí raided it in 1999, a decade after his retirement. 'When I was leaving my job, I packed some stuff in my bag and this was included,' he explained.

Redmond was a regular visitor to the Strawberry Beds house but it seems he never acquainted himself with its planning problems. As it happened, the house did not need to be demolished to make way for the toll bridge. Yet, as Rabbitte pointed out, compensation was paid out on a deal concluded by the Council with NTR. The house was used as a builder's site office before being sold in 1990 for £121,000, after the bridge was completed.

As previously noted, Tom Roche senior, chairman of NTR, gave Redmond £5,000 in 1989 — nothing to do with the Kennedy house, Redmond told the tribunal — and £10,000 in 1997. Redmond says he first met Kennedy in 1980 when acquiring land for a waste tip in county Dublin. Kennedy negotiated on behalf of an auctioneer who owned a suitable site in Waterstown.[41] Within months, the two men were business partners. Redmond loaned Kennedy £70,000 and contributed another £40,000 to Kennedy and his then partner, Limerick bookmaker Malachy Skelly. The money was used to buy land at Ballyowen Stud, near Lucan, for £1.3 million in 1980. The deposits put down by Skelly and Kennedy were £110,000 each, coincidentally the same amount loaned by Redmond. The debt is recorded in his diaries, though there was no written agreement or securities for the loan.

With the help of a prominent Fianna Fáil councillor,[42] Ballyowen was subsequently rezoned and sold three years later for £3.5 million. The Abbey Group, one of the Gallagher companies associated with Redmond's friend Paddy Tracey, bought the land. For several years, Redmond called into Kennedy's amusement arcade on Westmoreland Street to collect bundles of cash, which he said represented the interest payments on this loan. But Kennedy never repaid any of the capital, he says, although Skelly eventually gave him £10,000 in cash.

Kennedy also figures in the Jackson Way controversy. Around 1988, he was involved in the purchase of a 106-acre parcel of land in Carrickmines in south Dublin. The land was later registered to Jackson Way Properties, an offshore company fronted by nominee directors. Previously, this company had been known as Paisley Park Investments, an Isle of Man shelf company specifically set up in 1987 to buy the lands for about £540,000 from a South Dublin farmer, Robert Tracey.[43] Paisley Park was liquidated in 1994 and ownership of the lands passed to Jackson Way a year later.

Gardaí interviewed Tracey about his dealings with Kennedy during their 1989 investigation of planning corruption. In a sworn statement, Tracey said Kennedy and another man told him during the purchase negotiations that 'your land is zoned agricultural and it will stay that way unless we get it in hand — we have inroads with the planning authorities'. His statement continued: 'Both of them said "£20,000 had to be 'thrown in' to the Fianna Fáil party for starters. There are men who have to get £10,000 each…"'

Kennedy and his associate denied the allegation to Detective Superintendent Brendan Burns, who decided the alleged conversation may have been 'merely business tactics to impress the vendor. There is no evidence of a crime'.

Paisley Park hired Frank Dunlop to lobby for the rezoning of the Carrickmines land. The company paid substantial amounts of money to county councillors for votes on a rezoning motion in 1993, according to an allegation under investigation by the tribunal. Four years later, Fine Gael senator Liam Cosgrave led attempts to rezone most of the land for residential or industrial uses. These attempts failed, but under a compromise supported by Fianna Fáil and Fine Gael councillors, twenty-four acres north of the motorway were rezoned for industry. However, the council had other ideas for the rest of the land, part of which sat straight in the middle of the planned South-Eastern motorway scheme. Twenty acres were needed for the motorway, which was the last section of the planned C-ring scheme around Dublin.

Jackson Way later hired Liam Lawlor as a consultant. Lawlor's associate, the solicitor John Caldwell, denies owning the lands, but he concedes they are held 'to my order'. The company also took legal action to stop construction of the motorway, a move that threatened to cost the taxpayer millions of pounds. Jackson complained about access to its lands and pointed out that the motorway would divide the lands into two sections. It suggested an overpass might be needed to join the two parts. After a great deal of sabre-rattling, the company reached a 'non-financial' settlement with the National Roads Authority and the Department of the Environment just before the matter was due to come before the Supreme Court in December 1999. Only two years later did it emerge that the company's interpretation of a 'non-financial' settlement included a compensation claim for up to £90 million.

In May 2000, Jackson Way's solicitor, Stephen Miley, was summonsed to the tribunal and told to reveal the identity of his clients. On his clients' instructions, he refused to do so, citing client/solicitor confidentiality. Rejecting this argument, the tribunal said it believed the owners of Jackson Way and Paisley Park were the same, and were living in Ireland. It claimed the change of ownership was 'an elaborate charade'. In January 2001, in a decision of major importance for the way solicitors do their business, the High Court ordered Miley to reveal the identity of his clients to the tribunal. Miley appealed to the Supreme Court but this was struck out in March after the solicitor reached a compromise with the tribunal.

Today, Kennedy lives in tax exile, dividing his time between the Isle of Man and the south of France. On rare visits to Ireland, he is reputed to spend the night at his amusement arcade on Westmoreland Street, where thick steel doors ensure his security. Kennedy's anonymity remained perfectly preserved until spring 2001, when Charlie Bird of RTÉ News tracked him down one night on a rain-swept St Stephen's Green. Even then, Kennedy refused all invitations to comment; instead, he pulled the hood of his anorak down over his face and scurried away from the camera as quickly as he could.

4
Corruption Denied

'What we're dealing with here is not just a few backhanders, what we're dealing with is a nest of vipers.'
— Detective Superintendent Brendan Burns, who led the 1989 Garda investigation into allegations of planning corruption

The genteel columns of the back page of *The Irish Times* are normally filled with birthday greetings, discreet advertisements for country hotels and last-minute holiday offers. But on 3 July 1995, a very different advertisement appeared, sandwiched between a death notice and an advertisement for a suit sale.

Under the headline '£10,000 REWARD FUND', a firm of Northern solicitors, Donnelly Neary and Donnelly, appealed for 'information leading to the conviction of (*sic*) indictment of a person or persons for offences relating to Land Rezoning in the Republic of Ireland'. All information would be treated 'in the strictest confidence,' it was promised.

Donnelly Neary and Donnelly was acting on behalf of two anonymous clients. The pair, both thirty-something and with a background in planning law and environmental activism, concocted the idea in frustration at the continuing rumours of planning corruption and the failure of the powers-that-be to act. The reward was an ingenious stroke, dreamt up by dreamers with thin purses, let alone the £10,000 sum that was promised. With hindsight, given the stench that had emanated from planning in Dublin over the previous thirty years, it is amazing that no-one thought of 'smoking out' the rumours before this.

Much later, the two men were revealed as barristers Michael Smith and Colm Mac Eochaidh.[1] Smith, a tall, diffident figure from Loughlinstown in south Dublin, first developed an interest in environmental campaigning in 1992, when developers wanted to build a shopping complex near the home where he grew up. Smith's campaign of opposition propelled the young activist into a world of mailshots and protests and council meetings, and he learned a lot about the suspicious behaviour of some politicians. A non-practising barrister who lives on the income earned from a few buildings he lets, he became the youngest-ever chairman of An Taisce at the age of 33. Smith has always understood that effective protest requires a strong dose of imagination; when the Harcourt Street birthplace of Edward Carson faced the threat of demolition, for example, he promptly phoned the Democratic Unionist Party to enlist its help.

Mac Eochaidh, who has a Fine Gael background and is also from south Dublin, spent time in California and the European Commission in Brussels before starting a Bar practice dominated by environmental and planning issues. In 1996, the two men were involved in setting up Lancefort, a kind of vigilante company that contested large planning permissions and acted as the scourge of Dublin's developers for some years. Its most controversial campaign was the fight against plans to build a Hilton Hotel in the centre of Dublin. The development involved demolishing a number of listed and historic buildings to create a block that would dwarf its surroundings. Hilton eventually won in the courts, but the long and bruising legal battle was a major factor in its decision to pull out of the project. In September 2001, a smaller hotel opened on the site.

For years, there had been serious public disquiet about corruption in the planning system, as tribunal lawyer John Gallagher SC noted in February 2000.[2] Over three decades, there were successive waves of rezoning in Dublin, centred on the publication of each county development plan. The rezonings happened in a haphazard fashion, driven by the dictates of developers rather than the requirement of good planning. Intensive Garda investigations were undertaken in 1974, 1989 and 1993, yet little or nothing happened.

One early recipient of the benefits of land speculation was Charles Haughey, whose farm at Raheny was rezoned shortly before it was sold in 1967. But it was the 1970s before the matter first came to widespread public attention. At this time, two bright young politicians, Ray Burke of Fianna Fáil and John Boland of Fine Gael, represented north Dublin in the Dáil. Both men were councillors. Both men were auctioneers. And both men sold houses that were built on lands they helped to rezone in the council chamber. Allegations of conflicts of interest were made, but the careers of both men advanced unimpeded.

Boland, a four-time chairman of Dublin county council, was involved in at least three controversial land deals. As an auctioneer, he handled the sale of land near Dublin airport, the rezoning of which he had successfully piloted through the County Council. The land's value increased by over £1 million as a result of the decision. He was investigated by the Garda fraud squad in 1973 and 1974 and was interviewed by them on several occasions. The gardaí sent a file to the Director of Public Prosecutions, but no action was taken.

The first Garda investigation stemmed from an article written by Joe McAnthony in the *Sunday Independent*, which appeared to link a £15,000 payment by builders Brennan and McGowan to Ray Burke. In June 1974, McAnthony reproduced documents showing a £15,000 payment from the two builders to Burke under the heading 'Planning'. It was claimed the money represented his share of the proceeds when land at Mountgorry, near Swords, was sold. However, Burke claimed in his defence that the sale of the land had not gone through. As in the case of Boland, a file was sent to the DPP, but no prosecution was taken.

Gardaí also interviewed Brennan and McGowan about allegations surrounding the rezoning of land at Fortunestown, near Tallaght. This was after Dublin Corporation's plans to acquire 700 acres in the area by compulsory purchase order had been resisted by a consortium of six landowners, including Brennan and McGowan. Burke, who says there was 'absolutely nothing improper' about the episode, supported the developers' proposals for the land because 'they were in line with Fianna Fáil policies of promoting free enterprise'. This was the era of Jim Tully, the Labour Minister for Local Government noted for his bizarre and logic-defying planning decisions. Tully frequently overruled the planners and the councillors; indeed, on some occasions, he overruled councillors after they had overruled him. He gave approval to houses in nature reserves, housing estates in the remote countryside and other developments in the path of the proposed Dublin-Belfast motorway.

In 1974, the Kenny report on building land highlighted examples of the huge profits to be made on land speculation and the sophistication of the tax dodging mechanisms in use, even then. In one case, for example, a speculator bought an option on 88 acres at Balally in south Dublin for £440 and sold it less than a year later for £35,000. In 1980, gardaí launched an investigation into alleged planning irregularities surrounding An Bord Pleanála's decision to grant planning permission to a housing development in Killiney, County Dublin. The investigation centred on a senior member of the board who had made the decision. A file was forwarded to the DPP, who ruled that no prosecutions should be taken.

The rezoning frenzy rose to a new peak in the early 1980s. Huge areas to the north, west and south of the city were rezoned, even though there was no shortage of development land. Over a six-month period in 1982, 5,000 acres were rezoned, netting their owners an estimated £200 million in windfall profits.

The *modus operandi* of the councillors was by now firmly established. Fianna Fáil and Fine Gael councillors acted in concert. Most of the motions were proposed and seconded by a core group of half a dozen members, and the rest followed *en bloc*. Those who benefited included party supporters and election workers of the councillors voting through the rezonings. The advice of officials was ignored. *Irish Times* reporter Frank Kilfeather said that in twenty-three years of covering local authority meetings, he had never seen anything to compare to the activities of the Dublin councillors at this time. 'It makes one wonder why they are going through the charade of having a plan at all,' Kilfeather wrote.

A newspaper list of the top ten rezoners in 1982 included five Fianna Fáil councillors, four from Fine Gael and one Labour member. Some of the councillors faded into obscurity, but others went on to have prominent political careers. Liam Lawlor featured prominently on the list as one of those most active in rezoning and moving 'Section 4' applications. Section 4's were resolutions by councillors that forced the county manager to carry out their wishes whether he wanted to or not. It was widely used to force through planning applications which had been rejected by the officials, usually for good planning reasons.

Only one decision bucked this trend. In 1981, councillors voted to reverse an earlier decision to rezone 150 acres of land in Lucan. The reason for the change of heart was nakedly political; Fianna Fáil

TD Liam Lawlor had been unmasked as the owner of some of the rezoned land. Lawlor had left the meeting in April 1981 at which his fellow councillors pushed through the rezoning. But the news that he stood to gain over £300,000 from the move caused a huge public outcry. The Taoiseach, Charles Haughey, called in the Fianna Fáil group and told them to·reverse the decision. Lawlor lost his seat in the general election that followed.

So notorious had the councillors' behaviour become that the Minister for the Environment — none other than Ray Burke — was moved to complain in 1982 of their 'highly objectionable' activities. However, Burke shied away from any proposals to remove the power of councillors to rezone land.

In February 1989, the gardaí started another investigation into allegations of bribery and corruption in the planning process. By now, the man under investigation in the 1974 probe, Ray Burke, was Minister for Justice. A builder, Peter Loughran, complained to the Minister for the Environment, Pádraig Flynn, that he had been approached for money by members of An Bord Pleanála. At the time, he was seeking to develop a hotel in Sligo. Loughran was given immunity from prosecution and became the State's main witness in the trial of an official of the board, William Tobin. But the twenty-three-day trial turned into a disaster for the prosecution, and Loughran spent far longer in the witness box than Tobin. In the end, Tobin was acquitted of soliciting, receiving or obtaining sums of money in return for assisting with planning permission.

Gardaí investigated a wide range of allegations but, with no access to bank accounts, they ended up with little to show for their fifteen months of work, apart from the minor conviction of a building surveyor. The investigating Garda, Detective Superintendent Brendan Burns, came to the conclusion that 'what we're dealing with here is not just a few backhanders, what we're dealing with is a nest of vipers'. However, the lengthy report dismissed allegations of organised corruption: 'Newspaper articles suggested that bribery and corruption were endemic in the Planning Process. Whilst my enquiries were largely confined to the City and County of Dublin, I found this not to be the case'.

The investigation looked into other matters. There were allegations about George Redmond, Liam Lawlor (who emerged 'with his reputation unscathed,' the report concluded) and Charles Haughey, who was alleged to have gained from a pipeline installed across his lands in Kinsealy. Once again, nothing came of the gardaí's inquiries into these allegations.

The rezoning continued unabated. In 1991, Democratic Left TD Éamon Gilmore produced a report detailing the voting patterns of councillors over the previous six years.[3] Since the 1985 local elections, the Council had passed forty-one 'Section 4' motions. Over the same period it granted permission to 131 developments which materially contravened the council's own development plan. Over eighty per cent of these material contraventions were either proposed or seconded by Fianna Fáil councillors and most were voted through by a rump of Fianna Fáil councillors favouring rezoning. Of the 131 material contraventions passed, the manager recommended that the motion should not be passed on ninety-one occasions.

It wasn't as though material contraventions or the rezoning of land were bad in themselves. Often, they are necessary provisions to allow orderly growth of an area. However, as Gilmore pointed out, the problem in Dublin at this time was the frequency and the abuse of these provisions.

The journalist Frank McDonald had no doubts about what he saw unfolding in the council chamber:

It was as plain as a pikestaff to anyone who attended Dublin County Council's meetings that there was an unnaturally close relationship between certain councillors and their 'clients' — those who stood to make millions, in many cases, from rezoning decisions.

The council took on the atmosphere of a noisy real estate agency or pork belly futures market. Day after day, the small public gallery in the council chamber on O'Connell Street was packed with developers and their agents waiting, as it were, for their ships to come in.[4]

In July 1993, at the time the Council was making a new development plan for county Dublin, a series of articles appeared in *The Irish Times*. McDonald and his colleague Mark Brennock alleged county councillors had received bribes in return for their votes on rezoning. Under a banner front-page headline, 'Cash in Brown Paper Bags for Councillors', they quoted one developer's agent as saying: 'There is a certain number of people in that council chamber who put a value on their votes. They are the power-brokers who can bring five votes with you, or five votes against you, depending on how they're looked after'.

The two journalists interviewed a businessman who said he had handed an envelope containing £2,500 in cash to one councillor in a successful effort to persuade him to change his vote on a key rezoning motion. He offered the same amount to another councillor who turned it down because he wanted more. Another source said his son had been told to deliver £10,000 in a brown envelope to a man outside Holles Street maternity hospital to help persuade a reluctant councillor to change his vote on a rezoning in Tallaght.

None of the informants would agree to shed the cloak of anonymity, so the only councillor named was a dead one who couldn't sue. Seán Walsh had died in 1989, leaving almost £250,000 in banks and building societies in spite of having an outwardly modest lifestyle and no sizeable income. Walsh, who was a councillor for over twenty years and a Dáil deputy for thirteen years, had strong links to the building industry. Rather than deal with the allegations made, councillors rounded on the journalists for allegedly traducing the reputation of a dead colleague. Fianna Fáil TD Batt O'Keeffe described the claims as a 'new nadir' in Irish journalism.

The Minister for the Environment, Michael Smith, said he viewed the matter 'with the utmost gravity' and ordered a further Garda investigation in July 1993. Detective Inspector Michael Guiney and his team interviewed each of the seventy-eight members of Dublin County Council, but got nowhere. A file was sent to the DPP but no-one was prosecuted. The gardaí involved in each of these investigations stressed the difficulty of following up allegations of corruption. As Detective Superintendent Brendan Burns wrote in the 1989/90 report:

Bribery and corruption are furtive crimes engaged in by more than one person. All involved benefit ... Insofar as public officials are concerned, these crimes are all the more reprehensible ... Evidence to support criminal charges in this type of crime is almost impossible to obtain. Since both the giver and the recipient are equally guilty, it is usual that no information will be volunteered ... acceptable support of evidence must be obtained. Therein lies the difficulty.

But is this the full story? The subsequent success of the tribunal in digging up the truth seems to give the lie to this assertion. It is true the gardaí were hamstrung; for instance, they had no access to bank accounts, and they didn't have the power to offer immunity to those blowing the whistle on wrongdoing. Yet it is clear that the political will at the highest levels to act on persistent allegations about corruption was lacking. The 1993 Garda report was left to gather dust, just like its predecessors.

There was also no modern legislation on corruption that would adequately deal with the situation — the Prevention of Corruption Act dated from 1906.[5] As the Fianna Fáil TD, Willie O'Dea, pointed out in 1995, the laws in this area would make it 'virtually impossible' for the State to successfully prosecute a corrupt politician.

The Garda investigations, however inconclusive, failed to quell widespread concerns about the planning process. As Dublin county councillors embarked on another frenzy of rezoning in 1993, the Minister for the Environment, Michael Smith, tried to call a halt to their gallop. In May, in a speech to the Irish Planning Institute, he launched a scathing attack on the 'frightening degree of irresponsibility' of some councillors.

It is the taxpayers of this country who have to pick up the tab for the expensive extension of sewers, water-mains, etc. that can arise from inappropriate and ill-considered rezonings and it is a local community — and the new communities — that will suffer if social facilities and community services are not capable of meeting the demand that can arise from new developments.

Smith went on to single out the 'procedural and legal wrangling of extraordinary proportions' in Dublin County Council. 'The stage has now been reached where zoning has become a debased currency in the county Dublin area, where even desirable changes in zoning may

Rambo meets Ol' Blue Eyes, 1989.

Ray Burke arrives at the tribunal for his first day of evidence, July 1999.

Friends, business partners and benefactors of Ray Burke, builders Joseph McGowan and Tom Brennan.

George Redmond

A tale of two houses ... Briargate, which the tribunal says Burke got for nothing. He sold the house in Swords for £3 million in 2000.

George Redmond's house in Castleknock, which he sold for £750,000 to settle with the Revenue Commissioners.

James Gogarty leaves the tribunal, April 1999.

82-year-old Joseph Murphy senior arrives to give evidence in Guernsey, September 1999, accompanied by his son Joseph Murphy junior (left) and his solicitor.

Michael Bailey at play.

Tom Bailey with a thoroughbred sheep he bred and auctioned for charity. Tom once paid £94,000 for a purebred Suffolk sheep, but much of the funding for his hobby came from under-the-counter payments. (Frank Fennell Photography)

Turvey House in Donabate, north Dublin. JMSE bought the Turvey estate in 1968, but by the time this photograph was taken in 1977, the house was derelict. James Gogarty claimed George Redmond 'stuck his neck out' when it was pulled down in controversial circumstances in 1987. (The Irish Architectural Archive)

be tarred with the same brush as those which arise on the prompting of individual landowners or developers.'

In February 1993, Trevor Sargent of the Greens stood up during a rezoning debate at Dublin County Council and took an envelope from his pocket. A developer had written to him looking for the support of his party for a rezoning proposal. The envelope contained a cheque for £100. Sargent held up the cheque and asked if anyone else had received a similar contribution.

The question caused pandemonium. 'Withdraw, withdraw,' shouted Sargent's fellow councillors. Sargent was told to sit down and did so. Fianna Fáil and Fine Gael members crowded around him, trying to get the cheque. One councillor grabbed him around the neck. The meeting was adjourned. The developer who sent the cheque later explained to *The Irish Times* that he sent the money so the politician 'might at least read it before throwing it in the bin'.

Also in 1993, Labour Minister of State Joan Burton called on Fianna Fáil and Fine Gael to come clean on the issue. She referred to the unseemly sight of property developers and their agents 'crowding the council's ante-chamber and gallery, ticking off lists of councillors as they arrive and vote for decisions that multiply at a stroke the value of lands they own or control.'[6] Burton said the public was 'entitled to know from each and every councillor what campaign contributions, what hospitality and what assistance, direct or indirect … they or their parties received from these developers, landowners, associated builders and their agents'.

The reaction of her fellow councillors? Burton was sued by no fewer than forty-two of her colleagues. Solicitors acting on their behalf insisted that there were 'absolutely no grounds to suggest bribery or corruption in Dublin County Council,' and called on her to apologise and retract her allegations. They went on to refer to 'the distress and embarrassment caused to them, their families, friends and associates' and sought an affirmation that they had 'always dealt with rezoning applications … with the utmost integrity and having regard only to appropriate planning criteria'.

This was the background against which Smith and Mac Eochaidh decided to seek information through the classified columns of *The Irish Times*. The dogs in the street knew something was wrong with the planning system, yet nothing was being done about it. Even the Minister for the Environment was saying that rezoning in Dublin was a 'debased currency', yet county councillors carried on regardless.

The two lawyers tried unsuccessfully to engage a legal firm in the Republic. In the end, they had to go to a college friend in Northern Ireland to find someone willing to take on the brief. Donnelly Neary and Donnelly, the Newry solicitors acting for the anonymous lawyers, explained their clients' rationale: 'It is widely believed that the rezoning process is influenced by those who stand to become multi-millionaires if the tracts of land they have assembled are rezoned. Those behind the reward believe it is regrettable that the State has never sought a prosecution in this area.'

The advertisement garnered media attention but the politicians were unimpressed. Labour's Brendan Howlin, then Minister for the Environment, said he was 'totally committed to rooting out corruption' but wasn't prepared to do so 'on the basis of threats from anonymous sources'. Howlin was later made aware of the more serious allegations and supplied with a phone number of the sponsors of the advertisement, but did not make contact with them.

Fianna Fáil's Noel Dempsey, who was to succeed Howlin in the environment portfolio, said the advertisement would leave a 'cloud' hanging over the planning process in Dublin and over public officials and politicians. 'There is a widespread suspicion among senior politicians that the can of worms may be so large that they dare not prise it open because this might bring down the political establishment,' Frank McDonald commented in October 1997.

Within a month of Smith and Mac Eochaidh's advertisement, more than thirty people had contacted Donnelly Neary and Donnelly. They included James Gogarty, emerging from retirement with a grudge in his heart and an astonishing story to tell. Gogarty said he was in Ray Burke's house in June 1989 to witness the handing over of £80,000 to the minister by his then employer, JMSE, and a building firm, Bovale Developments. The money was paid to ease the way for the rezoning and development of lands owned by JMSE in north county Dublin, he alleged.

Two months before Smith and Mac Eochaidh's advertisement appeared, Gogarty had embarked on the odyssey that culminated in his appearance at the Flood tribunal four years later. A year had passed since Joseph Murphy junior's late-night phone-call to his home, but Gogarty was still simmering with rage. Having failed to convince the gardaí to prosecute Murphy, he started civil proceedings. When his attempts to serve a summons on Murphy in Dublin and London were unsuccessful, Gogarty changed tack — with dramatic effect.

In May 1995, he wrote to his local TD in Dublin North-East, Tommy Broughan of Labour, unburdening himself for the first time of a confused and confusing mix of personal gripe and sensational political allegation. Broughan asked the Minister for Justice, Nora Owen, in the Dáil why no prosecution had been brought against Murphy. But according to Gogarty, nothing happened.

He turned to Michael McDowell, then a Progressive Democrat TD, who recommended he find a criminal lawyer. Gogarty was incandescent by this stage, and prepared to make the wildest allegations against those who he felt had let him down. In his letter to McDowell, he accused Owen of 'double standards' and of thwarting an investigation by the courts. He also accused the gardaí of 'widespread corruption' and claimed 'decent' politicians, investigative journalists and judges shared that view. In a letter to Joe Higgins TD in 1997, he complained about Owen's 'repeated and callous' dismissal of his calls for an inquiry into Joseph Murphy's behaviour.

Gogarty never provided a shred of evidence for his allegations against Owen and the gardaí, which did not feature in his affidavit to the tribunal. Owen, who only became aware of the accusations made by Gogarty when the letters were read at the tribunal, denied that she had 'thwarted' any investigation of the gardaí as Minister for Justice in 1996.[7]

When Smith and Mac Eochaidh offered their reward, Gogarty was among the first to write to solicitors handling the matter. Donnelly Neary and Donnelly put him in touch directly with the two men. Over two meetings, Gogarty poured out his entire story. At this stage, he was still fixated on his pension dispute and his grudge against the Murphys. Smith and Mac Eochaidh tried to persuade the pensioner that this agenda would be best served by attracting publicity for his allegations about Burke, Redmond and corruption in planning. At first, Gogarty resisted, but with time his references to corruption grew more specific.

In the years that followed, the frustrated pensioner sent his hand-written missives to the Taoiseach, the Tánaiste, Government ministers, TDs of most parties and the gardaí. Broughan worked diligently on his constituent's behalf but to no effect.[8] Half a dozen letters and a series of parliamentary questions to the Minister, Nora Owen, met with brief, anodyne responses. Raheny gardaí told Broughan it would be difficult to sustain a prosecution against Murphy junior for the intimidation alleged by Gogarty. After Gogarty told the TD for the first time in April 1996 about the payment to Ray Burke, Broughan contacted the Fraud Squad. By now, large sections of the political system were aware of the nature of Gogarty's allegations, and where to go for more detailed information about them. There is no evidence, however, that his complaints were taken seriously.

Alone against the world, Gogarty presented a very nervous face at this time. Broughan recalled that he would often become agitated during their meetings and on one occasion he came close to fainting. Only a pot of tea could settle him. At a meeting in September 1997, Gogarty finally showed the TD the Bailey letter, but would not let him retain it or make a copy. He said he feared for the TD's safety while the letter was in his possession and warned Broughan to 'keep away from the window'.

Smith and Mac Eochaidh began leaking information to the media, before putting the pensioner in direct contact with journalists. A proposed arrangement with the *Sunday Times* foundered when that newspaper 'outed' the two activists. Eventually, Gogarty brought his story to Frank Connolly, a dogged investigative reporter with the *Sunday Business Post*.

Gogarty's allegations began to seep into the public domain from 13 August 1995, when the *Sunday Business Post* carried its first story about payoffs to 'a Coalition politician and three former Fianna Fáil office-holders'. Connolly first met Gogarty at the end of March 1996 in Donnelly Neary and Donnelly's offices in Newry, and subsequently wrote a story about 'a senior Fianna Fáil politician' who was accused of receiving two substantial payments in return for planning favours. The following month, an article identified Gogarty, without naming him, as 'a former company executive' who was present when £80,000 was allegedly handed over to a politician.

The bottle was open, but the genie took a while getting out; Gogarty's truculence and inaccuracy, legal worries and the complexity of the allegations meant that newspapers trod carefully before going to print. The *Post* declined to publish details of the letter Michael Bailey wrote in June 1989 promising to 'procure' planning permission on the Murphy lands, because of libel worries and Gogarty's refusal to give the paper a hard copy.

Half of Dublin knew Burke was the politician at the centre of the allegations, before the *Sunday Tribune* became the first newspaper to name him in July 1997. Confusingly, the *Tribune* identified Burke's donor as Michael Bailey of Bovale Developments. As we now know, although Bailey was present when Gogarty gave Burke at least £30,000 on behalf of JMSE he denies making any payment himself. The error allowed Burke and others to dismiss the report, and Fianna Fáil put it about that Gogarty was 'a headcase'.

However, in August, the *Post* correctly identified JMSE as the donor of the £30,000. The 'outing' of Burke was a major vindication for Gogarty. 'Up to now, it was one man against many, and now the ranks were broken and it was accepted that there was at least £30,000 paid over,' he explained later to the tribunal.[9]

Around this time Gogarty was offered immunity from prosecution in return for cooperation in the form of a signed statement to the gardaí.[10] However, his mistrust of the police remained deep, and he refused to sign a statement. He upped the ante by demanding a sworn inquiry. The Garda investigation went nowhere. Meanwhile, Fine Gael announced that none of its members had done anything improper.[11]

⬥⎯⬥

By 1997, Burke was the most senior politician in Fianna Fáil. Only one other figure had been in the Dáil longer, but no-one had held as many ministerial offices as the brash, abrasive fixer from north Dublin. The scent of controversy hadn't gone away, of course, but always Burke had been able to shrug off the questions that dogged his career.

If he was worried about storm-clouds on the horizon, Burke wasn't showing it. He'd already established his credentials as a survivor. Hadn't he backed George Colley in the 1979 Fianna Fáil leadership contest won by Charles Haughey, and still been retained as a minister for state? He became a full minister less than a year later. In 1983, he was removed from the front bench after ending up on the wrong side of an anti-Haughey heave, but was back in favour within a few years. In 1989, after he failed to bring in his running mate in Dublin North, there was speculation that he would be dropped. Instead, he was promoted, and given two portfolios. Finally, hadn't Bertie Ahern rescued him from the political darkness in 1994, only two years after he was banished there by Albert Reynolds?

True, the rumour machine was working overtime, egged on by a drip-feed of allegations from Gogarty. However, at the time of the general election campaign in June, neither he nor any other politician had been publicly named in connection with the scandal.

The election proved a disappointment for Burke and for Fianna Fáil. The party's vote stayed stuck at 39 per cent and a government could only be formed in coalition with the Progressive Democrats. Labour took a seat in Dublin North as Burke once again failed to deliver a second seat for Fianna Fáil in this crucial three-seater.

In opposition, Burke had been spokesman on foreign affairs and Bertie Ahern now had to decide whether to appoint him to this ministry. In spite of the ongoing drip-feed of Gogarty-inspired rumours in the media, the issue barely arose during the election campaign. Asked at a press conference about the allegations, Ahern said that he had 'gone to that member' and 'gone through it in detail on four separate occasions. Insofar as I possibly can be, I am satisfied'. Then, shortly before polling day, Fianna Fáil broke its silence when its director of elections, P.J. Mara, spun the line to journalist Frank Connolly that Burke had received a 'political contribution' but there was no wrongdoing.

When Ahern met Mary Harney in Buswell's Hotel on 11 June to finalise arrangements for the new Government, he told the Progressive Democrat leader of his intention to appoint Burke to the Cabinet. Harney was better informed than most; not only had Gogarty written to her, but PD deputy Michael McDowell had come to his leader with a fuller account of Gogarty's allegations. Harney expressed concern about the rumours floating around, and asked Ahern to investigate them before making the appointment. But she reassured the Taoiseach that the PDs regarded Burke's fate as an internal Fianna Fáil matter.

Bertie now had a decision to make — whether or not to pick Burke for the Cabinet. Around this time, Gogarty wrote to him calling for a judicial investigation into his allegations, but whether Ahern got this letter is unclear. Then Harney came back to the Taoiseach with new information. Through PD sources, she had learned of an allegation that Burke got £60,000 in return for planning permission on the Murphy lands.[12] The source of the story was a senior executive in JMSE, Gay Grehan, whose wife Mary had been an unsuccessful PD candidate in Louth.

Two sources in JMSE — Grehan and Gogarty — were now indicating that some kind of payment had been made to Burke. Ahern had been provided with this information, and he had been written to by Gogarty. He had also discussed the matter previously with Burke, who had denied there was any substance to the allegations.

With characteristic caution, Bertie Ahern decided to find out more about the allegations before making a decision. However, the limited investigation he now set in train was to add greatly to the confusion surrounding the Burke payment. The fallout would also destroy the ambitions for Taoiseach of one of his colleagues, without ever getting to the bottom of the mystery. The Taoiseach decided to send his chief whip, Dermot Ahern (no relation), to London to interview Joseph Murphy junior. He himself would talk to Burke and to the third party present in Burke's house in 1989, the builder (and Fianna Fáil supporter) Michael Bailey.

Dermot Ahern met Murphy for two hours in a London airport hotel on 24 June. He says he put three questions to the JMSE chairman. Was Murphy or his father at any meeting attended by Gogarty and Bailey at which a large amount of money was paid over? Did Burke give any undertaking in relation to the Murphy lands? Did any meeting take place between Burke and a Murphy company representative? Murphy says the three questions were: Did JMSE pay Burke money in 1989? If so, were any favours asked? Were any favours given? Whatever form the questions took, Murphy gave an emphatic 'no' to all three.

And so it was that Dermot Ahern came back to Dublin with the strange news that Murphy and his company were denying the payment of any money to Burke, a fact Burke and many others knew to be untrue.

While Ahern was in London, the Taoiseach put similar questions to Michael Bailey. Murphy and Bailey were interviewed simultaneously to prevent them speaking to each other in advance about the questions asked. Bailey told the Taoiseach that Gogarty had given Burke 'a political donation'.

Bertie Ahern contacted Burke on the night before the Cabinet was appointed. He told Burke about Dermot Ahern's trip to London and then asked him if he had done anything for the donation from JMSE. Burke says he told the Taoiseach he hadn't done anything for it.[13] It seems to follow that the Taoiseach must have known that a) Burke received money, and b) he was being told conflicting stories about the source of that money.

This is confirmed by Mary Harney's evidence to the tribunal.[14] She says the Taoiseach decided: that Burke had received money; that the sum involved was £30,000; and that it came from 'Gogarty/JMSE'. He told Harney that Burke kept £20,000 for his own election campaign in Dublin North and forwarded £10,000 to Fianna Fáil headquarters.[15]

But what was the money given for? Why such a large contribution? Were any favours asked for or given? What about the conflicting versions? Why were JMSE and Bovale both denying the payment? Why wasn't Murphy contacted again after it was decided that JMSE had given money? Why weren't Gogarty or Grehan interviewed? If the accounts given by Harney and Bailey are correct, how could the Taoiseach later tell the Dáil: 'On the day that I appointed the then Deputy Burke as Minister I was working on the understanding that no money had been given to him'?[16] None of these questions was answered at the time. Perhaps some of them could be accounted for by simple misunderstandings, but no-one bothered to sort the mess out.

With the agreement of the PDs, Ahern duly appointed Burke as Minister for Foreign Affairs; Dermot Ahern says he came back to Leinster House from his London trip to find Burke waiting ahead of him in the queue to see the Taoiseach. The new Government began its work to the background din of continuing rumours about Burke.

Behind the scenes, desperate attempts were being made to limit the damage caused by Gogarty, who had now been given immunity against prosecution. Michael Bailey made frantic efforts to effect a truce between Gogarty and Murphys. He later denied a claim by Joseph Murphy junior that Bailey had suggested they pay Gogarty £100,000 to extricate Ray Burke from the effects of 'a dispute between two old men'.[17] But Bailey did ring JMSE's financial controller Roger Copsey in Moscow, hoping he would intercede.[18]

Within weeks of the Government's formation, the news broke about Dermot Ahern's visit to London. A curious Burke rang him to see what he knew. When told that JMSE was denying having paid the money, Burke's response was: 'Well, who gave me the money? It must have been Bailey'. Burke later described this as a 'throwaway remark'.[19]

Dermot Ahern and Joseph Murphy junior met a second time, at Murphy's request, a week after their first encounter.[20] The date was 1 July, five days *after* Burke was appointed to the Cabinet. Murphy, tight-lipped and suspicious at their first meeting, was positively garrulous on this occasion. He repeated his denial that JMSE had paid any money to Burke. Ahern says he asked Murphy whether Gogarty could possibly have taken money out without the company knowing, but was told this could not have happened. Murphy then made his claim about Bailey's suggestion of a £100,000 payment to Gogarty. He says he turned down the invitation.

Murphy's evidence about the Fianna Fáil chief whip was to prove highly damaging for Dermot Ahern when it emerged at the tribunal in 1999. It portrayed a politician who was vain and ambitious, and inclined to shoot his mouth off about others around him. When they had first met in June 1997, Ahern was on the brink of his first full Cabinet post. He told Murphy he expected to be made Minister for Justice (he eventually got the Social, Community and Family Affairs portfolio). Murphy claims he made a number of unguarded remarks about the Fine Gael politician Nora Owen ('the most dangerous politician of them all') and the journalist Frank Connolly ('a dangerous bastard' and a member of 'INLA/IRSP'). Ahern denied the Owen remark and couldn't recollect making the comment about Connolly, who followed the minister into the witness box to decry his remark as 'a disgraceful suggestion' that could endanger his life.[21]

Within hours of his second meeting with Dermot Ahern, Murphy discovered that his company had, in fact, made a payment to a politician.[22] He went straight from lunch with the minister to the office of Roger Copsey. JMSE's financial controller told him that 'yeah, there was some kind of contribution' and it would be necessary to check the records. Given his earlier denials, the news must have come as a shock to Murphy. Yet it took him over two months to pass it on to Ahern, and this only happened when the Minister initiated contact. The reason for the delay, he explained later, was that he wanted to wait until he had the full information and the 'jigsaw puzzle' was complete. Also, his 'priorities changed' after his wife was taken to hospital and his son fell ill.[23]

Just why Murphy went straight to see Copsey is unclear; after all, Ahern hadn't told him anything new at their second meeting. 'I just decided to go and see him,' Murphy told the tribunal.

On 10 September 1997, the day Burke made a statement in the Dáil, Ahern rang Murphy, who explained that JMSE had found evidence of two payments of £20,000 and £10,000, matching the sum paid to Burke. But Dermot Ahern knew all this by now. The reason for his call had to do with Burke's Dáil speech scheduled for that afternoon. The new Government had a precarious existence and it would stand or fall depending on Burke's performance.

Murphy claims the Minister was looking for information on political donations by JMSE to other parties that would make good 'ammunition' to fire at the Opposition later that day. Embarrassingly for Ahern, he has no memory of this call, although it undoubtedly took place.[24] Neither can he remember telling Murphy that Fianna Fáil wanted to avoid a tribunal 'at all costs'.

Dermot Ahern's memory was already causing him difficulties. Five days before the conversation with Murphy, the Fianna Fáil chief whip stated on RTÉ television that he had not spoken to Murphy since the meeting in London. The remark angered Murphy, who started legal proceedings for defamation against Ahern. Murphy's evidence to the tribunal in December 1999 further undermined Dermot Ahern's credibility. In it, he recounted his conversations with the minister in embarrassing detail, and contradicted Ahern's evidence on more than a dozen points.

It was May 1998, almost a year after his investigation, before Dermot Ahern finally sent a copy of his investigation report to the Taoiseach 'as a matter of courtesy'.

⋘•⋙

In July 1997, a fortnight after the Government was formed, the *Sunday Tribune* reported the gossip that had been circulating around Dublin for weeks; that Burke had received £30,000 from a leading firm of housebuilders, Bovale Developments, in 1989. The story was garbled — we know now that the source of the money, insofar as has been established, was Joseph Murphy Structural Engineering — but the report did correctly identify the amount and the recipient. More importantly, for the first time, the 'senior politician' had been named.

At this stage, Bertie Ahern made his famous comment about having been 'up every tree in North Dublin' to find out about the payment before Burke was appointed to Cabinet. But as James Gogarty would later tell the tribunal, 'they went up every tree in north Dublin but they didn't come to me'.[25] The article prompted Bailey to ring Burke that Sunday evening, and the two men discussed their annoyance at the story.[26] Telephone records showed they were in regular contact between 1994 and 1997, but neither could remember anything out of the ordinary about their conversations.

Burke did what he always did, reacting with a mixture of bluster and misinformation. He issued a public statement on 7 August, saying he had done nothing 'illegal, unethical or improper'. He related for the first time the story of how Bailey and Gogarty came to his house in June 1989. 'Gogarty told me JMSE wished to make a political contribution to me and I received from him in good faith a sum of £30,000 as a totally unsolicited political contribution.'

Burke continued: 'At no time during our meeting were any favours sought or given. I did not do any favours for or make any representations to anyone on behalf of JMSE'. He told the Taoiseach the money was an election contribution, and said a 'substantial portion' had been passed on to Fianna Fáil (this wasn't the case). Burke described himself as 'the target of a vicious campaign of rumour and innuendo'. Ahern accepted his assurances and kept him in his Cabinet. A week later, and notwithstanding the fact that he had just acknowledged getting money from Gogarty, Burke started libel proceedings against the former JMSE executive.

Burke's statement raised more questions than it answered. The Opposition clamoured for more information. In the press, the drip-drip of allegations continued. Under growing pressure, Burke made a personal statement to the Dáil on 10 September 1997. In an emotional occasion, he rounded on his attackers, defended his personal integrity and that of his father and added a few new — and, with hindsight, misleading — details. This was his famous 'line in the sand' speech, in which he repeated earlier denials of wrongdoing and wrongly stated that £30,000 was the largest contribution he had received.

Confirming that he had received £30,000 from Gogarty on behalf of JMSE in 1989, he added that he had contributed £10,000 to Fianna Fáil headquarters and handed over about £7,000 to his local party organisation. The rest of the contributions he received were used to cover 'personal election expenses'.

Once again, Burke survived, with many observers admiring his performance under pressure. Fianna Fáil, meanwhile, held its counsel. Above all, it wanted to avoid setting up a tribunal. As Dermot Ahern told Murphy on the day, if Burke's speech didn't work, the party would 'have no problem putting him out to grass'.[27]

After fielding questions from his fellow TDs for several hours, Burke must have thought he was through the worst. Fianna Fáil and the PDs voted down an attempt by the Opposition parties to have the matter investigated by the Moriarty tribunal that was being established at the time.

But the media speculation refused to die down. Around this time, Gogarty's son Éamon attended a friend's wedding, where he met an acquaintance, John Ryan, who was then editor of Magill magazine. As they waited for the bride to arrive, Éamon Gogarty said he had something of interest to show Ryan, and he took a few sheets of paper from his inside pocket.

It was the letter in which Michael Bailey offered to 'procure' planning permission for more than 700 acres of JMSE land in return for a 50 per cent share of the action. Obtaining planning permission would be 'notoriously difficult, time-consuming and expensive,' Bailey warned, as he outlined the steps needed to effect the necessary votes by county councillors. The letter was dated 8 June 1989, on or about the day of the £30,000 payment by Gogarty to Burke, witnessed by Bailey. Ryan memorised what he could, went down the back of the church and jotted a few quick notes. A day or two later, he met Gogarty again and was shown the letter for about forty-five seconds. Before then, he hadn't heard the word 'procure' used outside 'the oldest profession,' he says.[28]

The excerpts, which appeared in the October edition of *Magill*, caused uproar. A day later, the newspapers published the full text of the letter. Burke's work in placating his fellow TDs was undone. He complained of a new attempt to smear him, and the Government described the letter as a 'normal business document, using standard commercial language'. However, behind the scenes, support for the embattled politician was ebbing away and the PD leader Mary Harney was pushing hard for an independent inquiry.

Harney met Bertie Ahern in late September and the two leaders came to the conclusion that a tribunal was needed to stem the drip-feed of allegations about Burke that was damaging their parties. Within days, the Taoiseach announced the terms of reference for a new tribunal. In one of the wilder predictions in Irish political history, he predicted it would complete its work within three months. The Opposition was strangely unenthusiastic; Fine Gael leader John Bruton claimed the proposal to have an inquiry 'into all sorts of planning matters in north County Dublin is simply a smokescreen'. Bruton, delivering his own hostages to fortune, said there was no evidence 'in the public domain' of payments to any other politician and he challenged the Taoiseach to produce any evidence he had.

Yet on the same day Donnelly Neary and Donnelly, the Newry solicitors acting for the sponsors of the £10,000 reward for information on planning corruption, revealed that they had received fifty-two allegations about planning. Some were frivolous, the firm admitted, but six had been forwarded to the gardaí and more were worthy of investigation. Former Dublin county councillors were behind three of the allegations.

Gogarty met gardaí on numerous occasions throughout 1997 and his solicitors told investigating detectives from the National Bureau of Criminal Investigation that he was willing to make a statement. However, Gogarty refused to sign a statement until he was given round-the-clock protection.

After some wrangling over the terms of reference, the Dáil agreed to the establishment of the new tribunal. Burke was to remain as Minister for Foreign Affairs, though it must have been clear that his days were numbered. The end came within a month, when *The Irish Times* published a story about the manner in which Burke, as Minister for Justice, had issued passports to a Saudi Arabian businessman and his family under the 'passports for sale' scheme. On 7 October, he resigned from the Cabinet and the Dáil, ending the Burke family's half a century possession of the Dublin North seat. 'I want to clearly restate that I have done nothing wrong,' Burke said in a resignation statement. The Taoiseach, Bertie Ahern, said an 'honourable man' had been 'hounded' from office. With his next move, he agreed to Opposition demands to set up a judicial tribunal into planning allegations and the Burke payment.

Back in November 1987, Burke had told the *Sunday Tribune*: 'If politics can be described as a disease, then I'm terminally ill. I love it. The wheeling and dealing is in my blood'. Now in indefinite retirement, Burke was cured.

5
The Great Unravelling

'My life was seamless. I was a politician from the time I got up in the morning until I went to bed at night.'
— Ray Burke in the witness box at the Flood tribunal,
July 1999

Establishing a tribunal was one thing; finding a High Court judge to preside over it was another matter. The Government struggled for a time to find someone willing to take on the task before appointing Mr Justice Feargus Flood as 'Chairman and Sole Member of the Tribunal into Certain Planning Matters' in November 1997.

At 69, Flood was well past the normal pension age and near enough to the retirement age for judges, which then stood at 72 years. A diminutive character described by colleagues as a 'perfect gentleman', Flood had been a High Court judge since 1991 without attracting much attention. He was born in Ballyshannon, County Donegal, but otherwise his background was typical Law Library — son of a banker, education at Castleknock College, UCD and the King's Inns, home on the Hill of Howth. Mild-mannered, inscrutable and a touch pompous, he was considered in his days as a practising barrister to have Fianna Fáil leanings.

As Flood began scouting for premises and staff with the necessary expertise in planning, the start-up of the tribunal was delayed by an unseemly row over fees. Lawyers approached by the tribunal first sought a flat fee of £2,100 a day, whether the inquiry was sitting or not. They later dropped this demand to £1,500 a day. Agreement was finally reached with the Minister for Finance in December to pay senior counsel £1,450 for sitting days, and £1,350 for non-sitting days, as well as a £25,000 'brief fee' or retainer. After the first fifty days, the rate for sitting days would drop to £1,350. Amazingly, no-one thought to apply an economy of scale by further reducing the daily rate if the tribunal continued longer than expected. The issue of costs, and in particular lawyers' fees, was to dog the tribunal intermittently throughout its life.

The team appointed by Flood included John Gallagher, a former Garda from Mayo turned planning lawyer, and Pat Hanratty, another senior counsel with considerable planning experience. Offices were found in Dublin Castle where the Printworks Hall, an enormous hangar-like room converted from a printing factory, was rented as a venue for the public hearings.

For the first half of 1998, nothing much happened in public. The tribunal held its first sitting in January, but this was only to hear applications for legal representation from a variety of parties. Flood visited Gogarty at his home briefly. He acceded to Gogarty's demand for 24-hour security, an arrangement that was to continue until the last day of the pensioner's evidence to the tribunal.

The lawyers began their mammoth task in private. Detailed questionnaires were sent to serving and former members of the Dáil, the Seanad, Dublin County Council, Dublin Corporation, An Bord Pleanála and local government officials. Of 406 forms sent out to Dáil and Seanad members, 390 were returned. More than 300 orders were made against various parties, often meeting with great resistance. Faced with a mountain of files and paperwork, the tribunal developed its own computerised document retrieval system, which has since been used by other inquiries.

Flood and his team quickly realised that the terms of reference they were working to were extremely narrow. He asked the Government to alter this remit to allow the investigation of matters dating from before June 1985.

In March 1998, developer Michael Bailey and his wife Teresa went to the High Court to challenge a tribunal order directing them to produce details of their bank accounts. This was to be the first of many legal challenges to the tribunal. The High Court rejected the Baileys' application in May but this was overturned by the Supreme Court in July. The court said the tribunal had given inadequate notice. Its orders were also deemed invalid because they impinged upon the rights of others not named on the order. Thus, for example, in the case of a man sharing a joint account with his wife, the tribunal was now required to issue separate orders for both persons. The tribunal had to return the documents it had received from the Baileys, though it was free to make new orders, provided they were correctly addressed to each affected person. The delay involved was considerable, and months of work were lost.

In May 1998, *Magill* revealed that Fitzwilton, the holding company controlled by the millionaire businessman and newspaper magnate Tony O'Reilly, had paid Burke £30,000 in 1989 through a subsidiary company, Rennicks Manufacturing. It was clear now that the £10,000 that Burke said he paid to Fianna Fáil came from this sum, not the Gogarty contribution. It was also clear that there was a lot more to Burke's finances than the former minister had publicly revealed.

In response to the ensuing political controversy, the Government agreed in June to widen the tribunal's terms of reference to allow for the investigation of *all* payments to Burke. The June 1985 watershed was also dropped. These changes transformed the tribunal which, from a narrow inquiry into a specific payment, became a massive trawl through the darker margins of Irish society. Without them, for example, the investigations into Century Radio could not have proceeded. They added years to the life of the tribunal but also smoothed the way for later revelations from Frank Dunlop and others.

By October 1998, the tribunal had been established for a year but had not yet heard any evidence. News broke about the allegations by Luton-based property developer Tom Gilmartin about payments to Pádraig Flynn and Liam Lawlor, but the tribunal was still getting to grips with the Gogarty allegations. Lawyers for Murphys and the Baileys, sounding a note they were to repeat right through the hearings until the delivery of final submissions, pleaded for more time to prepare their case. Uncertainty prevailed about Gogarty's intentions and the state of his health. Flood was already complaining about unnamed people who were 'less than wholehearted' in their cooperation with the tribunal.

However, once Gogarty finally appointed lawyers and delivered his 45-page affidavit to the tribunal in October 1998, the atmosphere changed. Up to then, the tribunal's unseen opponents had been happy to see matters dragged out as long as possible. After all, what possible threat could an 81-year-old suffering from heart problems, diabetes, arthritis, blackouts and deafness pose to some of the most powerful figures in Irish politics and business? Now that Gogarty had made his accusations formally, however, the push was on to discredit and destroy the tribunal.

Mysterious leaks began to appear in the national newspapers. Gogarty's affidavit was splashed over the front page of the *Sunday Independent*.[1] Most of the details were already public knowledge, but new material involved allegations of intimidation of workers at a JMSE site in Moneypoint, Count Clare, in 1981. Hardly coincidentally, they cast Gogarty in a poor light.

Government backbenchers and unnamed parties under investigation began to mutter about the unfairness of it all. Just a few weeks before Gogarty was due to begin his evidence in November, Ray Burke's lawyers wrote to Flood demanding a formal investigation of the leaks. JMSE said the leaks were a 'grave injustice' which must undermine the tribunal. The Taoiseach said it was 'a very serious matter'. The *Irish Independent* reported that the public hearings were 'in jeopardy'. Lawyers for Michael Bailey joined the torrent of criticism, saying they were 'shocked and horrified' by the leaks. Gogarty's affidavit was couched in 'scabrous terms' and 'littered with falsehoods and untruths,' roared Colm Allen SC, one of the tribunal's more colourful characters.[2] He too called for a Garda investigation.

Flood was forced to react as the clamour threatened to destabilise the tribunal before it had begun. Journalists who published confidential material were warned that they did so 'at their own peril'. High Court proceedings would be taken. It was all an unwelcome echo of the Beef tribunal, which identified massive fraud but threatened imprisonment only against Susan O'Keeffe, the journalist who uncovered the scandal. Later, Flood called in the gardaí to investigate the leaks.

Flood also pursued the *Sunday Independent* for its copy of the Gogarty affidavit. Thus it was that thirteen months after the tribunal was established, the first witness to give evidence was not a politician with a reputation to lose, or even a developer with a few secrets to unpack, but a little-known newspaper executive with next to nothing to tell. Michael Roche, managing editor of Independent Newspapers, hadn't even seen the affidavit and couldn't help the tribunal, nor could Jody Corcoran, who wrote the article.

Much, much later it emerged that Michael Bailey, in spite of his repeated denials of any contact with journalists, had been in contact with Corcoran in the *Sunday Independent*. Garda investigations established a series of calls from phones owned by Bailey to Corcoran around the time the newspaper published Gogarty's affidavit. The first call, lasting eight minutes, took place on the day before Corcoran first disclosed details of the document, and ten further calls followed in the same month. Citing legal advice, both Michael Bailey and his brother Tom refused to answer Garda questions.

During their investigations, the gardaí interviewed ninety-eight people, all of whom denied leaking the documents. Yet the leaks continued. Barely a Sunday passed without a highly charged and selective account of the various allegations appearing in the newspapers. In December, Flood wrote to newspaper editors to demand they refuse to publish any confidential information provided to the tribunal.[3] The information was being 'deliberately and systematically drip-fed to elements of the media,' he said, in a 'conscious attempt to undermine the tribunal'.

Most of the leaks and critical reports appeared in the newspapers published by Independent Newspapers. 'Mr Justice Flood said that in its attitude towards the tribunal, the Independent Newspapers group had behaved as if it was above the law,' *The Irish Times* noted in an end-of-year editorial.[4]

Eventually, the flow of information tapered off, but the damage had been done. Countless witnesses withheld or delayed their cooperation, claiming that any information they provided would immediately find its way on to the front pages. JMSE opted not to submit full affidavits, arguing that they would only be leaked. The uncertainty about Gogarty's health and willingness to give evidence persisted as the pensioner quailed at the accounts he read in the newspapers. The tribunal was off to a disastrous start, largely due to circumstances beyond its control, even before the public hearings began.

The tribunal accelerated the hearing of Gogarty's evidence. Given his age and bad health, it was decided to take his evidence first, 'out of turn', rather than waiting for all the evidence to be gathered and formally presented. It was to prove a controversial decision and, with hindsight, an ill-judged one, but at the time it seemed essential to capture Gogarty's evidence as quickly as possible.

Then, when the date of the first hearing was set for January 1999, George Redmond made a last-ditch effort to stop the tribunal in its tracks. Just before Christmas, Redmond went to the High Court to argue that the allegations against him should be heard in private. The court rejected his arguments, and the Supreme Court delivered a further rebuff in January. Just hours before Gogarty was to take the stand, lawyers for Ray Burke, and for Michael and Tom Bailey, filed minimalist statements denying Gogarty's allegations. Fifteen months after it was set up, the tribunal was finally able to open for business.

⋘⊱⊰⋙

On 12 January 1999, a frail-looking 81-year-old made his way to the witness box for the first time. His lips creased in righteous dudgeon, Gogarty negotiated the short walk from his solicitor's car to the tribunal hall with the aid of a walking-stick. Dozens of flash-bulbs caught a wan, bespectacled figure, tallish and thin and white-haired, with a permanent look of disgust about him. Ireland was about to get its first tribunal whistle-blower, and an unlikely one at that.

In true tribunal style, the first morning disappeared in legal argument, as the lawyers for Bailey and Murphys railed against the decision to hear Gogarty's evidence out of turn without a prior opening statement from the tribunal legal team. It was afternoon before Gogarty made his way to the witness-box and swore to tell 'the truth, the whole truth and nothing but the truth'. Within minutes, the pattern for the coming months was set, as the witness meandered through memories of his early years, interspersing his testimony with vicious accusations against his former employer, Joseph Murphy senior, and wild allegations against politicians and lawyers.

Displaying an impressive command of detail for events many years past, Gogarty overcame a shaky start to give a comprehensive account of his early years and his almost feudal relationship to 'Senior'. Seemingly deaf — especially when the questions were proving awkward — he ranged over the memories of a long life and career in a jumbled and often haphazard fashion.

From the start, his evidence was entertaining, though it was often hard to see what it had to do with the tribunal. On the first day, Gogarty's digressions took him to Sellafield — built with steel discreetly sourced from Murphy's companies in Dublin — and the Gaiety Theatre, where George Redmond enjoyed free tickets from the owners, Murphys. He assailed Joseph Murphy senior with allegations, claiming he had trouble with drink, suffered from 'nervous problems' and had considered committing suicide. Murphy 'would have no problem going through a bottle of brandy,' Gogarty claimed a few days into his evidence.

Garrett Cooney, the high-profile senior counsel engaged by Murphys to lead their defence, locked horns with the witness from the start, accusing him of defaming people 'left, right and centre' in front of the media. Cooney, who had made his name in a series of celebrity libel trials, approached the tribunal with a sense of wounded righteousness exceeded only by Gogarty's. Relentlessly, he cavilled with the tribunal's approach to the investigation and Gogarty's every utterance.

Gogarty's fifteen minutes of fame turned into fifteen long weeks of evidence. Because of his ill-health, the tribunal sat only in the mornings but even then frequent breaks were necessary. Before the tribunal started, it had been predicted that Gogarty would never enter the witness box; when it finally got under way, the lawyers were expected to tear him apart. Unseen enemies leaked unfavourable stories about him in the newspapers. Lawyers for Michael Bailey promised 'some big ambush'. Both Bailey and the Murphys employed expensive public relations executives to promote their versions of the story to any journalist who would listen. Gogarty stood alone in a world of crack lawyers and spindoctors.

Yet something amazing happened, as this elderly David started to turn the tables on the assembled Goliaths. Gogarty admitted his part in wrongdoing and expressed regret for this, but he held fast to his story about planning corruption. With time, he developed the skills to fend off the criticism thrown at him in the box. From the start, he displayed a razor-sharp mind, one which could remember the All-Ireland finalists in some distant year or the date of a crucial company meeting a decade earlier. Slowly, the 81-year-old began to get the better of the lawyers, at least in the popular mind.

'I came here to the tribunal to get the truth, warts and all, and if I did wrong I am ready to take my place in the queue to pay for it,' he declared early on in his evidence,[5] and repeated the line for effect at regular intervals thereafter.

The bad-tempered jousts between the witness and Garrett Cooney made for compulsive listening when they were re-enacted on Vincent Browne's night-time radio programme on RTÉ. Gogarty's attacks on 'lawyers on £1,350 a day' and 'crooked solicitors' earned him a personal fan club, an ever-growing collection of retired people who came to cheer for the man expressing the collective frustration of Ireland's *petit bourgeoisie*.

Even when the action wilted, other events intervened to maintain the sense of theatre. On one occasion, a solicitor discovered a gun near the tribunal hall. An absent-minded Garda detective assigned to security at the tribunal had forgotten the weapon after a visit to the toilets. As the proceedings halted in disarray, the colour-writers recalled the old Warren Zevon song, 'Send lawyers, guns and money/The shit has hit the fan ...'

Gogarty's lack of due respect struck a chord in society. As the chairman of a tribunal rather than a judge, Flood could do little to prevent the jokes, the insults, the cheers and the applause that became the daily diet of the tribunal. Most famously, Gogarty pounced on Cooney's unfortunate reference to the witness's 'long rambling speeches from the dock'. 'From the dock?' Gogarty replied, quick as a shot. 'Put me in the dock, that's where they want me, in the dock. Oh, Jesus, oh, Mother of God.'[6]

There were moments when you could hear a pin drop in Dublin Castle; for example, when Gogarty reported Joseph Murphy junior's alleged threats to 'break every fucking bone in your body'; or when he related the alleged conversation with Michael Bailey on the way to the famous meeting with Ray Burke. 'Will we get a receipt?' Gogarty says he asked. 'Will we, fuck' goes Bailey's alleged reply.

His ability to wound and cause offence was unerring. He claimed falsely, for example, that Joseph Murphy junior had a conviction for assaulting a girl during a rugby dance in the Berkeley Court hotel in 1989 and had been fined £100. But what actually happened was described in a short report in the following day's *Evening Press*. 'The court heard that Mr Murphy had "consumed a considerable quantity of alcohol" after coming up to Dublin for the rugby match on Saturday and had suddenly lifted up the hotel's extinguisher and fired it at the crowd of rugby fans,' the newspaper reported.

Cooney turned Gogarty's lack of accuracy, rather than Murphy's japes, into the issue. Murphy was charged with malicious damage after a 'silly and trivial' prank with a fire extinguisher, Cooney said.[7] Some of the water from the extinguisher that Murphy set off landed on the mink coat 'of a lady guest' which was on a chair. The hotel management insisted he be charged, but the district judge who heard the case applied the Probation Act and Murphy was required to pay £100 to the poor box. Gogarty refused the lawyer's invitation to apologise.

Gogarty also attacked Roger Copsey, the financial controller of JMSE, pointing out that he was fined £15,000 by the professional body for accountants in England over his involvement in the collapse of a bank in the Isle of Man.[8] And he managed to zero in on George Redmond's legendary reputation for meanness by alleging the official had asked him if JMSE 'had any painters to do a job on his house'.[9] But his phenomenal recall could desert him under hostile cross-questioning, as Cooney found out, and the witness would fall back on formulaic responses such as 'I couldn't swear to it' or 'You'll have to ask …'

With time, the legal disputes between the parties grew shriller. Gogarty had made a detailed sworn affidavit, so the tribunal wanted fuller statements from those who figured in his allegations. The aim was to prevent anyone 'pulling rabbits out of hats' during cross-examination. But the other parties continued to play their cards close to their chest; Burke, for example, refused to consent to his Dáil statement of September 1997 being circulated as a statement to the tribunal.

With Gogarty insisting that each and every detail of his pension battle be covered, Murphys demanded that all the evidence favourable to their position should also be adduced in evidence. Colm Allen SC, for the Baileys, justifiably claimed that only forty-five minutes of the first ten days' hearings had been taken up with relevant evidence.[10]

JMSE's lawyers branded Gogarty 'a malicious and artful liar' with 'a keen eye on a headline'. It would be 'a pointless exercise' to allow such a person to see the questions for cross-examination, they argued.[11] Garrett Cooney depicted Gogarty as a wrecker of reputations, a man who would destroy others for selfish, personal reasons, and someone with a 'tendency to accuse people in the wrong when he doesn't get his own way'.

Cooney's cross-examination of Gogarty was catty and combative on both sides, though leavened with the odd dash of humour. On one occasion, Cooney was quizzing the witness about a document he had been handed, when Gogarty shouted: 'I can't listen to you and read this bloody thing'. A frustrated Cooney appealed to the chairman, saying: 'I'm not sure if this is the Peacock or the Abbey'. To laughter from the public gallery, Gogarty retorted: 'No, the Gaiety,' a reminder that the Murphy group once owned that theatre. 'I suspect,' said Cooney, 'it may have been the *Folies Bérgères*.'

On another occasion, Cooney told the witness to stop looking at his legal team. 'I'm not, I'm looking at you, I've a pain in me face looking at you,' Gogarty replied, to more laughter from his fan club in the public gallery. 'Beauty's only skin deep, Mr Cooney,' Flood purred as counsel shook his head.[12]

Cooney grew more frustrated by the day. Here was a lawyer of forty years' standing complaining that Gogarty's answers were 'aggressive' and 'inclined to be funny'. He accused the 81-year-old witness of trying to sabotage his cross-examination, and warned that he would 'seek a remedy elsewhere' — lawyer-speak for the High Court.[13] Gogarty, theatrically, offered to go to Mountjoy, and his lawyer accused Cooney of throwing a tantrum. An exasperated Flood declared: 'If you want to go to the High Court, you are welcome to go now.' 'What is going on here? Are you going to give us a chance to defend ourselves?' Cooney asked a short time later.

Suddenly, Flood was demanding an apology for Cooney's 'insulting and insolent' remark and, when he didn't get it, he adjourned proceedings to ringing applause and cries of 'hear, hear' from the public gallery. Flood rubbed salt in Cooney's wounds the following day by demanding that the senior counsel withdraw from the tribunal. The hearing was again adjourned as an unrepentant Cooney vowed to take the matter to the Bar Council.

It seemed the tribunal couldn't sink much lower. In sixteen months of existence, it had made little headway in explaining the Burke payment. Its hearings were a morass of claim and counter-claim. Three of the principal legal teams — for Redmond, the Murphys and Burke — had withdrawn for differing reasons. One witness, Redmond, had been arrested and the main witness, Gogarty, was sick. And now Cooney and Flood, two of the most senior figures in the Irish Bar, were locked in an unseemly spat that had little to do with the matters under investigation.

For the public attending the tribunal and those who listened nightly to actors Joe Taylor and Malcolm Douglas re-enacting the proceedings on RTÉ radio, it was better than the theatre. 'It's the best free show in town. What better way to while away the winter?' one tribunal 'lifer' told *The Irish Times*.

The Bar Council, unhappy at the unfavourable light cast on the profession by the dispute, effected a compromise resolution between the two men. Cooney returned to the tribunal, where he issued a short statement that expressed regret at what happened but stopped short of an apology. The legal wrangling continued as before.

Michael Bailey's lawyers were due to cross-examine Gogarty in March 1999, the week of the Cheltenham races. Fortunately for Bailey's passion for horses, Gogarty became 'acutely distressed' after a Sunday paper ran a story claiming he paid to have workers intimidated during a strike at the Moneypoint generating station in 1981. His questioning was postponed for a week. The two Bailey brothers grabbed their unexpected release to fly over to England and see their horse, *Linden's Lotto*, run (and lose). Back at the tribunal, there were the by now ritual condemnations of the latest leak, the assertions by lawyers that *their* clients were not responsible and the decision to refer yet another leak to the Garda.

Bailey's senior counsel, Colm Allen, had earlier promised 'some big ambush' of Gogarty, so the witness and everyone else at the tribunal were on tenterhooks for the start of his cross-examination. But Gogarty proved more than a match for his portly, bearded inquisitor. His repartee was smooth and played to the public gallery. When Allen referred to him as the tribunal's 'star' witness, he responded: 'If you put any more stars on me, I'll be up in Heaven'.[14]

Allen suggested he was 'utterly indifferent' to corruption. The only reason he was there was to 'damnify' his former employers. 'Isn't it as plain as the rather substantial nose on my face that all you have sought to do is to damnify anyone who gets in your way?' Allen asked. 'First of all, your nose is nearly covered with your bloody moustache and your beard,' Gogarty replied. Allen apologised for his 'hirsute' appearance.

The cross-examination continued in this vaudevillian manner, typified by Allen's comment on the episode in which Gogarty asked about a receipt for the payment to Ray Burke and was allegedly told by Michael Bailey: 'Will we, fuck'. 'Which I presume, wasn't an invitation?' Allen added, to belly laughter from the public gallery.

It wasn't long before Allen and Gogarty were trading insults by the dozen, to the amusement of the public and the dismay of the chairman. Allen repeatedly branded the witness a liar and Gogarty was happy to return the compliment to the man he mocked as 'a second-rate barrister'.

Gogarty showed his continuing knack for delivering a good line, even if his musical knowledge was a bit shaky: 'The truth is out there,' he declared at one point, 'just like in that famous song. The answer is flowing in the wind'. On another occasion, when Allen accused him of 'traducing' Charles Haughey, he responded: 'Just go over to the other [Moriarty] tribunal and you will find all of that'.

The tribunal was in a difficult position, caught between a truculent witness and a legal team that had revealed almost nothing of its client's story. It was all 'brilliant theatre, but it was also demeaning and largely pointless,' I wrote of one particularly lively day's evidence.[15]

Towards the end of his cross-examination, Allen unveiled his long-promised 'ambush'. Michael Bailey would say he paid Gogarty £162,000 as a 'finder's fee' for his help in securing the purchase of the north Dublin lands.[16] Up to now, Gogarty had been claiming Bailey tried to buy his silence on an attempt to bribe Ray Burke. Now Bailey was claiming that Gogarty sought a bribe of his own. He depicted the tribunal's main witness as a voracious, disloyal employee determined to take a substantial cut on a land deal he essentially controlled.

Gogarty rejected the claim as 'a damn lie' and accused Bailey of 'having cleaned up and taken the Murphys for a ride'. The proceedings grew even more fractious. When Gogarty's counsel Frank Callanan intervened on a number of occasions, Allen delivered one of his more puerile attempts at humour. 'Mr Callanan is beginning to jump up and down with the frequency one would normally associate with the bloomers of members of the oldest professions,' he declared.[17] The day ended with Gogarty telling Allen 'don't be shaking your fist at me' and Allen protesting that he was just putting on his watch.

Right to the finish of Allen's cross-examination, witness and counsel crossed swords. 'Bullshit, bullshit,' were Gogarty's final words to the senior counsel, and there ended one of the most bizarre cross-examinations in Irish legal history.

Gogarty left Dublin Castle that day like an old matinée idol, one hand gripping his walking-stick and the other raised in acknowledgement of the cheers from a waiting throng of well-wishers. Queen Mother-like, he waved at the crowd as his driver took him away from the well-heeled, mostly elderly, fans in the public gallery to whom he was 'the people's champion'.

The rest of Gogarty's cross-examination was an anti-climax. Flood told George Redmond's solicitor, Anthony Harris, he was 'wandering around like an Arab in the desert' and 'babbling like a brook' during a brief cross-examination. He ruled out questions from gardaí who had been the subject of allegations by Gogarty on the basis that the witness had 'clearly and unequivocally' retracted any allegation of wrongdoing. There were lengthy delays caused by legal proceedings over the Conroy affidavit and the row between the tribunal and the Criminal Assets Bureau over George Redmond's records.

Ray Burke's new legal team completed their cross-examination of Gogarty in half an hour, largely thanks to a restrained approach taken by senior counsel Joe Finnegan. Sticking to the facts and avoiding the name-calling that characterised previous questioning, Finnegan set out Burke's version of the 1989 meeting in calm and measured tones. 'Mr Finnegan, a good man,' Gogarty remarked at the end. Yet even Finnegan couldn't gloss over the fact that Burke's story was changing. He had told the Dáil in 1997 that the JMSE contribution was 'entirely in cash'. Now, a month after the company produced the evidence that the contribution included a cheque for £10,000, Burke was agreeing with this version.

By the end of his evidence, the gloss had started to chip off Gogarty's performance. A good memory couldn't hide the fact that he was deeply embroiled in the whole seedy affair. He had an offshore account just like so many others, even if he did settle with the Revenue during the 1993 tax amnesty. For all his allegations of a web of planning intrigue and corruption, his direct experience of senior politicians was confined to a single meeting with a Government minister. The 'Mother of God' routine grew tiresome with repetition and his performance owed more to Boucicault than *Mr Smith goes to Washington*. Gogarty's repeated jousts with Cooney merely served to delay proceedings even further. And, truth be told, proceedings weren't really going anywhere at this stage.

Few people shared Gogarty's belief that Ray Burke got £40,000, and not £30,000, from the Murphys, or his contention that Joseph Murphy junior attended the meeting in Burke's house. The inconsistencies in the versions Gogarty gave to various solicitors, gardaí and politicians were amply highlighted by Garrett Cooney and others. He first told a journalist he gave Redmond £25,000, but later claimed the amount was £15,000. He told the TD Tommy Broughan and the journalist Frank Connolly that the JMSE managing director Frank Reynolds was at the meeting in Ray Burke's house in 1989, but later said he wasn't. There was no basis for his sweeping claims of Garda corruption, which he wisely steered away from in the witness box. His draft statement contained groundless claims about Charles Haughey and Bertie Ahern that were not contained in his sworn affidavit.[18] He claimed that he had no contact with Bailey between 1992 and 1996, but the telephone records proved this wasn't the case. And why was his name entered in George Redmond's 1988 diary on thirteen occasions? Gogarty originally said he only met Redmond twice that year.

The Murphys and the Baileys claimed that Gogarty was seeking cuts of his own on various land deals, and they produced a variety of scribbled notes in seeming confirmation of this argument. Cooney argued impressively that Gogarty was determined to blacken the name of the Murphys.

But equally the thrust of Gogarty's main allegations still stood. There *was* a payment to Burke, as Gogarty had always insisted. It was only after he went public with his allegations that both Burke and Redmond admitted to receiving money, though not to the extent or in the manner first alleged by Gogarty. JMSE undoubtedly paid Burke a huge sum of money for no clear reason. Although it was Gogarty who handed over the payment, it is hard to accept the company's contention that he was on a 'frolic' of his own when so many other JMSE executives were involved in preparing, collecting or authorising the money.

Gogarty finally completed his main evidence at the end of April 1999. The scourge of lawyers and unlikely champion of the common man took his leave from Dublin Castle, waving to well-wishers as his Garda escort sped him back to the anonymous retirement in north Dublin whence he was plucked. The massive public gallery dissolved, their hero gone. 'I don't know if I'll be here every day from now on. If the weather keeps up I might go swimming,' one of the regular attendees, Peter Zambra, told *The Irish Times*.[19]

❖

With the departure of the main actor, a succession of minor characters came to Dublin Castle to deliver their often flawed memories. The hearings delved deep into the affairs of JMSE and Gogarty's demand for a pension, and shed far too little light on the actual payment to Burke. There were more delays caused by legal disputes and High Court proceedings, the row with the Criminal Assets Bureau and the campaign for the European elections.

Up to then, the tack adopted by Gogarty's opponents was clear. Inconsistencies in his story were repeatedly highlighted and flaws in his character alleged. Everything possible was done to shoot down any other evidence which chimed with his version of events. Thus, for example, huge efforts were made to rule the Conroy affidavit off-side, because this backed up Gogarty's thesis.

However, Gogarty wasn't the only voice from within JMSE that was 'singing' about the payment to Burke. Back in June 1997, when the government was being formed, PD leader Mary Harney had been tipped off about the payment by a party source with connections — very close connections — to the company.

Gay Grehan was a former director of JMSE whose wife Mary achieved national prominence after she carried out medical research linking the Sellafield nuclear plant in Cumbria to an abnormal level of childhood cancers in County Louth. A GP, she stood unsuccessfully for the Progressive Democrats in the county in the 1997 election. Ironically, as Gogarty revealed, while Mary Grehan was campaigning against Sellafield, her husband's company in Dublin provided the steel used to build the much-criticised nuclear plant.

After the election, when the PDs were negotiating to form a

government with Fianna Fáil and it was clear that Ray Burke was the subject of continuing controversy, the Grehans contacted Harney. Harney says Gay Grehan told her Burke got £60,000 from JMSE and Michael Bailey, though he didn't have first-hand knowledge of this.

On 30 November 1998, before the start of public hearings, tribunal lawyers Des O'Neill and Pat Hanratty travelled to Dundalk to interview Grehan at his home. The two men had carried out dozens of such interviews as part of the process of gathering information and the swearing of affidavits. Hanratty asked the questions and took the notes, while O'Neill observed or tried to clarify matters when this was needed. Most of these interviews were fairly humdrum, but this one wasn't.

O'Neill and Hanratty returned to Dublin believing they had heard something extraordinary. Grehan first found out about the Burke payment from the company accountant John Maher five or six months after it was made in June 1989, according to the draft statement Hanratty drew up for Grehan.[20] 'Bailey/Bovale' made a similar payment (i.e. £30,000) and the purpose was 'to ensure that planning permission was granted in respect of the development of the land being purchased by Michael Bailey'. It was 'highly unlikely' that Gogarty would have paid cash 'unless some other party was present'. This was a sensational account. It appeared to show that JMSE managers knew all about the Burke payment, that the money was given in return for planning favours, and that Gogarty was not the prime mover behind the transaction.

There was only one problem: Grehan wouldn't sign the statement. Hanratty paid a second visit to Dundalk on 21 December, and produced the draft statement for the couple to read through. He says Grehan agreed with the contents, with one exception, but asked to think about it overnight.

When Hanratty called the following day, Grehan said he wanted to consult his solicitor. The tribunal lawyer promised to ring after Christmas, but Grehan then instructed his solicitor to handle all communications with the tribunal. When Grehan's statement arrived from his solicitor, it bore no resemblance to Hanratty's draft. Now Grehan was saying he learned about the Burke payment in late 1996, when allegations were beginning to appear in the newspapers anyway. He attributed some of his knowledge to Gogarty rather than

John Maher, and he made no mention of a £30,000 matching payment by Bailey. In any case, his understanding of events was entirely based on 'rumour and hearsay'. In essence, Grehan was now saying nothing new. A crucial prop for Gogarty's version had been kicked away almost as soon as it was put in place. The tribunal was back where it started.

In fact, it was worse off, because the two statements became the focus of a huge legal row. Grehan turned up at the tribunal in May 1999 with a top senior counsel, Denis McCullough, but it was Garrett Cooney, for JMSE, that launched the main attack on his behalf. In a heated standoff with the tribunal, Cooney battled to have the draft statement ruled out of order. After Mr Justice Flood ruled against him, Cooney accused Hanratty and O'Neill of 'dubious ethical standards' — an extraordinary allegation for one barrister to make against another — and vowed to bring his grievance to the Bar Council. Mr Justice Flood gave his two staff members the opportunity to come to the witness box to deny Cooney's charge and clear their names. Thus it was that the tribunal found itself interrogating its own staff instead of pushing ahead with investigations into corruption.

Grehan's testimony only added to the confusion. In a bizarre appearance in the box, the former JMSE director contradicted his own evidence and that of Mary Harney. Grehan first said Hanratty's draft statement was 'totally incorrect' and spoke of his amazement and shock when he received it.[21] But under cross-examination he proceeded to agree with large parts of it and admitted that he may have 'inadvertently' provided tribunal lawyers with other information they included in the statement. Thus, Grehan said he might have 'inadvertently' told Hanratty that he knew about the Burke payment in 1989. He may have 'inadvertently' said he learned of the payment from John Maher. And Mary Harney may have 'misunderstood' him when he rang the PD leader in June 1997.

Grehan first said he did not identify the 'unnamed politician' to Harney, but later changed his mind and said he did name Ray Burke. If Grehan's evidence was to be believed, it appears he rang one of the State's leading politicians, whom he barely knew, to tell her, not what he knew from company sources, but what he read in the newspaper at the time. The first he knew about the payment from JMSE was when Burke admitted it in the Dáil in September 1997, he now claimed.

When he returned to the box in November, Grehan explained that the first he, Maher and Frank Reynolds knew of the £30,000 paid to Burke was when the journalist Frank Connolly came to them with the allegation.[22] The problem here is that in 1997, Connolly was investigating allegations of a payment of £40,000, not £30,000. The conflict between Cooney and the lawyers was defused after Mr Justice Flood pointed out that Grehan had admitted 'inadvertently' giving wrong information to the tribunal lawyers. Hanratty and O'Neill couldn't therefore be accused of getting their facts wrong.

Grehan was now saying he rang Harney to 'reassure' her that JMSE had paid the money but it was not for a planning matter.[23] So whereas Harney thought she was getting 'important information' from a key source in the company, Grehan says he was just giving 'reassurance' and his knowledge was based on 'rumour and hearsay'.

Grehan left the company in November 1997 just as the tribunal was being set up, but denied this was because there was more bad news 'coming down the tracks'. His departure was 'merely coincidental'. He got a severance payment — amount undisclosed — in 1997 and two further payments in 1998 and 1999. The last payment was made a month after his first appearance in the witness box in May. That, he told the tribunal, left 'nothing unresolved' between him and the company.[24]

With Gogarty's evidence being taken first because of his age and infirmity, it wasn't until September 1999 that Mr Justice Flood made the opening statement that lawyers for Murphys and the Baileys had been demanding for months. And it wasn't until February in the following year that tribunal lawyers made their opening statement setting out the background to the tribunal and its proposed lines of inquiry. Senior counsel John Gallagher outlined the reasons for the delays afflicting the tribunal: elderly, sick or plain uncooperative witnesses on the one hand, document mountains, constant legal challenges and the widening of the terms of reference on the other.[25]

By February 2000, the tribunal had sent over 400 questionnaires to Oireachtas members, 200 to county councillors, 138 to An Bord Pleanala officials and 514 to local authority officials. Some 210 people had been interviewed and 63 witnesses called over 149 days of evidence. And the tribunal was only really beginning.

In the run-up to his appearance in the witness box, Ray Burke kept well away from Dublin Castle. He seldom ventured beyond north Dublin and appeared aloof and even indifferent to proceedings at the tribunal. But in reality he was following the evidence closely, his political antennae alive to the growing power of Flood's inquiry. In June 1997 he shredded over half a ton of confidential documents, though he later said these did not include material of interest to the tribunal. There were rumours of Burke trying to strike a deal by offering information in return for a promise of immunity from prosecution. Somewhere along the way, Burke parted company from his legal team. He remained unrepresented for much of Gogarty's evidence before new lawyers were engaged in time to cross-examine the elderly witness. Later, Burke lost a second senior counsel when Joe Finnegan was made a High Court judge.

Finally, more than 600 days after the tribunal was set up to investigate the allegations circulating about him, Burke entered the witness box in Dublin Castle in July 1999. The former minister was confident, even cocksure, as he cantered through his denials of the allegations made by Gogarty. He lost no opportunity to assert the height of his political stature or the length of his experience. After all, here was a man who was elected on the first count in nine general elections and three local ones; someone who claimed a central role in creating the Celtic Tiger; a politician who, far from being a tool of developers, used his influence to fight against rezonings by Dublin county councillors.

Clearly carefully prepared, and relying heavily on a number of binders he brought with him to the stand, Burke fixed his gaze steadfastly on the tribunal chairman, and away from the media and John Gallagher SC, who was asking the questions.[26] He told the Dáil in 1997 he got £30,000 in cash from Gogarty, but now he acknowledged, without admitting any error on his part, that the amount comprised £20,000 in cash and a cheque for £10,000 in two 'fairly reasonably-sized envelopes'.

Here was a complete stranger coming to his house to give him at least £30,000, on behalf of a company he had nothing to do with. No receipt was given, or asked for. Burke couldn't remember counting the money. He couldn't remember the denominations of the notes. He never wrote to express his thanks. It was 'not in the least unusual,' he insisted. As he told it, the business community was falling over itself to give money to Fianna Fáil for rescuing the State from economic ruin. And who better to give this money to but one of its most senior ministers and the 'standard-bearer' of the party in north Dublin?

In spite of Burke's ebullience, the cracks in his story quickly showed. On his second day of evidence, it emerged that he got £35,000 from a then unnamed donor just a week before the Gogarty payment in June 1989. So the Gogarty money was not the largest contribution he had received, as he told the Dáil in September 1997.

'My life was seamless. I was a politician from the time I got up in the morning until I went to bed at night,' Burke exclaimed at the end of his third day of evidence.

Too true. And nowhere was the join between the personal and political in his life more invisible than in his financial affairs. In fact, Burke's evidence to the tribunal quickly revealed his Dáil statement as an exercise in artful wording and clear untruths. Here was the man who told TDs he obtained a £35,000 overdraft in 1989 for 'family reasons' — the refurbishment of his home, building a tennis court for his children and a change of car for his wife. He raised the issue of the overdraft to call attention to his 'financial straits' at the time. 'Does this sound like someone who was awash with cash?' he asked his Dáil colleagues.

But at the time of this speech, as the tribunal established, Burke had £127,000 in one of his bank accounts.[27] At the tribunal, he admitted that the overdraft was actually paid back from political funds, largely those donated by Rennicks Manufacturing in June 1989.

In 1997, he addressed the Dáil on the £30,000 he got from JMSE. 'The money received was expended,' he said and, 'I received subscriptions which were spent on my campaign.' This was untrue. Even as he gave evidence to the tribunal, ten years after the heady days of June 1989, the money that was sloshing around his accounts had still not been dissipated.

Burke then constructed a Chinese wall around the donations he received. He told the tribunal that £118,000 was still lodged in a 'political fund' which was the subject of legal and accountancy advice. The fund included some of the £30,000 given by James Gogarty in 1989. Because he had retired from political life, he could not longer benefit from the money.

But when is a 'political fund' a 'political fund'? No-one in Fianna Fáil headquarters knew of the existence of this 'political fund'. The first anyone outside Burke's constituency knew of it was in 1998, when Burke told the Taoiseach, Bertie Ahern, of its existence — though not its size — on the night of the by-election to replace him in Dublin North. It is of interest, too, that after his retirement, Burke's bank manager recorded the fund as a personal asset.

Sometimes, you just have to ask the right question. But then as Burke said in a different context when giving evidence to the Beef tribunal: 'If the other side don't ask the right question, they won't get the answers'. Back in 1997, Jim O'Keeffe asked in the Dáil if the Minister had lodged money in an overseas bank account since 1989. Burke reacted angrily and refused to answer questions about 'my particular account'. 'I have bared my soul to the House today and I find that particular question offensive in the extreme … I have no overseas bank account.'

But O'Keeffe continued to press.

O'Keeffe: Is the Minister confirming that since 1989 he has not opened or lodged money in an overseas bank account? I refer in particular to an account in the Isle of Man.

Burke: As I have already said, the answer is no.

This was technically correct. Burke hadn't opened an overseas account since 1989, nor had he lodged money in such an account since that date. But he did have an account in Jersey between 1984 and 1994. Burke told the tribunal in July 1999 that £95,000 was lodged into this account in 1984. The money consisted of political donations raised from supporters in the UK. At the tribunal, he fended off further questions on these payments, saying they were 'matters for the Revenue'. In fact, as recounted in a later chapter, the money came in massive lump-sum contributions from offshore companies owned by the builders Brennan and McGowan.

Many more errors and inconsistencies in his Dáil statement were exposed during his evidence to the tribunal. He didn't just receive contributions during election campaigns, as he claimed. He never did give two drafts to his local organisation, as stated. The JMSE money wasn't paid entirely in cash. It wasn't 'the largest contribution I have received during any election campaign either before or since 1989'. Oliver Barry gave his politician friend £35,000 just a week before James Gogarty came knocking on his door with £30,000.

This was a particularly clever phrasing, which hid the fact that Burke believed he had received not one 'exceptional contribution' of £30,000, but three. He later told the tribunal that he mistakenly remembered the Barry payment as £30,000. Much later, too, the tribunal would discover that even the Barry payment of £35,000 wasn't the largest contribution that Burke had received.

In his evidence, Burke suggested a reason for his secrecy. TDs' salaries were inadequate to cover campaign expenses, he said, and deputies were reluctant to declare funds raised locally to the party for fear that headquarters would demand a cut. The picture painted is of a loose collective of politicians cooperating out of mutual convenience, rather than a cohesive political party with a unifying philosophy.

Even as late as July 1999, in his evidence to the tribunal, the former minister was still insisting that the 'broad thrust' of his Dáil statement and answers was correct. The statement was made 'in the raw heat of a highly emotional trauma which I was going through at that time,' he explained.[28]

You get an insight into Burke's fraught relationship with his party bosses from the tussle over the Rennicks money. Fianna Fáil was expecting a contribution from Fitzwilton in the weeks before the 1989 election. When party fundraisers contacted the company, they were told the money had been paid through a subsidiary, Rennicks Manufacturing, to Burke. So they contacted Burke, who presented them with a bank draft for £10,000 (out of £30,000 received) at a fundraising lunch in June 1989. When it was discovered that he had only paid over part of the money, Burke was confronted with a demand for the balance. 'That's as much as you're getting. Good luck,' Burke replied.[29]

The last of the three parties to the June 1989 meeting to give evidence was Michael Bailey. The main defence advanced by Michael Bailey and his brother Tom against Gogarty's claim that they bribed politicians to get land rezoned is to point to the ultimate fate of the lands. Just seventy-four acres of the 700 or so acres of north Dublin land had been rezoned since the Baileys bought them in 1989, and only nine acres had received planning permission, their lawyers told the tribunal in 1999.

Some 316 acres were under corn, and sixty-three were being used as grazing for horses. Fifteen acres in Finglas were being developed as a technology park. The Baileys sold on 225 acres in Donabate, including the site of the former Turvey House, at agricultural rates. Some of this land was then developed as a golf course and for apartments. Finally, forty acres were used for road development in the area.[30] It didn't sound like a great rush to development.

In the light of all this, Michael Bailey's promise to 'procure' planning permission for the lands in return for fifty per cent ownership of the lands, as expressed in his 1989 letter to Gogarty, was 'a dead duck. It never flew,' in the words of his senior counsel Colm Allen. According to Allen, the only real proposition therefore on the table was for Bailey to buy the lands outright, which is what he did. But this explanation fails to account for the possible intent of the parties in 1989, when the Murphy group sold the lands to Bailey for £2.3 million. It is entirely possible that subsequent events could have blown earlier plans off course.

Further, this depiction of continuing rural bliss is misleading. The tribunal broadly agrees with Allen's account of the fate of the lands — as of March 2000, just twenty-four acres had been developed for a housing estate in Portmarnock and an industrial park in Finglas.[31] Other evidence, however, indicates that the Baileys were well on the way to turning muck into gold. On at least three occasions in 1993, for example, Dublin county councillors voted, against the advice of their officials, to rezone Bailey-owned land from agricultural to more valuable residential or industrial uses.

Then there was the remarkable tale of the £50 million 'technology park' Bovale Developments planned for their site near Finglas.[32] This ambitious project would employ 1,500 people, the company promised. The local chamber of commerce hailed it as 'a glimmer of light at the end of a dark tunnel'. Representations were made to the Minister for Finance, Ruairi Quinn, who met Michael Bailey in the presence of the local Labour TD, Roisín Shortall. Quinn was won over by Bailey's arguments and the site was given special tax designation as an enterprise area in the 1997 Finance Act. Yet only weeks later, it emerged that there were serious problems with drainage on the site. Putting these problems right through the construction of the north fringe sewer would cost £20 million.

Department of Finance officials expressed their shock at the news, and said they would never have granted designation if they had known about the drainage problem. Nonetheless, the local authority rezoned the site to reflect its new designation under the Finance Act. Within a year, the Baileys succeeded in having it further rezoned to highly valuable residential land.

The Baileys' second line of defence is to allege that Gogarty sought a massive 'finder's fee' — a bribe — for his help in securing the purchase of the north Dublin lands. This approach implicated the Baileys in wrongdoing but, more importantly, it placed a huge question-mark over the character of Gogarty.

The first anyone learned of Michael and Tom Bailey's defence against the Gogarty allegations was on 4 February 1999, when the *Irish Independent* published a story under the headline 'Gogarty faces quiz on £50,000 bank cash'. The story, by journalist Sam Smyth, claimed that Michael Bailey withdrew £50,000 in cash from the Anglo-Irish Bank in November 1989, saying it was the first of three payments to Gogarty to secure a land deal. A bank official was said to have made contemporaneous notes of Bailey's comments and this document was available to the tribunal.

So was this the 'big ambush' promised by Bailey's lawyers some months previously? The Baileys, the bank and the tribunal — the only three parties aware of the transaction — all denied having leaked it to the press. The import of this revelation was huge. Bailey was effectively saying he paid off Gogarty with three sums of £50,000, the first in cash and the last clearly the post-dated and unused cheque which Gogarty held on to. There was only one problem. There was no mention of Gogarty as claimed on the bank documents, nor could the officials recall his name being mentioned.

The tribunal broke off its questioning of Gogarty for a day to hold an impromptu investigation into the leak. The Bailey brothers suffered a torrid cross-examination by lawyers for the tribunal and for Gogarty, which exposed serious contradictions in their version of events. The following month, Colm Allen provided more details of the brothers' counter-allegation.[33] Gogarty, it was claimed, was looking for £150,000. Michael Bailey felt this was exorbitant but he coughed up anyway. In fact, he ended up paying £162,000, after Gogarty sought interest on what he considered delayed payment of the money.

At a meeting in the Royal Dublin Hotel in 23 November 1989, Bailey allegedly gave Gogarty a briefcase containing £50,000 in cash and two post-dated cheques for £50,000 each. Strangely, this was four days *before* the sale of the lands to Bailey was agreed. The two cheques, it was said, were meant as security against the cash that was to come. The rest of the money was paid in smaller cash payments over six years. As evidence, Allen produced petty cash vouchers for sums of £5,000, £10,000 and £15,000, allegedly for three payments to Gogarty in 1990.

There were a number of problems with this explanation, not least that it was a long time coming. For a start, the details were scant. Allen said he would produce bank records to show that a £50,000 cheque was cashed, but he was unable to provide any evidence linking this to Gogarty. There was even less evidence for the smaller cash payments. No dates and few circumstances were provided. Flood warned he might not attach a great deal of credence to the evidence. Then there was the response Bailey gave the first time he was asked about the £50,000 cheque in Gogarty's possession. In 1997, he had told the journalist Frank Connolly this payment was made to assist in the purchase of a Murphy-owned house in Baggot Street. There was no mention of a backhander or a payment relating to the north Dublin lands.

It was July 1999, and the week of the Galway Races, when Michael Bailey himself was called to give evidence. The timing might have seemed unfortunate for such an avid racegoer; however, Bailey had Celtic Helicopters on hand to whisk him down each evening to the racecourse in Ballybrit.

Bailey, his broad builder's shoulders fully occupying the witness box, started with his denials of Gogarty's allegations. They were 'a total fabrication … I couldn't believe that someone could fabricate such lies'. He even wrote the word 'L-I-E-S' in big writing in the margin of the affidavit when he first read it. He disagreed with everything that Gogarty said except for the fact that Burke got two envelopes.

His decision not to attend for interview at the tribunal, or to furnish a sworn affidavit, was taken on legal advice. 'I'm a bricklayer, not a legal eagle,' he remarked. Yet for a developer who had built thousands of houses, he appeared to know remarkably little about rezoning or obtaining planning permissions; at one point, he couldn't even say whether planning permissions expired after five years or seven.

In the witness box, he quickly developed contradiction into something of an art form. He contradicted the version of events he put out a few years earlier, he contradicted his statement to the tribunal and he contradicted his own evidence from question to question. He even contradicted the version put forward by his own counsel, Colm Allen.

One day, for example, he told the tribunal he never met politicians about planning matters. By the afternoon, he was detailing his attempts to lobby councillors on such matters. Depending on when you talked to him, Bailey was either not present at the meeting in Burke's home in 1989, in the house but not present when the money was handed over, or in the same room and a witness to Gogarty's payment.[34]

Taking a note out of Gogarty's copybook, he frequently resorted to exclamations of mock-horror, or challenged the barristers head-on. 'Jesus, Mary and Joseph, would you grow up, for Christ's sake. That is totally untrue,' he roared at Gogarty's counsel at one stage. Bailey professed a continuing admiration for his tormentor, Gogarty. 'If he died in the morning I would be the first man to be at his funeral.' 'I'd say you would,' replied Gogarty's counsel.

More seriously, Bailey admitted that the £50,000 cheque he slipped into Gogarty's breast pocket in 1990 was a backhander or 'under the table' payment. He also admitted lying when he spun the tale to the journalist Frank Connolly about the cheque being for a building on Baggot Street. After the initial £50,000 down-payment, Bailey says he paid Gogarty in 'dribs and drabs' over the years that followed. Gogarty would press him for money and he would cough up. 'One day I gave him £1,000 and he came back to me on the phone and told me I was £20 short.' A final settlement was reached in 1996 after Gogarty threatened to implicate the Baileys in media investigations into planning irregularities, Bailey claims. Gogarty sought £25,000 in interest but eventually settled for £12,000.

Bailey's explanation begged a number of questions. How were the alleged payments treated in Bovale's accounts? Were there any records, receipts or acknowledgements for this deal? What use were the post-dated cheques to Gogarty, when they expired after six months and Bailey could have stopped them at any time? Why did Bailey happily agree to pay this enormous sum before the land deal was even completed? Why did Bailey keep no record of the massive amounts he says he paid to Gogarty? After all, only a year before, he had accused Gogarty of 'gazumping' him on a smaller land deal at Swords, yet now he was happy to rely on Gogarty telling him how much was owed.

By the end of his first week of evidence, tribunal counsel Des O'Neill had laid bare a multitude of discrepancies in Bailey's evidence. The witness was reeling. 'Oh Jesus, chairman, I'm telling you honestly, chairman, this man has my head spinning with all the different questions he's asking me, I can't concentrate on it,' the builder exclaimed. The only record of any of the payments to Gogarty was kept in a small spiral-bound notebook with a kitten on the cover. The so-called 'pussy book' contained handwritten lists of under-the-counter payments made to a variety of people in the 1980s. Most of the sums recorded in the book are small, but three entries relating to Gogarty amount to £30,000.

The problem for Bailey was that none of the £94,000 listed in the 'pussy book' appears in the accounts of Bovale Developments. If the tribunal was to investigate the truth of Bailey's 'finder's fee' allegation, it would need to scrutinise the accounts of Michael and Tom Bailey and their companies, as well as those of Caroline Bailey, wife of Tom, who made the entries in the book.

Caroline, a former bank clerk who carried out the day-to-day accounting for the two brothers, was called to give evidence.[35] She told the tribunal that it 'signified nothing' that the entries for Gogarty were written in the 'pussy book' in black pen, when all the other entries were written in blue. Later, the tribunal had forensic tests carried out on the 'pussy book' but they failed to establish the authenticity of the book one way or another.

A figure of £50,000 in the accounts was linked to the acquisition of the Murphy lands. Perhaps, it was speculated, this had been paid to Gogarty. However, Caroline revealed that this referred to a £50,000 cheque paid into the couple's personal account, where it was used to fund Tom's sheep farm in County Meath. If it was used to buy sheep, it couldn't have been given as payment or security to Gogarty. A further hole had been knocked in the Baileys' story.

Like his brother, Tom Bailey was a true rags-to-riches story. The poor boy from County Roscommon who left school at fifteen, who toiled long hours as a bricklayer on the houses his brother Michael had started building in Dublin, was now fabulously wealthy. With his wife Caroline, he lived in a fine house on 185 acres of rolling land in County Meath. In his new life Tom took up gentlemanly pursuits such as sheep-breeding and cattle-rearing. From the witness box, Tom explained how he once spent £94,000 on a pure-bred Suffolk sheep, and 10,000 guineas on a stock ram. Using money withdrawn from the company of which he was a director, he paid £58,000 for a lot of sixteen sheep.

Much of this lavish spending was at least partly rooted in the evasion of taxes. At least £100,000 in cheques was kept out of the company's accounts, the tribunal learned, on top of the £94,000 in under-the-counter payments listed in the 'pussy book'. Needless to say the rest of the money allegedly paid to Gogarty was also kept off the books. Asked why he failed to tell his accountant about the £100,000 in cheques that were written to pay for his sheep-rearing hobby, Tom Bailey replied: 'I don't believe he asked me about them'.

Not for the first time, the tribunal was faced with a flat refusal of a witness to open up the books for examination. Having made their allegation about a finder's fee for Gogarty, the Baileys fought to prevent the tribunal examining their accounts in order to test the veracity of their claims. The 'finder's fee' allegation was 'a collateral issue only,' their lawyer claimed, and there was no need for the tribunal to investigate it.[36]

In February 2000, Tom and Caroline Bailey and Bovale Developments went to the High Court to stop the tribunal gaining access to their personal accounts. The court rejected their claim the following month, and a Supreme Court appeal was equally unsuccessful in April.

However successful they were as builders, the Baileys were certainly accident-prone when it came to keeping their accounts. The firm suffered an unlucky series of accidents over the years that severely reduced the amount of documentation it could produce to the tribunal.

In July 1998, they lost important records when a fire was started in a steel trailer they were using as a makeshift builder's canteen in Finglas. The documentation, which included a crucial cash payments journal, was stored there along with workmen's overalls and tools. The blaze occurred four months after the tribunal had demanded the documents, and on the very day the Supreme Court was to decide on the validity of a tribunal order seeking them. A district officer with the Dublin Fire Service reported seeing a man fitting Tom Bailey's description at the scene at 6 a.m. when the fire destroyed the trailer,[37] but Bailey denies he was present.

Meanwhile, copies of the same files had already been destroyed by water damage at their auditors' office in County Kildare in Christmas 1992, though no insurance claim was ever made for the documents that were said to have been damaged. As a result, no records for Bovale or its unfortunate directors have survived for the crucial 1989-90 period — the time when Michael Bailey is alleged to have paid money to Ray Burke.

Indeed, this run of bad luck started much earlier when, in March 1990, a fire believed to have been started by vandals damaged Poppintree House, which was part of the Murphy lands. Bailey, who had bought the lands the previous December but had yet to pay the money due, demanded that JMSE rebuild the house at a cost of £400,000. Murphys were disinclined to agree to this, given that they had only paid £65,000 for the land and buildings at Poppintree.

The tribunal's forensic examination of Bovale's accounts proved highly embarrassing to the Baileys. In 1989, for example, Tom and Caroline Bailey channelled £286,000 into their own personal account and £80,000 into Michael Bailey's account, when their taxable earnings were just £25,000. Some £180,000 passed through two personal accounts held by Caroline Bailey. In 1990 and 1991, £657,000 went straight from Bovale into the personal accounts of its directors.[38] Special bank accounts were set up for these purposes, and hidden from Bovale's bankers and accountants and the tribunal.

Tom and Caroline explained that the reason he withdrew so much money from the business was to realise his 'childhood dream' of building a flock of pedigree Suffolk sheep. Much of this money was wrongly recorded as payments to the ESB or Dublin County Council, when it was being channelled secretly towards other uses. Political donations were entered in the books as returned house deposits. Caroline Bailey admitted making up fictitious names to hide the donations in the cheque-book journal and mislead the auditor.[39]

At the time, the directors of Bovale were paying themselves small salaries of between £4,500 and £36,000 a year, according to the books. The company itself made a profit on paper of only £10,000 in 1989. It made further small profits over the following two years before going into loss for the next four years. By the end of the Baileys' cross-examination, Bovale's accountant had succumbed to the inevitable by advising the Revenue Commissioners that he intended carrying out a 'major review' of the company's books.

⌐⊰∘⊱⌐

Throughout the hearings, Garrett Cooney aggressively defended the interests not only of his clients but also of others whose rights he believed were being infringed by the tribunal. Why wasn't there an opening statement setting out the specific allegations being made, he repeatedly asked. Why wasn't the planning history of the lands set out first, before the evidence was heard?

The JMSE legal team fought a series of running battles with the tribunal. Detailed statements had been prepared for each of the company's executives, but in response to the series of media leaks before the start of hearings, it was decided instead to submit brief statements denying Gogarty's various allegations.

The tribunal spent over a year trying to get the documents it required from the company. At first it got little or nothing, then it was deluged with crateloads of 'dirty, musty' — and unindexed —

files,[40] more than 30,000 documents in all. Frustrated tribunal lawyers at one point accused 'somebody' of going through the files beforehand and removing key documents.[41] The Murphys' legal team denied that charge, saying 'we could not give what we do not have'. Agreement was later reached on an indexing system.

The Murphys, senior and junior, also showed great reluctance to disclose their bank accounts. They were not prepared to make details of their accounts available, in particular overseas accounts, their lawyers told the tribunal in May 1999. Joseph Murphy senior, the tribunal was told, held no bank accounts in Ireland or England.

However, after the tribunal found evidence that Murphy and his wife Úna did have accounts in Ireland in the 1980s, it demanded further information about their financial records for a period covering almost a quarter-century. Nine accounts in the Republic were discovered in the name of Joseph Murphy, his wife Úna or their children.[42] All were non-resident accounts and one had over £270,000 in it in the mid-1980s. Murphy's lawyers said the accounts might have belonged to Úna Murphy.

Cooney also fought hard to prevent the tribunal revealing the contents of the affidavit filed by former chief executive Liam Conroy in 1988 during his wrongful dismissal case in the Isle of Man. When Flood ruled the document admissible in March 1999, the company took its case to the High Court and then the Supreme Court, which ruled against it in June that year. The Conroy affidavit was finally read out at the tribunal in September 1999.

By the time he was due to give evidence, the 82-year-old Joseph Murphy senior was in feeble health. His last trip to Dublin from tax exile on the island of Guernsey in January 1999 had ended in the Blackrock Clinic. By the summer his doctors were saying he was unfit to make the journey to Dublin Castle. According to Garrett Cooney, his client suffered short-term memory loss and another unspecified condition that would necessitate frequent interruptions when he came to give evidence. A hearing accompanied by 'excessive publicity' could put his health under serious strain, Cooney argued.

Having sat 'back-to-front' to accommodate Gogarty, the tribunal now made special arrangements to facilitate its other octogenarian witness. Flood initially considered setting up a video-link or travelling to Jersey to take his evidence, but neither proved feasible. Instead, he decided to travel to Guernsey and hear Murphy's evidence in private near his home.

Murphy was effectively seeking a private hearing before the chairman, on home ground, something that had been denied to every other witness. The tribunal had an obligation to carry its work in public, but against this Flood had to consider the appalling vista of a witness possibly dying in the box. He ordered independent medical tests, but it is unclear if these were ever carried out. The media successfully challenged their exclusion in the High Court, which quashed Mr Justice Flood's order. However, the chairman, who was already in Guernsey, simply appointed himself as a commissioner to take Murphy's evidence in private.

The tribunal set up shop in the small meeting room of a former convent, now the Les Cotils Christian conference centre, in St Peter Port, the capital of the island. With the media still pressing for the right to attend, Flood took evidence from Murphy's doctor in Guernsey, who said his patient's life might be endangered by the presence of journalists when he gave evidence. Murphy's psychiatrist said he would suffer extreme stress from the presence of the media, whether their attendance was physical or by proxy, using a video-link.

Flood again ruled that the hearing should go ahead in private, even if Murphy's fear of the media was irrational. The way was finally clear for the 82-year-old witness to make his appearance on 1 October. Arriving in the front seat of a chauffeur-driven Mercedes, Murphy walked slowly and silently past the photographers to the tribunal hall to give his evidence. 'The impression was of a man crumpled by age, but someone who must have been immensely strong in his prime,' I wrote in The Irish Times the following day.

Because of his age and ill-health, Murphy spent only a few hours a day in the box, with frequent time-outs. As a result, his evidence took three weeks instead of the expected one. It then took a further week to read out his evidence back in Dublin Castle, a bizarre and mind-numbing performance carried out by the tribunal registrar Peter Kavanagh to an empty hall.

Not surprisingly, Murphy denied the allegations made about him by Gogarty and Conroy.[43] Gogarty 'haunted' him for months to sell the Murphy lands and then took backhanders on their sale, he claimed. Conroy was 'totally bananas' and made up the allegations in his affidavit in order to 'destroy' his boss. As for Ray Burke, Michael Bailey or George Redmond, Murphy said he'd never even heard of them until they were linked to his companies. He wasn't even aware of the late-night phone call his son had made to Gogarty.[44] He had never made a political donation in his life and wouldn't have given a penny to Burke.

Murphy died at his home in Guernsey in August 2000, before the tribunal had completed its investigations into his companies. He had been suffering from cancer for the previous two years. At the time of his death, the family fortune was estimated at £30 million.

Joseph Murphy junior followed his father into the box in December 1999. The passage of time had done nothing to dim his hatred for Gogarty, whom he accused of 'lies, blackmail and theft'. The JMSE chairman denied Gogarty's allegations; he wasn't there for the Burke payment (he was in London and at a funeral in Leitrim over the relevant period), he wasn't involved in negotiations with Bailey and he never knew George Redmond. Murphy also delivered his explanation for Gogarty's allegations; it was all because he [Murphy] had refused a demand from Gogarty for £400,000 to be lodged in an offshore account as part of his pension settlement. 'He said: "Mark my words, I'll get you",' Murphy told the tribunal.

Gogarty, he claimed, used the Revenue Commissioners, the newspapers and the gardaí to blackmail him. The two men had a few meetings to try to sort out things, but Gogarty was 'like a nuclear reactor going off'. Murphy, then a 30-year-old rugby player, said he felt 'threatened and intimidated' by Gogarty, who was 75 at the time. He claimed Gogarty shouted abuse at him, at one point referring to his deceased stepmother as 'a dead effing bastard'.

The foundation stone of JMSE's defence is that Gogarty was on a 'frolic' of his own in making a payment to Burke without the knowledge of the company. But the evidence produced to the tribunal shows that others must have known something about the payment. Gogarty asked the financial controller, Roger Copsey, to supply the money for a political contribution. Copsey expressed no curiosity about the request for £30,000 in cash; later, he couldn't even recall knowing which political party it was for.[45]

Copsey in turn rang the company solicitor, Denis McArdle, to arrange the transfer of funds. The managing director Frank Reynolds accompanied the accountant, Tim O'Keeffe, to collect the money from the bank, although Reynolds says he didn't know anything about the withdrawal or what it was for. O'Keeffe, who also says he didn't know what the money was for, wrote out the cheque for £10,000 which was added to the available cash, and Gogarty and Reynolds signed it.

Also difficult to explain is the recording of the £30,000 sum in the company books as a payment for 'planning permission' and 'land enhancement'. Tim O'Keeffe, the trainee accountant who collected the money from the bank, made the entries. He claimed the reference to a 'planning permission' in the accounts related to a different entry on the page, though any common-sense reading of the document indicated otherwise.[46] Roger Copsey told the tribunal there was no explanation 'whatsoever' why a political donation would be recorded in the accounts as 'enhancement' to the value of land.[47]

The money paid to Burke was deducted against tax as though it were a legitimate business expense. In September 1997, a month before the tribunal was set up, the company corrected the error with the Revenue Commissioners and repaid £12,000.

As early as 1991, the company auditor John Bates said he informed senior executives of the existence of 'unvouched expenses' for £30,000. It follows from all this that the company must have had some inkling that there was a question mark over a large unexplained sum in its accounts. Yet it never once made a statement saying it knew a payment had been made before Burke supplied the details to the Dáil in September 1997. In July 1997, the financial controller, Roger Copsey, first told Murphy junior that he remembered 'something about a political contribution' but could not recall the date, time, amount or recipient. The frailty of his memory is strange, given that JMSE seldom contributed to politicians. The company's next largest political donation was a mere £1,000.

Strange, too, is Murphy junior's failure to inquire of Michael Bailey what he was doing in Burke's house in 1989. From the time of the first newspaper allegations in 1996, Murphy and others in his company were well aware that the unidentified 'property developer' referred to in articles was Michael Bailey. Yet it seems that Murphy never asked Bailey whether he was at Burke's house or what he was doing there. Even at the time of the Ahern investigations in June/July 1997, with the political world in convulsions and storm clouds breaking over his company, he spoke to Bailey but again failed to ask him what tribunal lawyers called 'the central question'.[48]

Another mainstay of the JMSE defence is that there would have been no point in the company paying off a politician to get planning permission on the north Dublin lands when they were being sold. However, the company hadn't sold the land at the time the payment was made to Ray Burke in June 1989; the deal with Bailey wasn't struck until November and the sale wasn't completed until several years later.

Nothing better summed up the morass of confusion swirling about the tribunal than the efforts to find out when Gogarty made his payment to Burke. By the end of the evidence, we didn't even know what day it took place. We know the money was paid during the election campaign of 1989, when polling was set for 15 June. Burke himself can't remember the date. Michael Bailey's famous letter promising to 'procure' planning permission on the north Dublin lands was dated 8 June and it seems this was also the day the cash for the payment was withdrawn from JMSE's account in AIB Talbot Street.

Gogarty, in his initial contacts with the gardaí, suggested that 8 June was the day of the meeting. However, in his evidence to the tribunal, he put the date at 'a few days after' 8 June. Notwithstanding his certainty and his powerful recollection of so many other details, he refused to be nailed down to a single date. On learning that 8 June was a Thursday, he said he believed the meeting happened on Monday, Tuesday or Wednesday of the following week, or 12-14 June.

But in his affidavit, Gogarty also remembered Burke saying at the meeting that he had a radio or television appointment later in the day. The only day on which Burke appeared on television during this period was 8 June, when he appeared on a *Today Tonight* election special with Des O'Malley. Could Gogarty's reluctance to be tied down have anything to do with the fact that Joseph Murphy junior was in London on this date? Two days later, he came over to Ireland for a family funeral in Leitrim, and he left again the following Monday.

By the end of 1999, the tribunal was, to borrow the words of its chairman, 'wandering like an Arab in the Sahara'. It was over two years since Flood had been given the job of discovering 'who gave what to whom' in relation to a few hundred acres of land in north county Dublin. 'Two long years, and we are not a jot wiser as to what happened,' I wrote in frustration that November.[49] In fact, the tribunal was a lot worse off. The number of conflicting stories and counter-allegations had grown with each day of evidence; the result was a morass of lies and confusion. As the old phrase had it: Anyone who wasn't confused didn't really know what was going on.

This confusion extended to the core event under investigation; the meeting in Ray Burke's house in June 1989. As noted above, we didn't know the date of the meeting. We didn't know who was present. We didn't even know how much Burke got — was it £30,000, £40,000 or £80,000? And, of course, we didn't know what happened to the money he did get, or why it was given. There wasn't even agreement on how many acres the Murphys owned in north Dublin — was it 711 acres, 726 acres, or some other figure? At this stage, nothing had been heard of the tribunal's promised investigations into Pádraig Flynn, Frank Dunlop, Liam Lawlor and many others.

In truth, the tribunal had lost its way. Its first mistake was to agree to listen to Gogarty's grievances against his former employers. Once that happened — and it took four months — everyone else had to have a say. At length. With full legal representation, at the taxpayers' expense. Witnesses came and went, but left little wisdom behind them. The only events they tended to confirm were those that were documented elsewhere. Their stories relied on people who were dead, and couldn't contradict them. They had, unfortunately, kept no records or receipts.

Witnesses such as Batt O'Shea or Joseph Murphy senior, both of them 82 years of age, couldn't correctly identify the years in which they got married, let alone throw any light on planning corruption. Other witnesses, such as Michael Bailey or Gay Grehan, contradicted themselves by the hour. In 1999, the Dáil Public Accounts

Committee sidelined the lawyers and wrapped up its inquiry into non-resident accounts in five weeks, the same time it took the tribunal to get Murphy senior's evidence in Guernsey.

The legal teams for the various parties sat patiently through the proceedings. Why wouldn't they, when the meter was running? Lawyers as a breed never use a short word when a long one would do, but at the tribunal some counsel seemed to prefer a short book to a simple sentence. The sitting day — 10.30 a.m. to 4 p.m. — was relatively short, and punctuated by frequent breaks and interruptions. Five-day weeks were rare.

The level of opposition and foot-dragging was immense, it was true. Already, up to a dozen legal actions had been taken against the tribunal by various parties. Only later did the extent of non-cooperation from some quarters become apparent, as those under investigation withheld documents or flooded the tribunal with huge quantities of dusty files. By Christmas 1999, despite over 150 days of hearings, the tribunal was no nearer the truth behind Gogarty's allegations than when it started. Costs were running at over £5 million, and two of the main barristers had already shared £1 million of this.

It was all great fun, free theatre for anyone on a day off or between shopping trips. It was also an important exercise in democracy, and it was opening up the legal profession to public scrutiny. 'But every show gets pulled when the audiences drop off and the reviews are bad,' I wrote at the time.

The Gogarty module ended as it had begun, in a torrent of words and lawyers' excuses. Four times Mr Justice Flood had to extend the deadline for final written submissions, as the various parties made excuses for their tardiness. Shortly before Christmas 2000, the tribunal finally overtook the 226 days of the Beef tribunal as the longest-running inquiry set up by the State. Seven years after the Beef tribunal ended in July 1993, the cost of that inquiry stood at £19.5 million and the bills were still coming in. On the day following this milestone, the various legal teams made their final submissions on Gogarty's allegations. One strand of investigations had come to a close, but the tribunal itself was only getting into its stride.

6

The Art of Hiding
in Full View

'If I borrowed £600 or £6 million I don't see the bearing it has on the granting, the refusing, or the rezoning of different planning permissions in County Dublin.'

— Liam Lawlor, at the tribunal in December 2000

'Ashamed? No, I just saw it as something to be done. It was a major misunderstanding as I saw it. I just got on with what I had to do. No big deal there.'

— Liam Lawlor in May 2001, reflecting on a week spent in Mountjoy jail[1]

'I wouldn't have that man consulting on a shithouse.'

— Developer Tom Gilmartin's views on Lawlor

Cell F-6 of the medical unit of Mountjoy Prison is a grim place to make history. Its furniture is spartan — four bunks, an unpartitioned toilet and a table and chair. Its normal occupants are the bag snatchers, murderers and other criminals who find themselves locked up in the jail. Many of those in the unit are recovering heroin addicts. The doors of the cell close at 8.15 p.m. each night and remain locked for 12 hours.

At lunchtime on 17 January 2001, the doors of F-6 opened up to receive someone out of the ordinary as its newest occupant. Prison warders introduced Liam Lawlor, Dáil deputy and businessman, to his new home. For the first time in the history of the State, a politician would spend time behind bars in connection with the tribunals.

Two days before, Lawlor had been sentenced to spend a week in jail on contempt charges arising from his failure to cooperate with the Flood tribunal. Court 12 on the first floor of the Four Courts was packed to the gills when Mr Justice Thomas Smyth came in to read his ruling from handwritten notes. Lawlor sat impassively at the back of the court, his arms folded.

Most observers were betting on a fudge which would allow the TD more time to set his house in order. No-one dared to think that Lawlor or any other politician would be sent to jail — after all, not a single person implicated in the multiple scandals Ireland had lived through over the past decade had been locked up. Why should anything be different now?

This line of thinking was justified by past events, but it was wrong. Exasperated and angry, Smyth was determined to apply the full measure of the law to Lawlor. 'No-one is above the law ... there are no untouchables,' he declared. He lashed the defendant for trying to 'fob off' the tribunal, and for his 'bare, minimalist approach' to giving information. Reviewing the TD's lack of cooperation since 1998, he quoted *Macbeth*: 'Things bad begun make strong themselves by ill'. The TD's failure to appear before the tribunal was 'not unintentional'. As the judge's ninety-minute pummelling progressed, the defendant's fate became clear. Smyth was about to breach a new frontier in Irish public life. He accused Lawlor of 'blatant defiance' of the tribunal, then put it in context. 'That he did so as a citizen is a disgrace; that he did so as a public representative is a scandal.'

Lawlor was given a three-month sentence and fined £10,000. All but a week of the sentence was suspended on condition that he provided the tribunal with the documents it was looking for. The costs of the four-day hearing, estimated at over £100,000, were awarded against the TD. Smyth's ruling was the answer to all those who had legitimately asked of all the tribunals: 'But will anyone go to jail for it?' Seven days in Mountjoy mightn't seem all that much, but it was a start.

So it was that Lawlor found himself the unwilling occupant of F-6. It could have been worse; although the prison governor promised that Lawlor would not be given special treatment, he was allowed sole occupancy of the four-bunk room. F-6 was one of the few cells with its own toilet, so he was spared the indignity of slopping out.

In Leinster House, there was shock at the jailing of a TD, and some colleagues must have wondered 'who's next?' Lawlor himself was never a man given to brooding or self-doubt, but as the lights

went out at 10 p.m. that first night behind bars, even he must have
wondered where it all went wrong …

⋘⋙

What Ray Burke was to north Dublin, Liam Lawlor was to the west
of the city — a big-budget, parish-pump Fianna Fáil TD with his ear
to the ground and ever-so-close relations with the businessmen who
built houses and pulled pints in his area. The whiff of intrigue hung
about both men for years. To deal with the awkward questions, each
perfected the defence mechanism of impenetrable silence, inter-
spersed by savage bouts of verbal aggression.

The party used both men as political bootboys when it suited.
Burke's combative interviews on RTÉ were legendary. In the Dáil,
Lawlor was sent in to throw back the muck that came Fianna Fáil's
way, a task he performed with relish. When Fianna Fáil dumped him,
he started throwing dirt at his former colleagues. As Charles
Haughey once described Lawlor to a woman journalist: 'You might
not like him, madam, but he gets the job done'.

But whereas Burke was the minister who would never be
Taoiseach because of the allegations that dogged him, Lawlor was the
TD who would never be a minister, for the same reason. Whereas
Burke topped the poll in every election he stood in, Lawlor's hold on
the lower rungs of political life was distinctly shaky. On numerous
occasions, Lawlor lost his Dáil or county council seats, only to win
them back through doggedness and big spending at a later election.

Whereas Burke got over his difficulties with Charles Haughey
and others in the pursuit of personal power, Lawlor was destined for-
ever to play the role of the maverick in Fianna Fáil. In 1990, when
no-one else dared to raise a voice openly against Haughey, Lawlor
told the Taoiseach it was time to go. Long before he left in 2001, he
was already a 'semi-detached' member of the party.

If Lawlor excelled in anything, it was in the art of making money.
As early as the 1980s, he was the only backbencher to arrive at the
Dáil in a chauffeur-driven top-of-the-range Mercedes complete with
state-of-the-art car telephone. He bought a magnificent nineteenth-
century house, Somerton, surrounded by extensive lands in Lucan,
earning himself the nickname 'Lord Lucan'.

Like Burke, Liam Lawlor was a 'family man' when it came to making friends in business; his earliest contacts were inherited ones. For example, he knew the businessman Jim Kennedy through his parents who, like Kennedy, hailed from County Laois. His father was also friendly with Tom Roche of National Toll Roads, who was to make large payments to the TD during his career.

Born in Dublin in 1944, Lawlor grew up in Crumlin and attended the Christian Brothers in Synge Street. Sport was his main passion in the early years; he played hurling for Dublin and Leinster and ran marathons in Dublin and New York. But he was also steeped in politics. With his family, he attended Fianna Fáil ardfheiseanna as a child and went to his first cumann meeting as a teenager. He studied engineering in Bolton Street and married a fellow student whose father ran a refrigeration company. After his apprenticeship Lawlor went into the same business. As he tells it, Lawlor's story is a rags-to-riches tale forged by hard work and a burning ambition to succeed. He bought a £200 van and drove around servicing refrigeration machinery. He then built up companies providing equipment and service to refrigeration and air-conditioning users. His companies also designed computer rooms and insulated offices and factories. Business prospered during the economic boom that accompanied Ireland's entry into the Common Market.

But Lawlor wanted to succeed in politics as he had in business. A member of Fianna Fáil since he was sixteen, he stood for a seat on Dublin County Council in 1974 but was beaten by Brian Lenihan. It was to be the start of a long-running political conflict between Lawlor and the Lenihan family. Lawlor's perpetual misfortune was to share a constituency for so long with the most popular politician in Fianna Fáil.

Lawlor swept into the Dáil in the party's 1977 landslide election victory under Jack Lynch. At 33, he was one of the youngest TDs to be elected that year. Two years later, he secured a seat on the council. Meanwhile, his business continued to thrive and at one point his companies were employing several hundred people. Shortly after entering the Dáil, he secured the contract to install air conditioning in An Post's central sorting office in Sheriff Street. Later, he sold off his main refrigeration business to an English company so he could concentrate on politics.

A brash, sharp-suited politician with a taste for expensive cars and Georgian houses, Lawlor developed something of a reputation as a 'poor man's Haughey'. Constituents visiting his constituency office in Somerton could rubberneck the Mercedes parked outside. He ran expensive election campaigns and publicity machines, and funded them with £250 a plate fundraising dinners. Lawlor himself estimates that he spent a total of over £250,000 on campaigning in all elections since 1977. His posters and leaflets were always bigger and better than anyone else's and they were also highly personalised. He would deliver bags of coal to constituents at election time, but take them back if he discovered opposition supporters in the house. During petrol rationing in 1979, there was a fuss when he had 300 gallons of fuel delivered to his company while thousands of motorists queued at the pumps. Serving as a TD proved no bar to his expanding business activities, as Lawlor put himself about as a consultant in various areas. The Mercedes, the mansion and the expensive tailoring gave Lawlor the look of importance, and his patter filled in the rest.

It was the refrigeration business that brought him into contact in the 1960s with Larry Goodman, then well on the way to becoming Ireland's biggest and most controversial beef baron. During the battle between Goodman and Killeshandra Co-op for control of Bailieboro Co-op, Lawlor emerged as Goodman's chief lieutenant. He organised the canvass of shareholders that eventually swung the battle in Goodman's favour. In November 1987, he was rewarded with a seat on the board of Goodman's company, Food Industries. Much later, it emerged that a Goodman company paid over £300,000 into the accounts of one of Lawlor's companies, Advanced Proteins, around this time.

Politically, though, he was less successful. Already, the rumour machine was working overtime about the wealthy young TD, and he never progressed beyond front bench spokesman rank. From early in his political career, it was evident that his politics were of the *mé féin* variety. He comforted Charles Haughey during the latter's years out in the cold in the 1970s, but then he was greedy and 'too clever by half'. In 1979, he backed George Colley in the Fianna Fáil leadership contest, having heard a rumour that Colley would give him a cabinet seat. Haughey triumphed, and never forgave him.

On the council, Lawlor was already making his mark as a supporter of developers and appeared regularly on the list of the top ten major rezoners. As councillors embarked on a rezoning frenzy — embracing a total area of land three times the size of the Phoenix Park — Lawlor proposed or seconded major rezonings in Tallaght, Finglas, Brittas, Clonsilla and many other areas around the fringes of the city.

In April 1980, Dublin County Council rezoned 150 acres in Lucan for housing, against the advice of its officials. Only fourteen out of thirty-six councillors took part in the vote, with the Fianna Fáil group supporting the motion on a whip. The decision was hugely unpopular, even before it emerged that Lawlor himself owned over twenty acres of the land. In his defence, the TD claimed that he was not present when the vote was taken; he had left just before his party colleagues pushed it through. This was to become a familiar refrain over the years — a colleague once said of Lawlor that he had perfected the technique of hiding in full view. He argued that young people needed houses, though there was plenty of zoned land in the area already. The decision increased the value of the land from £6,500 an acre to £20,000 an acre, netting Lawlor a profit of more than £300,000 on land he had bought just a year before.

After massive controversy and an intervention by Haughey, the council rescinded the rezoning of his lands in the following year. As Frank McDonald noted at the time: 'It was the only time that public opinion — as opposed to the insistent importunings of landowners — had any real effect on the members of the council. And it was also the only time that the leaders of the two main political parties, Mr Haughey and Dr Fitzgerald, brought their errant councillors to heel and forced them to overturn a decision that became a public scandal.[2]

But this wasn't the end of the mystery surrounding Lawlor's twenty-three acres. Although a few feeble attempts were made to change their status again, in zoning terms the lands were tainted by their previous history. Lawlor had borrowed heavily to buy them in the confident expectation that they would be rezoned. Now, in the mid-1990s, he was under severe pressure from the banks, to which he owed £1 million. He was forced to sell the twenty-three acres.

Shearwater Properties, a company registered in the British Virgin Islands, bought them for £410,000 in July 1995 and Lawlor used this amount to settle with his biggest creditor, ACC Bank. Grim-faced, he would explain later that he had sold 'at a 90 per cent discount' in order to avoid another 'Liam Lawlor rezoning controversy'. Lawlor garnered some sympathy a number of years later when the lands were sold on again and the new owners succeeded in having them rezoned. 'I just didn't want the controversy over the rezoning. I just didn't want the hassle of it because it temporarily damaged my political career. But it is behind us now,' he told the *Sunday Tribune* in February 1998. Lawlor says the twenty-three acres are now worth £20 million.

But had Lawlor really divested himself of all interest in the lands? No-one would have been any the wiser if it hadn't been for the tribunal's investigations. It discovered that Lawlor continued to exercise a claim on the lands even after he had sold them. According to the TD, he made a deal with Harry Dobson, the owner of Shearwater, before the lands were auctioned, under which the two men would develop the lands for their joint benefit. He made this claim in a High Court action in 1997 to block Shearwater from selling on to another developer.

Dobson, a Scottish mining millionaire in his early fifties, made a fortune in Canada and then invested heavily in property, mining and bloodstock in Ireland. The owner of homes in London, Vancouver and Edinburgh, his wealth was estimated at more than $1 billion. 'Property deals are like buses in Piccadilly, there's one coming every five minutes,' he was once quoted as saying. In the 1970s, while scouting in Ireland for investment opportunities, he met Lawlor for the first time. It was shortly after the rezoning controversy over the twenty-three acres, and the TD suggested Dobson build an under-ground service pipe from the old village of Lucan to the vicinity of his lands at Somerton. 'I knew from my knowledge as a local repre-sentative that west Dublin would develop sooner or later. It was well known in the area that services would ultimately be required but that the local authority did not have the funding at that time to provide them,' Lawlor says.[3] More to the point, the development would also greatly increase the value of the lands above the pipe.

Dobson and businessman Jim Kennedy developed the project and Lawlor acted as a consultant. In the early 1980s, a pipe was laid from Lucan village to a point seventy yards from the boundary of Lawlor's twenty-three acres. The land under which the pipe was built was registered in Cyprus in the name of Pentagon Property Services.

Lawlor claims he was entitled to a one-quarter share of Pentagon for introducing Dobson to the project. His purpose in launching the High Court action against Shearwater was to enforce this claim.

Dobson rejected Lawlor's claim and suggested his action was motivated by unhappiness about their other dealings. In June 1997, Lawlor and Dobson reached a settlement through their advisers, under which Lawlor and Kennedy were given joint ownership of the pipe. Lawlor was also to get £50,000 'by way of consultancy fee' and a further £50,000 when full planning permission was granted for Clonburris Rail Park. This was a reference to Dobson's plans for a massive rail-based national freight distribution centre at Clonburris, near Clondalkin. Lawlor was to give 'help and advice as needed and requested to ensure the due grant of planning permission' for the rail park.

Shortly after, the agreement was amended to allow for the payment to Lawlor of £15,000 immediately and £85,000 within a month. This alteration was made 'so as to remove any semblance of a consultancy which we all agree does not exist,' according to the new agreement. Lawlor says he opposed the development at Clonburris, which was unpopular in the area. The £100 million project has since been abandoned in the face of local opposition to the traffic it would generate.

In April 1998, Lawlor got $30,000 from Shearwater, paid to one of his bank accounts in Liechtenstein. The tribunal believes another offshore company, Clearview Ltd, owns 50 per cent of Pentagon Property Services; Lawlor's claim is for 50 per cent ownership of Clearview.

During the High Court case, Shearwater pointed out that Lawlor had made no declaration of the interest he claimed in the pipeline in the Dáil register of TDs' interests. The politician then drafted an amended return, which was sent to the clerk of the Dáil. However, the clerk raised a number of issues which were not resolved and Lawlor's entry in the register stayed as it was. For four years, the TD's entry remained inaccurate. Then, in November 2000, RTÉ News broke the story, reporting that the pipes were the subject of a still unresolved dispute involving Dobson, Lawlor and a solicitor, John Caldwell. The station passed on its confidential information to the tribunal.

As the tribunal's inquiries grew ever more pressing, Lawlor finally declared a 50 per cent shareholding in Clearview in the 2001 register of interests. Questioned about the entry in June 2001, he publicly acknowledged his business dealings with Kennedy for the first time. Kennedy might have an interest in a company in which he was also claiming a share, he told *The Irish Times*.

To this day, Lawlor's entry in the register is inaccurate. In October 2001, a supplementary statement was published, and this listed some of the interests he claimed. Yet much of the information remained contradictory, confusing and incorrect.

❦

The row over the twenty-three acres and the presence of a H-Block candidate cost Lawlor his Dáil seat in 1981 but he won it back in February 1982. In the second election that year he lost out again, this time to Eileen Lemass, who had the backing of Brian Lenihan. He remained on the council and topped the poll in the 1985 local elections.

Lawlor should have become chairman of Dublin County Council in 1986 but, in an unprecedented move, Ray Burke insisted on staying on as chairman for a second term. After Burke left to become a minister in 1987, Lawlor became the most influential voice in Fianna Fáil on the council. He played a major role in marshalling other councillors for rezoning and Section 4 votes, though his personal involvement was less visible than before.

Sticking his fingers into an astonishing number of pies, Lawlor also served as an underwriter for Lloyds insurers for over a decade.[4] No tax was paid on the dividends earned until he discharged a £30,000 liability in the 1993 tax amnesty. He was also a member of the Trilateral Commission, the controversial international think-tank.

His activities came to the attention of the 1989 Garda investigation into planning corruption. The developer Tom Gilmartin, whose plans to build a huge shopping centre at Quarryvale in west Dublin had run into trouble, made a number of allegations to gardaí. Gilmartin claimed the TD told him he would need the support of eight local councillors to get the site rezoned.[5] Lawlor put him in touch with four councillors who each demanded £100,000 for support, he claimed.

Gilmartin also made an allegation concerning Lawlor and a Dublin garage-owner, but this led nowhere when the garage-owner told the gardaí he 'did not experience any difficulty in [obtaining] payment' for a Mercedes bought by the TD. The gardaí, who also examined the TD's links with businessman Jim Kennedy, concluded that Lawlor 'emerges from this enquiry with his reputation unscathed'.

There were further problems that year when his involvement with Food Industries was the subject of controversy. At the time, he was chairman of the Oireachtas Joint Committee on State-Sponsored Bodies, which was looking into the affairs of the State-owned Irish Sugar company. Food Industries, the Goodman-controlled organisation of which Lawlor was a director, was attempting to acquire Irish Sugar. In February 1989, he failed to attend a meeting of the committee that planned to question him about his links to Goodman's company. Amid allegations of a conflict of interest, he resigned his position on the committee. The affair highlighted the extent to which TDs were not required to disclose their business interests.

Living precariously on the interface between business and politics, Lawlor repeatedly represented himself as someone who could provide access to the powerful. For example, the Beef tribunal heard evidence that Lawlor travelled to Iraq on behalf of the Goodman organisation in 1989, but allowed Iraqi officials to believe he was a representative of the Irish government. A decade would pass before the full extent of his dealings with Goodman came to light. During his evidence to the tribunal in December 2000, it emerged that £900,000 was transferred into the accounts of one of his companies, Advanced Proteins, although Lawlor said it never traded. Some £365,000 of this came from Goodman International. The tribunal wanted to know what it was for.

Advanced Proteins was set up in 1984, with Lawlor and his wife Hazel as directors. Ostensibly, it aimed to find ways of creating wealth out of the animal blood regularly disposed of in slaughter-houses, by turning it into valuable proteins. The company picked up funding from Goodman, the EEC, the IDA and Argentina. However, the project went nowhere and the company never got off the ground. Instead, Advanced Proteins became a channel for money used in property speculation. Tribunal lawyers zeroed in on £203,000 transferred out of the company's account in November 1987. Lawlor said this was money returned to Goodman after it was decided not to purchase equipment from Argentina for the protein project. However, the money was returned, not to the Goodman group, but to Binchys solicitors. The lawyers talked to Goodman, who told them the true purpose of the transaction.

Coolamber House was a fine five-bedroom residence located across the road from Lawlor's home in Lucan. But as far as the TD was concerned, its real treasure was the fifty-five acres of agricultural land surrounding the house. Adjoining lands had been rezoned and once the Lucan by-pass was completed this property would be worth a fortune. Lawlor says it was 'an exceptional development opportunity' but he didn't have the money to buy the property when it came on the market in 1987. He discussed its potential with his friend, Jim Kennedy, and John Caldwell, a partner at Binchys solicitors. The three men agreed a strategy; Kennedy would deal with the planning issues and Caldwell would take care of the legal and tax aspects of the bid. It was Lawlor's job to raise the finance required.

In July that year, Lawlor approached Goodman with a copy of the Coolamber sales brochure. They struck a deal; the beef baron would put up the money and pay the interest charges in return for a share of the ultimate profits. Goodman says he knew nothing then about the shares held by Caldwell and Kennedy, but Lawlor disputes this.

Goodman arranged for an advance of £350,000 — the money that passed through the accounts of Advanced Proteins. He then covered this with a mortgage from the Bank of Nova Scotia, which was advanced to an Irish company, Southfield Property. An Isle of Man shelf company, Navona Ltd, was established to hold the lands in trust for Southfield Property Co Ltd. Goodman undertook, in a letter of comfort, not to relinquish 100 per cent ownership until the debt was cleared. Goodman had effectively bought the land, but he says he was never provided with a shareholding in Southfield. He says that company then sold its interest in the lands to an Isle of Man company, Vino Property Ltd, without telling him. In the early 1990s, Goodman International was put into examinership, and the beef baron sought to recover his costs — over £157,000 — from Lawlor. By then, the land had been sold on to Tiernan Homes at a profit of £1.5 million.

As in the case of many of his land deals, Lawlor denies having any shares in the venture, but accepts he expected a share of the ultimate profits. He denies any knowledge of Navona and Vino Property, and says he believed Goodman to be the owner of Southfield. However, Lawlor's record of the meetings he had with Kennedy and Caldwell appears to show he held a 41 per cent share. Kennedy was allocated a similar share, with Caldwell taking up the rest. Under a re-financing agreement, Kennedy took 50 per cent, Caldwell 25 per cent and Lawlor 25 per cent, which was held in trust by Kennedy. The notes also prove conclusively that Lawlor had a business relationship with Kennedy, something he was never keen to acknowledge publicly.

Lawlor says it is 'a matter of regret' to him that having introduced the beef baron to the deal, Goodman 'continues to be out of pocket on my account'. There can't be many occasions on which Goodman, who twice built a multi-million pound business from nothing, lost out so comprehensively in a business deal.

Coolamber became the subject of a huge controversy in the early 1990s when Tiernan Homes used the services of Frank Dunlop to get the lands rezoned. It was later developed as the Finnstown estate.

❖

Throughout the 1990s, Lawlor's continuing knack for courting controversy was apparent. Along with twenty-four other Fianna Fáil councillors, he voted for the rezoning of Quarryvale in May 1991. Lawlor says he voted for the proposal merely to 'allow Seán Citizen have his say' by putting the project on public display.[6] But his involvement went far deeper than a mere vote. Lawlor was closely involved with Gilmartin in the early stages, at the same time as he was picking up a £3,500 a month consultancy fee for assistance on Gilmartin's project at Bachelors Walk. His name pops up repeatedly in Gilmartin's account of his troubles. The Luton-based developer claims Lawlor is 'a hustler' who introduced him to George Redmond and claimed to be acting on behalf of the government on Bachelors Walk. Lawlor also had contact with developer Owen O'Callaghan, who was to bring the Quarryvale project to fruition.

He lost his council seat again in June 1991, along with many other councillors who voted to rezone Quarryvale. 'I'm a big fish in a small pond — it's only a temporary setback,' he observed.

Once again, he crossed swords with Brian Lenihan over voting preferences in Dublin West during the 1992 general election. After a row over forged election literature, he lashed out at his running mate in typical style: 'Mr Lenihan is consistent in his inconsistency. After all, he cost us the presidential election'. The count brought Lawlor within a whisker of losing his Dáil seat; he beat Tomás MacGiolla by fifty votes on the fourteenth count. One of the count officials was George Redmond, by then retired. The result confirmed Lawlor's image as a battler with an uncanny instinct for survival.

In 1993, three acres by his house in Lucan were included in the controversial rezoning of Airlie Stud. Lawlor claimed he was unaware of the change in zoning until told about it by *The Irish Times*. The rezoning increased the value of his holding by up to £250,000, but after further controversy, this rezoning was also rescinded.

He achieved his first front bench posting in 1995, when he was appointed party spokesman on arts, culture and heritage. This, however, was the pinnacle of his political career and there was no Cabinet seat for him when Fianna Fáil returned to power in 1997. By now, it was all bad news for the TD. In September 1999, he was stopped for drink driving and was disqualified from driving for a year.

As the Flood tribunal got into gear, Lawlor's past associations came back to haunt him. In March 1999, he issued a statement denying that he ever met George Redmond and Jim Kennedy together, or that he ever attended meetings between the two at Kennedy's amusement arcade in Westmoreland Street, Dublin. Charlie Bird of RTÉ had reported that a Fianna Fáil TD was a regular visitor to the arcade, always entering and leaving by a rear door. Redmond called to the premises regularly to collect sums of cash. Lawlor also denied any knowledge of Kennedy's house in the Strawberry Beds, with its unusual planning history.

⋘∙⋙

Lawlor's finances were complicated, and anything but orthodox. He used a multiplicity of companies, accountants, lawyers and friends to conduct his business, and kept few records. He entered into complex land and financial deals on the basis of verbal agreements, handshakes or short notes scrawled on pieces of paper. He was frequently at log-gerheads with the banks, some of which had to write off substantial portions of his debt. And in the 1990s, he moved his business inter-ests onto an international plane, as he followed other gold-diggers to the promise of easy money in the Czech Republic.

In 1987, his brother-in-law, Noel Gilsen, obtained a £25,000 lease on the TD's behalf, which was used to buy a Mercedes 280SE. The TD told his relation he was 'financially embarrassed' and couldn't get credit.[7] Two years later, the term loan was increased by £17,500 with-out Gilsen's knowledge. Lawlor used the money to buy a Mercedes 560 for £68,000. Someone forged Gilsen's name on the leasing agreement, and on a direct debit mandate to pay for the car. The repayments came from one of Lawlor's many companies, Economic Reports Ltd.

A taxi-driver friend, John Patrick Long, opened two accounts in his own name on behalf of the TD in 1997.[8] Lawlor had explained he was 'in trouble with the banks'. The politician used one of the accounts so heavily that the bank manager called Long in and said 'it was a bit much for a taxi-driver to have in the account'. In response, Lawlor wrote what Long called 'a letter by way of comfort' for the bank manager. In 1999, Long took out a credit card in his name and without signing the back of it, passed it on to Lawlor. 'When I got it was the last time I had it,' he told the tribunal in December 2000. 'There's only one Liam Lawlor,' he reassured the lawyers.

Lawlor's business links seem endless. He was involved in proposals to set up the European arm of a US telecommunications company, Wavve Communications. He sued builder Séamus Ross of Menolly Homes, claiming the builder owed him a 20 per cent cut of a £20 mil-lion housing development. This claim was rejected by the Supreme Court in November 2001. Another builder said he gave Lawlor £10,000 to look at a piece of property in Lucan in the late 1980s. 'It would have taken a day or two at the most,' the builder said. When he gave Lawlor the money, the TD responded: 'Is that all?'

National Toll Roads gave him two political donations amounting to £74,000 in the early 1990s. When Tom Roche, NTR's chairman, said he needed an invoice for his accounts, Lawlor obliged with a fake from one of his friend's companies, Industrial Consultants, which provided advice on refrigeration and cold stores in Nigeria.

By the early 1990s Lawlor's financial situation was, in his own words, 'dire'. The millstone of the twenty-three acres was still around his neck. He owed almost £1 million to the banks. In 1994, he suffered a run of embarrassing financial judgements, including £15,500 in favour of a financial services company and £18,500 in favour of a Dublin bank. The Irish Nationwide Building Society sought to repossess his home, Somerton. When these judgements were reported in the newspapers, there was further pressure from other banks to which he owed money. Lawlor says his friend and financial adviser, Luke Mooney, intervened to 'horse-trade' on his behalf with the banks. His largest creditor, ACC Bank, which was owed £640,000, settled for just £383,000, which was the amount raised after expenses from the sale of the Lucan land.

Lawlor cites another reason for his financial exposure. In the early 1990s, he responded to his financial crisis by looking for new ways of generating income. He couldn't rezone his land. His political career was moribund, with no prospect of promotion. He decided the place to go was the Czech Republic, then in the throes of a property boom following the end of Communist rule. Ambrose Kelly, who ran a design practice and was familiar to Lawlor from Quarryvale and other projects, was already active in Prague. Kelly, Phil Monahan of Monarch Properties and Gerard Jennings of Northern Ireland company Rotary International, put up the capital and Lawlor, as usual, operated as a freewheeling consultant. In December 1993, an apartment was hired in a Prague apartment block, from where an elderly Irish architect, Conor McElliot, carried out business on behalf of the owners.

The venture was formally established as The Irish Consortium in March 1995. The exact nature of Lawlor's involvement is disputed; he denies holding any shares in the company but the tribunal believes he owns one-third. Just as in the case of his deals with Harry Dobson and Larry Goodman, he claims to have a verbal agreement to a share of any profits. He also claims an option on a one-third share of its biggest project, the Alpha building. Meanwhile, out in Prague he put himself forward as the 'head' of the Consortium. Whatever his interest was, it did not appear in the register of TDs' interests in the Dáil at this time.

Frank Dunlop, who was also interested in the prospects offered by Eastern Europe, travelled there with Lawlor on several occasions in

1994 and 1995. Lawlor claims his only involvement with Dunlop was to introduce the lobbyist to other PR consultants. Dunlop clearly attended meetings of the Consortium but Lawlor says Dunlop 'merely sat in to get a flavour of the local practices'.

The TD, who was in opposition at the time, visited frequently, doing the rounds of property developers and estate agents. He had printed a business card that read 'The Irish Consortium — Liam A. Lawlor MP'. On one visit, representing himself as a key 'member of the ruling party in Ireland', he introduced Dunlop to the Czech trade and industry minister, Vladimir Dlouhy, and they talked about setting up a PR company in Prague, he claims. Dlouhy, who later resigned from the Czech government after being implicated in a corruption scandal, has no recollection of the visit and nothing came of the proposal.[9]

After a few years, Monahan withdrew and was replaced for a period by a Malaysian businessman, Loraine Osman. The former chairman of the Bank of Bumiputra, Osman was fresh from almost ten years in jail in Britain and the Far East after being convicted of thirty-six charges of corruption, theft and fraud in connection with a £600 million investment swindle. On his release, he started a number of business ventures with Irish partners, including an ambitious plan to develop the site of the Battle of the Boyne in County Meath into a luxury hotel and golf course. When permission was refused, the property was sold to new owners, who disposed of it to the Office of Public Works for a massive profit. According to Lawlor, Osman left The Irish Consortium after a disagreement with one of his partners.

The Consortium offered £7 million for the Alpha building, but the owners wanted £12 million and there were endless complications. It looked at other buildings in Prague and in other Czech cities. McElliott became ill and moved home — he died shortly after — leaving behind company documents and unpaid phone bills. Other files were left with a Czech lawyer, identified by Lawlor as Dr Richard Kavalek. 'Mr Lawlor might have some strange ideas sometimes but he is an honest man trying to do honest business,' Kavalek told *The Irish Times* in December 2000.[10]

Subsequently, Lawlor says he invoiced Dunlop for £38,000 for 'consultancy services' provided on their joint trips. (The tribunal believes this sum relates to the rezoning of Quarryvale.) According to Lawlor, the invoice was issued through a consultancy called Long Associates in London. He later admitted that he dreamt up the name Long Associates. The cheque was cashed in dribs and drabs, courtesy of a friendly publican in his constituency, Pat Murphy of the Sarsfield Bar in Inchicore.

To date, none of the Consortium's multi-million pound projects has come to fruition. Ever the optimist, Lawlor believes that with the imminent accession of the Czech Republic to the European Union they will ultimately prove hugely profitable.

Lawlor's claim that his Czech sorties failed to generate any profits may well be true, but they generated large amounts of money in other ways. He regularly recovered expenses from the Consortium for flights and other items; he was paid £12,000 one year and £9,000 another year. He also claims to own another Czech property company, Zatecka. This company denies Lawlor holds any shareholding but it did issue him with a credit card to pay personal and business expenses. The TD ran up bills totalling £164,000 on this card in just nine months in 2000. The tribunal is investigating other payments the company appears to have made to Lawlor.

Then there is the mysterious generosity shown by a Jersey solicitor, David Morgan, to Lawlor. The two men, who met through a mutual friend in the UK, discussed the possibilities offered by the Czech market and Morgan expressed an interest in investing in suitable opportunities. In 1995, when Lawlor was under financial pressure, Morgan agreed to loan him money. As usual with Lawlor, it was a 'gentleman's agreement', sealed 'on a handshake' with no written documentation. Longwater Investments, a Bahamian-registered company owned by Morgan and (after his death) his family trust, made two 'loans' totalling £600,000 sterling to Lawlor. The money was paid circuitously, through an account opened on Lawlor's behalf in Liechtenstein. Lawlor says the money went to help defray his debts back in Ireland. The tribunal later discovered that, contrary to Lawlor's indications, he had full control of the Liechtenstein accounts and that Morgan was merely his adviser.

Most of Lawlor's indebtedness to the Irish banks had been settled through the sale of the twenty-three acres near his home.

Although he only needed £153,000 to clear his outstanding debts, £604,000 was brought home from Liechtenstein to his Irish accounts. The Liechtenstein accounts — eight of them in all, although Lawlor insists they form one 'core account' — continued to receive money until 1999. Then they were closed and the money moved to Ireland or the US.

On the face of it, this was an extraordinarily good deal for Lawlor, involving a huge loan and no pressure to repay it. If only the Irish banks had been so facilitating! It isn't clear whether any of the Longwater loan has been repaid, although Lawlor told the tribunal in December 2000 that he had repaid £30,000. He says the agreement was that he would repay the loan as profits were generated on the Czech projects. He agreed not to sell the six acres around Somerton without consulting Morgan. And since there haven't been any profits, he hasn't had to pay any money.

Lawlor and Dunlop also collaborated in a proposal by developer Owen O'Callaghan to develop a national soccer stadium at Neilstown in west Dublin. O'Callaghan bought the site, which was designated as the town centre for Lucan/Clondalkin, in the late 1980s. However, Tom Gilmartin then purchased the lands at Quarryvale, a mile away from Neilstown, and began lobbying for a shopping centre there. After Gilmartin ran into difficulties, O'Callaghan took over the Quarryvale project. That left him with the Neilstown site. Together with Lawlor, Dunlop and Ambrose Kelly, he attempted to promote the site for use as a soccer stadium. Kelly drew up extensive plans and planning permission was granted. However, the project has stalled since. Lawlor still got £65,000 from Dunlop's PR company, he has told the tribunal.

⋘∘⋙

By the late 1990s, with the juggernaut of the Flood tribunal heading in Lawlor's direction, his instinctive reaction was to pick a fight. Already by October 1998, tribunal lawyers were complaining about the 'futile and argumentative correspondence' conducted by the TD through his solicitors.[11] In March 1999, in response to the tribunal's request for his bank accounts, he sent in a four-page statement, and attached a copy of the Census, an ESRI report, a Central Bank report

— everything except the phone directory and the information sought.

In June 1999, Lawlor responded to further inquiries by challenging the tribunal in the High Court. High-profile senior counsel Adrian Hardiman made the case that the TD was entitled to know the detail of the allegations against him before being called to the tribunal. It was an 'I'll show you mine if you show me yours' argument that Lawlor and others were to continue using over the next two years. Hardiman claimed that tribunal lawyers had more powers than gardaí dealing with subversives, a point that Mr Justice Kearns seemed inclined to accept. The judge remarked that the tribunal's power to make orders was 'very draconian'.

After an eight-day hearing, Kearns granted Lawlor's application to quash two tribunal orders directing him to appear before its lawyers in private session, and to swear an affidavit detailing his company interests. But the judge refused to quash a third order directing him to produce documents covering payments made by Arlington Securities Ltd and/or Thomas Gilmartin. On the steps of the court, Lawlor protested his willingness to cooperate. 'I don't know what, if anything, I'm being accused of. I've no problem answering questions, but I need to know what they are.' If details were put in the post on Monday, he would respond by Tuesday.[12]

The tribunal appealed, but the Supreme Court unanimously upheld the decision in October 1999. Lawlor had won a significant victory, though it turned out to be a temporary reprieve. Matters took a serious turn for the worse with Frank Dunlop's revelations of payments to politicians in April 2000. Although Dunlop did not publicly name those to whom he paid money, Lawlor was clearly identifiable as the 'Mr Big', a 'powerful individual' who was part of a 'core group' of councillors who whipped their colleagues into line on the rezoning. Dunlop claims he gave Lawlor £40,000 in cash, and £8,500 in two cheques.

Lawlor's identification as the chief beneficiary of Dunlop's generosity marked the beginning of a long fall from grace for the west Dublin TD. At first he reacted in typical style, with a flurry of denials. While other councillors ran for cover Lawlor, characteristically, rushed out a statement. In it, he denied being a member of the council when 'the Liffey Valley/Quarryvale shopping centre, as proposed by O'Callaghan Properties Ltd, was considered and voted upon by the then council'.

'I never at any time had any hand, act or part in seeking support for, or voting for the Liffey Valley project,' he stated. Characteristically, too, this statement was misleading. Lawlor *was* on the council for the first vote in May 1991, which he supported. At this stage, Quarryvale was being jointly developed by Tom Gilmartin and Owen O'Callaghan. Lawlor was no longer on the council by the time of the last Quarryvale vote in 1993, when O'Callaghan was in complete control of the project.

Then he went on the attack, claiming the Fine Gael leader, John Bruton, benefited from the Quarryvale rezoning and suggesting Bruton got money from Dunlop. A second cousin of Bruton's had once owned some of the land, but there was no more truth to Lawlor's accusation than there was to any of the other wild allegations he threw out.

Under pressure, he was forced to announce his resignation from the main ethics body of the Oireachtas, the Members' Interests Committee, which was then carrying out an inquiry into one of his party colleagues, Denis Foley. Fianna Fáil, concerned about the growing din surrounding the TD, called Lawlor in for interview on several occasions, but no action was taken.

By this stage, the tribunal already had documentary evidence for some of the payments from Dunlop to Lawlor. Lawlor claimed the monies were consultancy fees, but he did little to explain what services he actually provided. As for the payments he got from Gilmartin, he ascribed these first to consultancy services, then explained they were political donations. Later, he claimed that when Dunlop was starting his own business it was he [Lawlor] who gave him financial support.[13] But for the rest of Dunlop's work: 'I was out of the council and Frank's activities in the 90s had nothing to do with me'. This explanation, of course, took no account of the two men's activities in Prague, or their involvement in plans to build a soccer stadium in Neilstown.

Lawlor told the Fianna Fáil Standards in Public Life Committee in May that he received around £12,000 to £14,000 in donations from Dunlop. The total derived from minor payments for printing bills, contributions to golf classics, and the like. He denied being the

'Mr Big' referred to by Dunlop, or getting £40,000 in cash from the lobbyist. As usual, his denials were carefully worded: 'If Frank Dunlop has suggested to the Flood tribunal that I was supposed to have received £40,000 in his office, I state categorically I never received any such contribution from Frank Dunlop'. But he went on to detail numerous business discussions he had had with Dunlop in the role of a consultant. He estimated the value of these consultancy services at … £40,000. His evidence about the smaller Dunlop contributions of £5,000 and £3,500 conflicted with receipts Dunlop had already provided to the tribunal. He also told the committee he never had an offshore bank account and had no knowledge of Jackson Way Properties.

However, the committee said he had given conflicting accounts of his Czech dealings. The Irish Consortium invoiced Dunlop for £38,000, Lawlor had told one of the meetings of the inquiry. At a later meeting, however, he stated that the company had no dealings with Dunlop.

To the relief of Fianna Fáil, Lawlor resigned from the party as the report of the party's Standards in Public Life committee accused him of being uncooperative and contradictory in his evidence. Lawlor bade farewell to thirty-nine years of membership of the party with his usual denials: 'Any decisions I ever made as a public representative, either as a member of a local authority or as a member of Dáil Éireann, were made in the PUBLIC INTEREST and NEVER for financial gain'.

Up to this point, Lawlor had fared well in his legal battles with the tribunal. Bolstered by his success, he fended off all inquiries and acted as though he was immune to the tribunal's influence. Since 1999, tribunal lawyers had been seeking to interview him, yet he was the only one of over 100 present and former Dublin county councillors to refuse their request.

His confidence was misplaced. The High Court decision just meant that all the tribunal's dealings with the TD would have to take place in public. And before this could happen, the tribunal needed his financial records. The tribunal, slow but dogged, simply changed tack.

By mid-2000, Mr Justice Flood's patience was running out. In May, tribunal lawyers wrote to him regarding the main allegations he was facing. These included the payments from Tom Gilmartin and

Frank Dunlop, alleged bribes paid by companies in which he was involved with two other individuals, payments from National Toll Roads, and claims that he faked invoices from companies for goods and services that had not actually been provided. Information on his use of the 1993 tax amnesty was also sought.

In June, the chairman ordered the TD to produce his financial records. In July, *The Irish Times* reported that the tribunal had written to all the financial institutions in the State in search of accounts held by the TD. Lawlor's reaction was to demand a Garda investigation into the 'leak'.

In September, having 'failed to secure any meaningful co-operation,' Flood summonsed Lawlor to appear before the tribunal and to bring the financial records with him. However, Lawlor cocked a snook at the tribunal, telling this reporter in October that he had 'no intention' of appearing. 'I don't know what it is about and I don't propose to appear. They certainly didn't specify what it is about,' he told me.[14] On the morning of the summons, 'sources close to Mr Lawlor' let it be known that the deputy would be playing golf instead of giving evidence. In Dublin Castle, the allegations against the TD were read out to an empty witness box.

More than anything, this rash act of defiance brought the roof down on Lawlor. Many others had spun matters out for years through the devices of copious correspondence and expensive lawyers, but here was an elected TD sticking two fingers up at the legal system. It was politicians who had set up the tribunal, and now one of their number was blankly refusing to cooperate. Was this the way the ruling class treated its own investigations? As a clearly affronted Flood pointed out: 'A citizen cannot decide for himself to ignore a summons because, in his opinion, the summons is invalid.'[15]

Lawlor's claim that he didn't know what the tribunal wanted looked ridiculous when it emerged that he had received over fifty letters from its lawyers. In over two years, he had produced hardly a single meaningful document. The tribunal said his replies were 'long on verbiage and short on facts'.[16] He went on radio to declare: 'I asked every bank that I ever had dealings with to give them whatever they had'. This was simply untrue — even before the tribunal uncovered further undeclared accounts in Ireland and overseas. For months, he misled the tribunal about his efforts to get financial records from three banks where he was known to have accounts. On five occasions, his solicitors assured the tribunal that he was seeking the information, as they believed he was, only for the tribunal to discover the banks had not been contacted. At one point, the tribunal summonsed a number of bank managers for failing to provide information about accounts Lawlor held in their branches, only to find that the officials knew nothing about the tribunal's search. Lawlor had undertaken to request the information from the banks, but had never acted.

Flood immediately began High Court proceedings to force Lawlor to appear before the tribunal. Politicians, roused from their moral slumber by Lawlor's refusal to attend the tribunal, agreed an all-party statement expressing concern about the TD's behaviour.[17]

Lawlor found himself in October 2000 once again at the back of a crowded courtroom, his arms tightly folded and his mouth permanently puckered like a bull-dog. Once again, he engaged a top-dollar counsel, former attorney general John Rogers, to represent him. Rogers did his best, claiming Lawlor was being treated unfairly as 'an accused man', but he was fighting an uphill battle. In October, Mr Justice Smyth ordered the TD to appear before the tribunal within two weeks, and to provide all the documents it required.

It was a bleak judgement for the TD, who was criticised for 'choosing to rely on the letter of the law rather than its spirit'. Lawlor was given a timetable to produce documents going back to 1964 and costs were awarded against him.[18] Pointing out that the politician had over thirty years of experience in public life, Smyth quoted Edmund Burke: 'Those who would carry on great public schemes must be proof against the worst fatiguing delays, the most mortifying disappointments, the most shocking insults, and, worst of all, the presumptuous judgement of the ignorant upon their designs'.

It wouldn't be the last time that this judge would find himself quoting words of advice to the recalcitrant TD.

Incredibly, Lawlor tried to claim the ruling as a victory because it excluded documents from before 1964 — when he was a teenager. 'I didn't lose today — the order has been amended,' he blustered at a hastily convened press conference, before going on to rage impotently against the tribunal and Tom Gilmartin. For the first time, he acknowledged receiving £74,000 in 'political contributions' from National Toll Roads, something he had neglected to tell the Fianna Fáil inquiry. Once more, he played for time by appealing the judgement to the Supreme Court. However, as Lawlor tucked into his Thanksgiving turkey with his sons in the US, the court threw out his case without even requiring to hear the tribunal's arguments.

Also in November, RTÉ News revealed Lawlor's business relationship with the amusement arcade owner, Jim Kennedy. The TD had never acknowledged any business links with Kennedy, whom he claimed to know only as a friend and constituent. On this occasion, the normally garrulous TD declined to comment.[19]

Lawlor's four-day appearance in Dublin Castle in December 2000 was an extraordinary performance. The TD had clearly decided that attack was the best means of defence, and tore into the tribunal for 'time-wasting' and exceeding its powers. By the end of the first hour, Mr Justice Flood's patience had run out. He sent Lawlor home for the day to think about how he could give evidence in a civil manner.

On the second day, Lawlor was again sent home to 'reflect' on his evidence after the chairman twice expressed 'unease' about his evidence. Flood warned the witness he could be charged with hindering or obstructing the tribunal, an offence which carried a penalty of up to two years in jail, and/or a fine of £10,000. The flavour of Lawlor's bull-headed performance is conveyed in answers such as 'I don't propose to address this matter,' 'No, it's nothing to do with you' or, when asked to produce documents after lunch, 'Is there a mad urgency about it?' On the third day, after flatly refusing to answer questions about his interests in the Czech Republic, he received another warning.

Matters came to a head the following day. The tribunal revealed that £4.6 million had flowed through Lawlor's accounts since 1983. The source of £2.6 million of this money was unaccounted for, and the uses to which much of the remainder were put were unexplained.

When Lawlor declared that he 'didn't propose' to answer questions about his credit cards, Flood had had enough. 'I don't intend to sit here for any longer,' he declared, and referred the matter to the High Court. He also sent a file to the Director of Public Prosecutions. Lawlor left Dublin Castle saying 'I have nothing to hide'.

The contempt proceedings came before Mr Justice Smyth in the High Court in January. Lawlor turned up this time with two senior counsel, John Rogers and the veteran criminal specialist, Paddy MacEntee. Rogers bowled a googlie by arguing that Smyth should be prevented from hearing the case because he had once written an opinion for Green Property when it was campaigning against the rezoning of Quarryvale.

If Smyth was to be debarred for a piece of work he couldn't even remember carrying out, then most of the Irish judiciary would be unable to hear a case involving Lawlor or most other prominent individuals. Smyth dismissed the challenge. For once, Lawlor did not appeal.

For the court hearing, Lawlor switched to apologetic mode, far removed from his combative performance at the tribunal. But he wasn't admitting guilt — rather, he had 'totally misinterpreted' the High Court order, his legal team argued. By now, they pointed out, Lawlor had coughed up serious amounts of information — forty-two boxes of documents, details of £1.5 million in donations he received going back over twenty-five years and an apology.

But, as the tribunal pointed out, of the 2,120 pages of documents sent in by Lawlor with his first affidavit in December, 2,000 were simply reproduced from documents supplied by financial institutions. Lawlor already knew the tribunal had this information. As for apologies, it was simply too late.

Meanwhile, Lawlor resigned his position as vice-chairman of the Oireachtas Finance and Public Service Committee rather than face a vote of no confidence he was certain to lose. He stepped down with little grace, lashing out with allegations about the Fine Gael, Labour and Progressive Democrat leaders before he left. He stayed on as an ordinary member of the committee, and of two others. He also refused to resign his Dáil seat, but Fianna Fáil de-selected him by choosing two newcomers to contest the Dublin Mid West constituency in the next election.

Smyth pondered the matter over the weekend before delivering his historic verdict on 15 January. Lawlor was given a three-month sentence and fined £10,000. All but a week of the sentence was suspended on condition that he provide the tribunal with the documents it was looking for. The costs of the four-day hearing, estimated at over £100,000, were awarded against the TD. Lawlor left the Four Courts without a word of comment.

The judgement sent shock waves through the political system. But the Government was slow to condemn its former colleague. Bertie Ahern said his jailing was unfortunate 'on a personal basis'. The fact that Lawlor's vote was needed in a tight Dáil must have been furthest from his mind.

At 12.25 p.m. on 17 January — over ninety minutes early — Lawlor evaded the waiting photographers to arrive at Mountjoy jail through a back entrance. He was given sole occupancy of a four-bunk cell at the end of the medical unit wing and spent the week catching up on paperwork.

But even jail could not shield Lawlor from further humiliation. His three mobile phones were handed over to the tribunal. The Taoiseach said he should resign his Dáil seat unless he cooperated fully with Flood. The *Sunday World* published creased and burned copies of his financial records, which it claimed to have found near a bonfire at his home on the day before he went to jail. Tribunal and Garda investigations were called, and Lawlor later accused journalists of trespassing.

He left Mountjoy the following Wednesday in the back of his gardener's van, again successfully escaping the attentions of the media, and travelled straight to his office in Leinster House. Before long, he had adjourned to the members' bar, where 'howls of laughter' could be heard, according to the next day's *Irish Times*.

On his release, a newspaper poll found that 85 per cent of people wanted him to resign. He did step down from two Oireachtas committees — again, before he was pushed — but steadfastly refused to resign his seat. In a Dáil debate on his behaviour, he staunchly defended his position and, once again, smeared other politicians with allegations. Asked later if he was ashamed about his week behind bars, Lawlor said: 'Ashamed? No, I just saw it was something to be done. It was a major misunderstanding as I saw it. I just got on with what I had to do. No big deal there.'[20]

Lawlor's cooperation with the tribunal came up for review in the High Court at regular intervals following his release. It soon became apparent that the tribunal was not happy with the quality of documentation it was getting. As ever with Lawlor, quantity wasn't a problem — over 150 folders had been submitted. An astonishing 101 bank accounts had come to light. But was this all the TD had? And was it relevant to the matters under investigation? And where were the explanations for the transactions contained in the documents?

In July, the tribunal waved the whip again. Lawlor had still not met his obligations, it told the High Court. There was a dearth of information about the manner in which Lawlor settled his crippling debts in the mid-1990s. Lawlor had sought information from 272 parties with which he had financial dealings but, curiously, his financial adviser Luke Mooney was not one of them. The tribunal also wanted to know more about the Morgan trust and its loans to the TD.

For a third time, Mr Justice Smyth found against the TD. In July, he sentenced Lawlor to another seven days in prison and fined him £5,000. Ruling that he had not cooperated fully with the tribunal, he declared that 'the rot has got to stop'. On this occasion, the learned judge quoted from Balzac: 'Nothing causes deeper sadness than an unmerited fall into disrepute from which it is impossible to rise again'. Once again, costs estimated at over £100,000 were awarded against the TD.

The threat of imprisonment was averted by an appeal to the Supreme Court, but only temporarily. In December 2001, the court delivered yet another shattering judgement for the TD. In a unanimous ruling, the five judges confirmed Mr Justice Smyth's decision and suggested that Lawlor's sentence could have been even stiffer. One judge even accused him of lying in his affidavits. Worse still, they ruled against him on costs, leaving him with an estimated legal bill of over £300,000 from his legal tussles with the tribunal.

Yet the judges too came in for ferocious criticism after they agreed to defer Lawlor's one-week sentence in Mountjoy until after Christmas. Whereas 'ordinary decent criminals' usually have to start serving their jail terms immediately, Lawlor's wish that he be allowed to spend the holiday with his son's family in New York was granted.

In January 2002, he finally began his sentence, yet again evading the attentions of photographers with the help of the Garda. Inevitably, Lawlor's new familiarity with the jail gave him a new nickname — Lord Mountjoy. Just as before, he was segregated from the rest of the prisoners, this time in a single cell in the basement of B-wing. Even behind bars, it seemed, there was one law for the rich and powerful, and another for the rest of us.

Yet even this wasn't the end of Lawlor's ignominy. He was barely out of jail before the issue of his continued cooperation with the tribunal came up again for scrutiny. Once more, Mr Justice Smyth heard the case in the High Court and the tribunal argued that he was not complying.

Tribunal lawyers said there had been 'a significant and continuing failure' by the TD to meet his obligations. They outlined eleven specific concerns, many of them relating to bank accounts controlled by Lawlor in Liechtenstein, the US and Ireland.

Yet again, fresh information emerged. The court heard that solicitor John Caldwell had transferred £350,000 to Lawlor in 1995. A fortnight later, the politician lodged a similar amount in his bank in Liechtenstein. Shortly after, £157,000 of this was withdrawn to clear his debts with the banks in Ireland.

Then there was the revelation that his son Niall Lawlor operated a number of accounts on his father's behalf in the early 1990s. The TD managed to forget about these — and the £322,000 they contained — until reminded by his son. At the time they were opened, the banks were closing in on the financially strapped politician, and this provided a way of keeping money beyond their grasp. The tribunal also demanded more information about lodgements made by Lawlor into his son's accounts in the US.

Many of the most startling revelations came from Lawlor's own legal team. In total, he had received almost £1.5 million in political donations and consultancy payments during his career, the court was told. The largest contributor was Lark Developments, a building company that gave Lawlor £100,000. The TD also claimed to have received £80,000 from the meat processor Kepak. The company said it knew nothing about the payments, which may have come from its founder Noel Keating, who died in the early 1990s.

Then there was £60,000 from Frank Dunlop and £51,200 from another builder, Seán Mulryan of Ballymore Properties. The latter company said that apart from £1,200 given as a political donation, the rest of the money related to its involvement with Lawlor in property projects in Central Europe. Not for the first time, we learned that Lawlor generated false invoices in return for these payments. Two invoices for £20,000 each were issued in the name of Long Associates, a name he says he 'chose at random' and £10,000 was invoiced by King and Company, an estate agency in Prague in which Lawlor had no interest.

It was already known that Lawlor had issued fake invoices to process payments of £74,000 he received from National Toll Roads, but now further payments from that company were revealed. These included cheques for £10,000 and £3,000 from NTR's chairman, Tom Roche senior, a £1,200 contribution in 1993 and £1,000 paid during a charity golf classic.

Lawlor didn't bother attending the start of the hearing until he was ordered by Mr Justice Smyth to do so. After his lawyers failed in an attempt to argue that the court had no jurisdiction in the case, it grew clear that he was in trouble. The verdict came in February 2002, at the end of a long week of legal argument, and once again the judge found against the TD. This time, Mr Justice Smyth delivered pearls of wisdom from Dr Johnson, Dryden and Machiavelli before consigning Lawlor to Mountjoy for one month. He was also fined £10,000.

'The defendant seems only to bestir himself when the matter comes into a court listing,' the judge remarked before a stony-faced Lawlor departed into the murk of a rain-lashed Dublin. He opted not to appeal to the Supreme Court, which could have imposed an even heavier sentence, and slipped into Mountjoy a few days later, for the third time in thirteen months.

Yet within days, Lawlor was out again, if only temporarily. As his colleagues in the Dáil united to call for his resignation, he went to the High Court to demand his temporary release for the period of the debate. In a twenty-minute contribution, he apologised for his actions, but said his non-compliance with the tribunal was 'unintentional and non-malicious'. His contribution made no difference to the result — not that Lawlor had any intention of resigning, anyway. Within a few hours, he was back in Mountjoy.

7

Radio Fianna Fáil

'Irish national radio like you've never heard it before.'
— James Stafford of Century Radio promises big things at the
oral hearings to award new licences, January 1989
*'That's the minister, Ray Burke — he's the one who's going to give us our
licence.'*
— An English visitor recalling how Oliver Barry, co-founder of
Century Radio, pointed out the Minister for Communications in
the Horseshoe Bar of the Shelbourne Hotel in 1988. Barry denies
making the remark.

Achilly day at the National Concert Hall in Dublin in
January 1989. The occasion is the oral presentations made
by the various bidders for the first national commercial
radio licence. Four groups are in the running. The decision rests with
the ten members of the Independent Radio and Television
Commission, set up by the Minister for Communications, Ray Burke,
only four months earlier.

The ritzy world of Irish entertainment is well represented —
theatre impresarios, showband managers, disc jockeys, radio pirates
and the like. But away from the stars and smiles up at the front, the
sober suits and serious money of financial investors are much in
evidence. Commercial radio is the dot.com of its day. You couldn't
throw a stone in these circles without hitting one of the big names
of Irish business — Smurfit, Desmond, McEvaddy brothers, Crean
and, on his first big outing, Denis O'Brien. It was television that first
earned the description of 'a licence to print money,' but commercial
radio has always attracted the same get-rich-quick aspirations.

None of the bidders has had to publish their applications and
none has done so, so their ownership and plans remain a mystery to

the public. Cameras and radio microphones are excluded — this from a 'public' hearing to decide the future of radio and television — and only selected print journalists are allowed to attend. And they certainly aren't allowed to ask questions.

Once the hearing begins, the promises rain down like confetti. Century Radio — dubbed by some as 'Radio Fianna Fáil' because of its connections in high places — leads the way. It promises 250 jobs, two regional studios, education programmes and documentaries. The station will be 'an alternative to RTÉ but will not duplicate RTÉ'. There will be 'a phrase a day' in Irish. Something for everyone in the audience. It will be 'Irish national radio like you've never heard it before,' promises Century's co-founder, James Stafford.

The chairman of the IRTC, former Supreme Court judge Séamus Henchy, chips in a question about ownership. Stafford tells the hearing that only he and Barry own the company and shares have not been offered to any other party. No mention, then, of the involvement of John Mulhern, a son-in-law of the Taoiseach, Charles Haughey, nor of offerings to any other potential investors. Next question.

Stafford and Barry promise to get their station on air within four months. At this moment, Century has no physical existence, not even a bent clothes hanger in the air. No-one on their team has ever run a radio station before, let alone set one up. There's no explanation of how this deadline is to be achieved. Next question.

Century's application looks good on paper. It boasts it can get a signal out around the country for a cost of only £375,000, whereas its two main rivals are budgeting over £800,000. Less money spent on engineering means more money available to balance the books during the difficult early years, so Century scores well here. There's only one problem; Century has said it isn't viable beyond the £375,000 figure. But RTÉ, which will carry out the transmission work, has agreed with the Department of Communications on a fee of £692,000.

Century's promotional video hints heavily that a certain big name broadcaster will be joining the new station. People have read the tabloid headlines about Gay Byrne's supposed £1 million deal with Century, so everyone is suitably impressed. No questions are asked, which is a shame really, because Byrne had walked away from the deal a fortnight earlier.

The other applicants make their pitches. There are three other bidders: veteran pirate broadcaster Chris Carey; a consortium of former RTÉ journalists and their backers; and Radio 2000, chaired by Denis O'Brien. Carey, unable to shake off his wideboy image, is first out. Most observers believe the race is between Century and Radio 2000.

The hearing over, Barry fields questions from reporters while Stafford dodges the cameras. Journalists play pundit, and most give Century the thumbs-down. A week later, the Commission meets again in Cork, and Century is awarded the licence. For O'Brien, the disappointment of losing is tempered a month later when he wins one of the Dublin licences.

Two seemingly unrelated events happen the following May; a general election is called, and Frank Sinatra comes to town. Ol' Blue Eyes fills Lansdowne Road stadium early in the month, and meets Ray Burke at a party afterwards. Sinatra's voice is shot, but the crowds are happy and the concert is a huge success for its promoter, Oliver Barry. The showbiz impresario's bank accounts bulge with the profits.

Barry is a life-long Fianna Fáil supporter, and a friend and neighbour of Burke. When the general election is called, he resolves to share some of his good fortune with his long-time buddy. On the morning of 26 May, he goes to his bank at O'Connell Street in Dublin and takes out £35,000 from the Oliver Barry/Frank Sinatra savings account.[1] The amount is in cash, which he stuffs into his briefcase. He does a few errands, eats some lunch. Then he walks across town to one of Burke's departmental offices — neither man can remember which one. The two men meet briefly. Barry opens his briefcase and hands Burke the bundle. Burke thanks his friend and says the money will ensure Fianna Fáil wins a second seat in his constituency in Dublin North (it doesn't). Asked to explain the payment years later, Barry describes it as a 'no strings attached, bona fide political donation'. Five days later, Burke lodges the money to his personal bank account.

Throughout the 1970s and 1980s broadcasting was one of the most controversial issues in Irish politics. The airwaves teemed with dozens of pirate broadcasters and there were numerous calls to set up local radio stations. RTÉ's response to the loss of its monopoly was lethargic. It set up Radio 2 (now 2FM) in 1979, but this barely stemmed the pirate tide. Meanwhile, journalists at the State broadcaster found themselves in repeated conflict with Fianna Fáil over allegations of political bias.

Legislation to shut down the pirates was drawn up in 1977 but took more than a decade to enact. Fine Gael and Labour brought forward proposals for local radio when they came to power in the 1980s. However, they spent so much time arguing over the contents that they were never implemented.

Fianna Fáil returned to power in February 1987. A month later, Ray Burke was given the job of sorting out the mess in broadcasting. Burke, whose relations with RTÉ were already fraught, wasn't noted for any prior interest in the area. Yet he was to hold the communications portfolio up to 1991, through three changes of administration and one of the most turbulent periods in Irish broadcasting. During the election, Fianna Fáil had proposed the setting up of a network of local and community radio stations. It was Burke's task to deliver on this promise. It was also to be 'payback' time for RTÉ; after years of testy relations between its journalists and Fianna Fáil politicians, Burke wanted to provide the party with an alternative outlet for publicity. 'Levelling the playing pitch' became the cliché of the day.

The Minister asked his officials to submit their proposals for legislation. By September 1987, a memo to government had been prepared, setting out the objectives of the legislation. Neither the memo nor its summary referred to a national radio licence. However, an appended note on the legislation referred to the possibility of introducing a franchise for a national commercial radio service at some time in the future. Where this first mention of the proposal came from isn't clear.

On 6 October, the Government gave Burke the go-ahead for the licensing of local and community stations. There was still no mention of national radio. But within weeks, the proposal for a national station moved from the distant future to the present tense. On 28 October, Burke told the senior civil servant responsible for the legislation of the Government's intention to have an independent national commercial radio service in addition to local radio. He later claimed to have raised the matter 'informally' with the Cabinet on this date. There was, however, no documentary evidence to indicate that this happened, nor had the Department done any work on such a proposal.

As far as the main official dealing with radio was concerned, the idea of a national station 'came out of a clear, blue sky'. So did a new stipulation that the new stations should provide a minimum 20 per cent of news and current affairs in their output. This would ensure the politicians got an alternative outlet for publicity to RTÉ.

Things then moved quickly. A Bill that had been hanging around for more than six years was whipped into shape in weeks. The proposal for a national station was tacked on to the Bill that had been prepared. Burke got final Cabinet approval on 16 November.

There was still some unease, though. The Department of Finance was concerned that the licences were being given out for nothing. The Minister for Finance, Ray MacSharry, wrote to Burke in December saying they should be awarded by tender to the highest bidder. This would generate extra funds for the Exchequer, he argued. Burke rejected MacSharry's argument, saying this would mean only the 'well-heeled' would be able to afford to get involved. His option, in contrast, would give everyone 'an equal chance to get access to the airwaves'.

As it turned out, the successful bidders, Century Radio,[2] were as 'well-heeled' as you could get — its founders were a millionaire businessman, a high-profile showbusiness promoter and the wealthy son-in-law of Charles Haughey.

At this stage, too, Burke was proposing that the power to award licences should rest with the minister. As the Bill stated: 'the minister shall have regard to, but shall not be bound, by the advice of the advisory committee'. It took considerable pressure from the Opposition, which railed against the possibility that this power could be abused, before Burke backed down and agreed to set up an independent commission.

Oliver Barry, the public face of Century during its rise and fall, was a businessman well versed in the vicissitudes of the entertainment business. A life-long Fianna Fáil supporter, Barry was best known as the manager of the Wolfe Tones and, later, as the promoter of a series of successful, middle-of-the-road pop concerts. Born in Banteer in County Cork in 1940, he was educated in nearby Fermoy and worked for a time in his family's wholesale fruit and vegetable business. He moved to Dublin and a spell as a laboratory assistant before venturing into the showband scene in the 1960s. Before long, he was representing acts like The Freshmen, Earl Gill and, later, Stockton's Wing and Bagatelle. In 1966, he signed the Wolfe Tones, who were to become Ireland's most successful — and controversial — ballad group.

He was always close to the GAA and in the 1970s, he raised hundreds of thousands of pounds for the Association at a series of concerts at Páirc Uí Chaoimh in Cork, designed to clear the Association's debt. The chairman of the Cork county board of the GAA was Donal O'Sullivan, who was later appointed to the IRTC and adjudicated on Century's application for a radio licence. James Last, Prince, Frank Sinatra, Status Quo, Steve Collins and the Tall Ships all owe their appearances in Ireland to Barry. His plans to bring U2's Popmart tour to Lansdowne Road for two dates in 1997 ran into determined opposition from local residents, but Barry won that battle in the courts. Barry experienced personal tragedy at the height of his business success. In January 1997, his 24-year-old son Brian died when the parked car in which he had fallen asleep caught fire.

Charles Haughey appointed him to the RTÉ Authority in the mid-1980s, where he met and became friendly with the broadcaster, Gay Byrne. It was then that Barry developed the idea of setting up a rival commercial station and met many of those he would later try to woo to Century. The chairman of the Authority was Fred O'Donovan, a showbusiness impresario who was later appointed by Burke to the IRTC.

An accomplished networker, well liked across the political spectrum, Barry maintained a variety of business interests outside the entertainment scene. Even during the worst of his financial woes at Century, Barry was able to invest £250,000 of his own money in developing a golf course near his home at Hollywood Rath in West Dublin.[3] He also developed a small housing estate nearby.

Politics was Barry's other main passion. He was closest to Ray Burke, but he also knew Charles Haughey, Jack Lynch and Albert Reynolds and boasted frequently about his political 'clout'. He used his promotional skills to help organise Fianna Fáil Ardfheiseanna and once thought of standing for election for the party. Barry 'likes politics, he was always involved in politics of many hues,' John Mulhern commented at one point, disapprovingly.[4]

One day at the end of 1987 or the start of 1988, Barry was on the morning train to Cork when he ran into another friend with strong connections to Fianna Fáil and the Haughey family. 'I was reading in the paper that there were going to be commercial licences and Oliver Barry happened to be on the train,' John Mulhern recalled.

Barry told his travelling companion of his plans for a national radio station built around Ireland's most famous broadcaster, Gay Byrne. Mulhern expressed an interest in getting involved, and later introduced Barry to his friend James Stafford.[5] The three men agreed to take one-third stakes in the new venture. Like Stafford and Barry, Mulhern had no direct experience of running a radio station, but that didn't prevent him coming on board. Mulhern invested £300,000 in 1989 and a further £310,000 in late 1990, but kept out of any visible involvement in the day-to-day running of the company.

Mulhern said his involvement was kept secret because the other two wanted 'a position of power' within the company. 'I was dealing with two friends. I assumed my interests were being looked after.'[6] He claimed he was unaware of the IRTC's requirement that all investors in the new stations be publicly disclosed. Barry admitted the concealment was 'innocently wrong,' but only after it had been revealed publicly over a decade later.

The involvement of Mulhern, the director of a large food distribution business, was never disclosed. Barry and Stafford say they kept quiet about his role because it was felt that publicity about the involvement of the Taoiseach's son-in-law would damage Century's bid. Mulhern never owned shares in Century, allowing Stafford to claim that he hadn't mislead the IRTC by saying no-one else was involved. But it was clear he was kept fully informed about and participated in most decisions regarding the company. When more money was needed, he put it in.

Aside from the money he put in, Mulhern brought his connections to the venture. For over twenty years, he had been friendly with the financier Dermot Desmond and the government press secretary P.J.

Mara, whose names were to crop up unexpectedly at various times during the Century saga.

Stafford, his clipped phrases and stiff bearing revealing his education in an English public school, took over the day-to-day running of the project. The scion of a prominent coal and shipping family in County Wexford, he already had a proven track record in business failure. Having started from a position of great comfort, his career was pockmarked by speculative ventures, many of them spectacularly unsuccessful. He was just 25 when he came to Dublin in the early 1970s to carve out a career in the property world. In typically grand fashion, he installed himself in a penthouse suite in the Gresham Hotel, which was owned by his family at the time.

In 1974, his property business collapsed when recession struck. The value of the sites he had acquired at relatively high prices plummeted overnight. Undaunted, he moved into the oil business, and emerged in 1980 as one of the founding directors and major shareholders of the speculative oil exploration company, Atlantic Resources. But he later resigned from the company and sold his shares after a disagreement with the then chairman, Dr Tony O'Reilly.

Another high-risk project was Atlantic Satellites, which secured an exclusive licence to provide an Irish satellite television network. The idea, which was before its time, was to set up a home-shopping channel. Stafford teamed up with the Hughes Corporation in the US, but nothing much came of the project. It did, however, launch the business career of then unknown Denis O'Brien, who set up Esat originally to provide services for Atlantic Satellites.

Stafford had been a friend of Charles Haughey for thirty years — his mother worked as a publicist for the young TD — and in 1988 he invested £100,000 in a mining company set up by Haughey's son Conor. He once suggested to Haughey that the Government should set up a financial services centre in Dublin but again, this was an idea before its time. Another long-time friend was John Mulhern, and he was best man at Mulhern's wedding to Eimear Haughey in 1990.

Stafford could be a prickly individual to do business with, even if you were on the same side. Vincent Finn, RTÉ's director general, said Stafford's idea of a difficult person was one who contested whatever proposition Stafford was making. Mulhern commented acidly: 'Usually when there was a whinge you heard it from Mr Stafford.'

Barry and his team were quick off the blocks. He began hatching plans in 1987, around the time Burke was bruiting the necessary legislation. It helped that Barry had at his disposal a secret report on the future of local radio, drawn up in the mid-1980s.[7] Marked 'strictly private and confidential,' it was meant only for the eyes of the Minister for Communications, his department and the commission that drew it up. Barry canvassed his ideas with Gay Byrne and on 6 November 1987 he and Mulhern met the broadcaster. The issue of a national radio licence was discussed.

Meanwhile, Burke had first raised the idea of a national licence with a civil servant a week earlier, on 28 October, but at this stage, there were no formal proposals for national radio. The first evidence of a Cabinet decision on the matter dates from 16 November.

The coincidence of dates is interesting, but Burke denies discussing the matter with his friend. If Barry learned about the national franchise, it wasn't from him. 'If they did [know], they didn't know it from me. Nobody knew about this other than members of the Government and the officials in the Department, until publication.'[8] If Barry had a vision, though, it was formed in a tunnel. With no experience of running a radio station, he moulded his concept around one man, Gay Byrne.

Byrne had been Ireland's best-known and most popular broadcaster for more years than people could remember. But the 'housewife's favourite' had suffered some reverses latterly, most notably when his personal accountant embezzled a lifetime's savings. Byrne certainly had a financial incentive to leave RTÉ after almost three decades.

Barry and Byrne knew each other from the corridors of RTÉ, they moved in the same showbiz circles and they were good friends. Barry invited the broadcaster along to a planning meeting in the Shelbourne Hotel. Byrne remembers that Stafford, Enda Marren, a lawyer with Fine Gael links, Mulhern and a leading accountant, Laurence Crowley, were also present. Byrne said he was told Century would be 'a licence to print money'. It would produce so much money 'you would have to get wheelbarrows to carry it around'. But

Century's investment was in Gay Byrne, as much as in any new radio station. 'If you have Gay Byrne, you have a licence to print money,' was Stafford's view.

Byrne remembers urging the others to bid for a Dublin or Cork licence instead of the national one because this would involve 'far less money, far less hassle and fewer people'.[9] It was sensible advice, with hindsight, but the others were fixated on the national prize. In spite of his doubts, Byrne stayed on board through most of 1988, and the project was built around his persona. News of his involvement leaked out and made for good tabloid headlines. This did no-one any harm; Century gained its reputation as a front-runner from its association with Byrne, and RTÉ responded by offering improved terms to its star broadcaster.

The only problem was that Byrne hadn't finally committed. In fact, his doubts were multiplying. He realised he was comfortable where he was, with a national audience in RTÉ. He began to doubt the viability of the project. Most of all, though, he could see all the blame coming down on his shoulders — 'muggins' behind the microphone — if the venture failed.

Barry thought his friend was just playing hard to get. He filed Century's application, with a programme schedule tailor-made for the broadcaster, in mid-December 1988. Just before Christmas, he called up to Byrne's house on the Hill of Howth for a final decision. Barry took an envelope from his inside pocket and slid it onto the table. 'That is the amount we discussed,' he told Byrne and his wife.

It was — and more. The envelope contained a bank draft for £1 million. The two men had discussed a figure of £1 million, but this was for a three-year contract. Now Barry, in a last, desperate throw of the dice, was offering a cool million upfront. Stafford would later say he didn't know about his partner's £1 million offer to Byrne. But he agreed: 'Gay Byrne was an absolute winner. Even at £1 million, he was good value'. However, Byrne was cagey. 'I do not want that in my house overnight. I wouldn't sleep a wink. Please take it away,' he told Barry. He promised a decision quickly. A few days later, he told Barry he was staying in RTÉ.

Burke pressed ahead with the legislation to set up commercial radio and television, and to put the pirates off the air. The Radio and Television Act became law in July 1988 and the Independent Radio and Television Commission was established shortly after, in October. The Commission appointed by Burke contained the usual mixture of worthies and party hacks. Its membership included two judges, a union leader, a public relations guru, a few business people and a retired teacher.

Burke's influence on the Commission was evident from the start. The inaugural meeting was held in Newbridge House in Donabate, in the heart of the minister's constituency. One of its first decisions was to accept Burke's nominations for banker, solicitor and accountant to the Commission. The bank just happened to be the Ulster Bank in Dublin airport, which had been Burke's branch since 1974. It was here the politician banked many of his donations, and remitted £10,000 from the Rennicks payment to Fianna Fáil in 1989. The minister even called the manager on the day the decision was made to deliver the good news. Just what use a branch in Dublin airport would be to the IRTC offices in the city centre was hard to understand.

The solicitor involved, Michael O'Connor of John S. O'Connor, was also a constituent of Mr Burke's. He first learned of his appointment from his father, Pat. John S. O'Connor were solicitors to Fianna Fáil and had represented Éamon de Valera in his time. More recently, the principal of the firm, Pat O'Connor, had been Charles Haughey's election agent and achieved notoriety — and the nickname 'Pat O'Connor Pat O'Connor' — after he was charged with and cleared of double voting in the 1982 election. As for the accountancy firm, Burke chose it on the basis that one of the partners had done 'good work' for Fianna Fáil and deserved a 'thank you'.

Not for the first time, Burke relied on his family links to get what he wanted. One of the Minister's appointees was Donal O'Sullivan, a retired teacher from Cork, whose father had served in the Dáil with Burke's father. Before the IRTC's first meeting, he rang O'Sullivan, whom he barely knew, and asked to meet. As it happened, Burke was travelling to a party function in Mallow the following day, so he had the ministerial limousine pull up in Fermoy beforehand.

It was a short meeting. Burke asked O'Sullivan to propose certain people for positions that would appear on the agenda. O'Sullivan didn't know them, so he wrote the names down on a piece of paper afterwards. Their business done, Burke left in his usual hurry.

O'Sullivan duly did the minister's bidding, and the rest of the IRTC never knew Burke's hand was behind the nominations. For Henchy, equally oblivious to what was going on under his nose, it was 'a matter of no importance'.[10] Or, as O'Sullivan commented later: 'That's the way government works.'[11] Asked later about this exercise in croneyism, Burke had no apologies. He didn't benefit in any way. It was 'simple networking'. He was just doing a favour for constituents.

But if Burke saw nothing wrong in doing a favour for these constituents, would he not also help out another constituent, Oliver Barry? Burke emphatically denied he did any favours for his north Dublin neighbour. Burke had no recollection of discussing his plans for national radio and, later, Century's application with his friend. The first he heard about Century's bid was through general 'Dublin gossip' and 'chat', he said.[12]

Another early decision by the commission was to process applications for a national licence first, ahead of local radio franchises. This, it was argued, was because a longer lead-in time was required. Yet pirate radio was the scourge of the minister's department at the time, and it operated on a local level. The best prospect of getting rid of the pirates was to legalise local stations as quickly as possible. Then the commission opted not to have votes on the licence applications but to reach agreement by consensus, apparently out of a fear of leaks. This form of decision-making would not apply to other matters.

For cost reasons, the commission decided to dispense with the services of its accountants when considering the applications for radio licences, leaving its ten members without the benefit of independent financial advice on the merits of the various bidders.

In addition to hiding Mulhern's involvement, Century operated a further layer of concealment. The three promoters were secretly involved in a separate bid for a radio licence in Dublin. A leading accountant, Paschal Taggart, drew up the detailed proposal for Dublin One Radio. Taggart took a 10 per cent stake and the former Dublin GAA manager Kevin Heffernan took 5 per cent, but the remainder was owned by the three Century principals, who devised an elaborate scheme to disguise their involvement.

For Stafford, it was 'a second oar in the water', a fallback position if Century failed to win a licence. It isn't clear why Century hid its involvement in Dublin One from the IRTC; after all, Denis O'Brien also had 'two oars in the water' and suffered no ill-effects. The three men hid their investment in Dublin One from their own staff and their accountants. Monies spent on Dublin One were wrongly entered as the costs of starting up the business. The station's chief executive, financial controller and, later on, its chairman made a number of attempts to establish the destination of these monies, but got no clear answers.[13]

Taggart and Barry fell out over costings and Taggart pulled out. The bid was never made but, later on, there were disputes over outstanding bills. According to Taggart, Century was underfunded and had no chance of succeeding. Barry 'wasn't up to speed on the cost of running a Dublin radio station, so I wasn't surprised he didn't get it right for the national station,' was Taggart's verdict on the Century debacle.[14]

The closing date for applications for the licence was 16 December 1988. Of the four applications in by the deadline, Century had by far the lowest projected expenditure on transmission services. Its submission stated that the station would not be viable if it had to pay RTÉ more than £375,000 to broadcast its signal around the country. In other words, it was refusing to pay more than this amount. The minutes of a Century board meeting held immediately before the oral hearings recorded that '£375,000 is our figure. Commission will avoid that issue'. Another note read: 'RTÉ fee (unlikely to be asked)'. So did Century know that the IRTC would not ask any awkward questions about the transmission fee issue? Stafford insists he had 'no knowledge whatsoever' of what the Commission was going to ask.

Separately, RTÉ and the Department of Communications entered into talks on the issue. On 11 January 1989, a fee of £692,000 was agreed. But where did this leave Century? Should it have been ruled out of the race because it wasn't prepared to pay more than £375,000? Logically, the matter should have been sorted out at the oral presentations that took place the following day, 12 January.

However, Century wasn't asked this important question. A question was drafted but never put, seemingly because the Commission didn't want to 'tie the hands' of the winner in future negotiations with RTÉ.[15] Century, which had no breakdown or background for its £375,000 proposal, never had to face this potentially embarrassing scrutiny.

At the oral hearings in the National Concert Hall, the media's cameras and microphones were excluded and only selected print journalists were allowed to attend. Century's presentation was strong on celebrities — Terry Wogan and Chris de Burgh had been recruited as investors — but many observers felt its rivals had the edge in terms of programming. For most of the IRTC members, Century was the clear leader. A final decision was deferred to the next meeting.

On the day after the oral hearings, Stafford met Henchy and the secretary of the IRTC, Seán Connolly. It was, as Stafford underlined in subsequent correspondence, a 'very satisfactory' meeting. In other words, Century felt it had got the gig. It wasn't until six days later that the official announcement was made after a second meeting of the Commission.

Stafford also noted that Henchy and Connolly promised to 'challenge' RTÉ on the matter of transmission charges and to 'justify' £375,000 as the amount Century would have to pay RTÉ. Having picked the winner, the Commission was clearly determined to see it got a good start in life. Effectively, it adopted the Century figure and pressed the minister to direct RTÉ to reduce its fee appropriately.

Unknown to Century and the IRTC and everyone else involved in the process, Gay Byrne signed a new contract with RTÉ on 16 January, just two days before Century was officially awarded the licence. The pearl at the centre of the new station's plans had just slipped out.

In the few days that elapsed between the oral hearings and the announcement of the successful bid, James Stafford received an unusual call. The financier Dermot Desmond expressed an interest in investing in Century. Desmond said he was acting on behalf of an investor, who he declined to name. However, Stafford rebuffed the financier, saying his offer would have to wait until after the franchise had been awarded.

Much later, it turned out that Desmond was acting for none other than himself. He explained later that he had wanted to get in on

Century cheaply before the licence was awarded rather than have to pay more to a successful bidder. 'I would camouflage my interest because if there's a price for Joe Public, there's a [higher] price for Dermot Desmond,' he explained.[16]

For Desmond, who revelled in his theory of 'contrary investment' in companies that no-one else would touch but were later successful, Stafford's answer was 'not good enough'. A few days later, he invested in one of the bidders for the Dublin licences, Capital Radio Productions. His instincts were as sound as they had been with Century, with Capital winning a franchise a month later. Desmond was to fine-tune his technique of investing in public sector communications franchises later in the 1990s, when his investment in the second mobile phone licence netted him a windfall profit of £100 million.

The IRTC's work was quickly mired in controversy when one of the failed applicants for a Dublin licence took a High Court action to have the decision overturned. Robbie Robertson of Sunshine Radio ran one of the slickest pirate operations, broadcasting from a hotel in Portmarnock, in the heart of Burke's constituency. Robertson 'went legit' and pulled out all of the stops to win a licence, for which Sunshine was a favoured contender. He failed, even though two licences, rather than the one originally expected, were handed out in Dublin.

Robertson took legal proceedings in which he pointed out that one of the IRTC members, Fred O'Donovan, had until a few months earlier been a shareholder and director of Esat Television, the main company involved in Denis O'Brien's rival bid. At the time, O'Donovan's daughter was dating O'Brien (it didn't last) and the two men were close personal friends, Robertson told the court. O'Donovan denied any conflict of interest and pointed out that he had taken steps to divest himself of 'a direct pecuniary interest' in Esat. Following a disagreement with O'Brien, he said he resigned as chairman and director of the company in July 1988 and sold his shareholding to another shareholder, Paul Power. Curiously, Power was the man who with Robin Rennicks delivered a £30,000 cheque to Ray Burke in June 1989. This money was a political donation paid on behalf of Fitzwilton, the investment vehicle controlled by Dr

Tony O'Reilly. The Flood tribunal is investigating this payment and, in particular, the success of O'Reilly-linked companies in securing MMDS rebroadcasting franchises.

The High Court challenge to O'Brien's licence award failed. The judge said that O'Donovan had successfully divested himself of his shares and there was no real likelihood of bias on his part. In any case, O'Donovan told *The Irish Times* in July 2000 that he did not participate in the IRTC vote on Capital's appreciation.[17] Robertson endured a difficult time for a few years before moving to Lanzarote to run a bar. O'Brien set up 98FM, and embarked on a business roll that was to culminate in the sale of his share in Esat Digifone for a personal profit of nearly £230 million in 1997.

The other Dublin licence award also has an indirect connection to payments to Ray Burke. It went to Capital Radio Productions, broadcasting today as FM104. The chairman and 9.8 per cent owner of Capital, Liam Conroy, was chief executive of the Murphy group of companies until June 1988. This is the company which paid Burke £30,000 in June 1989.

⋘⋙

As a national station in a sparsely populated country, Century faced a considerable technological challenge. It could set up its own set of antennae around the country, at great expense, or 'piggyback' on someone else's network. The obvious alternative was to use RTÉ's transmission system, but RTÉ was the new station's main competitor. It was always going to be a recipe for friction. The State-owned broadcaster, responding to directions from the Department, agreed to talk to Century.

At first, the talks proceeded along the usual lines for such negotiations, with RTÉ demanding £1.14 million for the use of its transmission network, and Century expressing its 'shock' at such a charge. 'It was the normal huckster shop negotiations you get in Ireland where no-one believes the other's price and fairy tales are told,' Fred O'Donovan commented later.

But the face-to-face haggling expected by RTÉ never materialised, and a meeting of the two sides in mid-November — two months before Century even got the franchise — was to be their last. Century had a different approach in mind, hinted at in a comment blurted out by Stafford in one meeting: 'We'll see what the Minister says about that.'[18] RTÉ dropped its proposed charge to £914,000, but Century continued to play hard-ball. It offered to pay £375,000 and maintained that anything more would make the project unviable. This was just huffing and puffing; internal documentation showed the company regarded this price as 'a steal'.[19]

Under pressure from Burke, who said he had a 'problem' with its demand, RTÉ further reduced its asking price. By the time of the licence hearings in early January 1989, RTÉ and the Department of Communications had reached agreement on a price of £692,000. On Burke's 'strong urging', this was further reduced to £614,000. In February, Burke wrote to the IRTC chairman, Justice Henchy, saying the agreed charge was 'not unreasonable in Irish circumstances'. So the Department was happy. For RTÉ, it was 'a done deal'.[20] Burke, seemingly, was happy. But Century wasn't.

Barry and Stafford pressed home their political connections. They met Burke in February 1989 and told him they wanted the price set at £375,000. They even complained directly to Haughey about RTÉ's proposed charges and pleaded with the Taoiseach to 'give them a break with the ball'. Barry met his minister friend for dinner in the Coq Hardi in Dublin on 7 February, when the matter was 'probably' discussed.[21] Burke 'marked our card,' as Stafford later explained. Burke himself couldn't do anything, but he did suggest a plan. Century should go to the IRTC and urge it to seek a directive for £375,000 from the Minister.[22] Under the legislation, the Minister could intervene if requested to do so by the IRTC.

The evidence supports this version of events. In February, Century's solicitor noted that 'the minister will give a directive for £375,000'. This was a full month before Burke actually issued a directive. Three days later, Century wrote to the IRTC asking for a directive to reduce the charges. The Commission forwarded the letter to Burke, who issued the directive against the advice of his officials on 14 March. He said it 'followed discussions' with the IRTC. In fact, the commission members were not consulted and no formal decision or request was made.

The decision came as a bolt from the blue to RTÉ. 'Absolute shock and disbelief' is how the director general, Vincent Finn, described his reaction. The station pondered a legal challenge, but thought better of it. Challenging the directive would only be portrayed as RTÉ trying to hold on to its monopoly, and the Minister's mind was fixed. Burke says he wanted to get the station on the air as quickly as possible. As for the figures he agreed to in February, these were 'binned' because they were 'never a runner'.

The directive gave Century the best possible start, even before it went on the air. According to the tribunal, it saved the station £600,000 a year compared to the amount agreed in January, and £222,000 in once-off charges.

In May 1989, just two months after Burke's intervention in the transmission dispute, Barry made his £35,000 cash donation to Burke. Barry claims the politician, then in the throes of a general election campaign, had looked for £30,000, saying it was to help secure a second Fianna Fáil seat in north Dublin. The promoter was taken aback. He was used to helping his friend out with small contributions and canvassers and transport to get the voters out on polling day, but this was in a different league.[23] Burke, who reaped almost £100,000 in other contributions during this period, denies ever asking for money. He wasn't surprised to get a donation from his friend, but he was surprised at the amount involved.[24]

The election campaign was on a knife-edge at the time, with closely fought constituencies such as Dublin North expected to make all the difference. A second seat for Fianna Fáil would mean a swing of two to the Government. Century had its licence by now, but Barry could see what effect the election result might have. Fianna Fáil had championed commercial radio over RTÉ and community radio. Burke had championed Century in its battle with RTÉ over transmission fees. An alternative government involving Labour and Fine Gael mightn't be so kind. For the battles to come, Century needed a friendly face in power, and it needed access. Burke offered both. 'Radio Fianna Fáil' knew which side its bread was buttered on.

Barry said he decided to make the payment on behalf of Century. The curious decision to bump the amount up to £35,000 was his, he later explained. The contribution was to be part of his £275,000 investment in the company, he determined.[25] Barry and Burke agree that no receipt was asked for, or given. No record was made of the payment on either side. Burke included the cash in a lodgement of

£39,500 he made to his personal account on 31 May.

Burke was Minister for Industry, Commerce and Communications at the time of Barry's payment. Only a week later, he collected £30,000 from Rennicks Manufacturing, on behalf of Fitzwilton, and at least £30,000 from Gogarty. After the election, Burke was returned to Cabinet with responsibility for the split portfolio of justice and communications.

Barry paid the money, but on whose behalf? Was it a chummy dig-out from a friend, or a corporate contribution from a company that had regular dealings with the Minister? The money trail, which shows the cost was borne ultimately by Century, points to the latter explanation. Barry claims both Stafford and Mulhern agreed in advance to the payment, which he says he made on behalf of Century. His two colleagues say they only learned about it later. Mulhern says he heard about it from Stafford 'a considerable time later,' probably by the end of 1989.[26]

Stafford originally told the tribunal he only learned about the payment from newspaper reports. In evidence, however, he dated his knowledge to March 1991, almost two years after Barry made the contribution to Burke. He explained the discrepancy by saying he knew but didn't 'actually' believe a payment had been made. Barry owed him £29,000 and he thought this was just another story told by his partner to avoid having to repay the debt.

However, Century's accountant Tom Moore said that within six to nine months of the launch of Century in January 1989, Stafford told him that Barry 'wished' to make a cash payment to the Fianna Fáil politician. In other words, Moore was saying, Stafford knew about the payment in advance.

Another piece of evidence appears to indicate that Stafford knew about the payment. Barry's investment in the station was 'shy' by the amount he paid to Burke. So how come Stafford, who watched every penny spent, never raised the matter with his business colleague? When asked about this, Stafford's explanation was that 'it escaped his attention' that Barry was short.[27] Barry went to great lengths to ensure he was repaid for the money he gave to Burke before Century folded in 1991. Surprisingly, given their differences, Stafford supported him in these efforts.

As the launch date approached, Barry and Stafford worked desperately to get everything ready. Negotiations on a transmission contract with the IRTC had been traumatic and relations were irretrievably soured.

Barry still hankered after Gay Byrne. 'I thought once we got the licence we'd get him back in. Money talks in that business, you know,' he said much later. Byrne wasn't for moving, though, and Barry had to search elsewhere. He tried hard to lure another high-profile personality away from RTÉ. Marion Finucane was courted, unsuccessfully. Terry Wogan and Chris de Burgh were on board as high-profile investors but that wasn't much use to the schedule, aside from Wogan's limited involvement from London. Century ended up with Marty Whelan and a bunch of relative unknowns.

Meanwhile, the advertisers were adopting a 'wait and see' approach. Century's outgoings were growing rapidly, and there was little enough money coming in. Barry and Stafford quietly dropped their promises for educational programmes and documentaries. But there was still the expensive requirement for all the new stations to provide a specified minimum of news and Irish-language programmes on the schedule.

Once again, Burke intervened on the station's behalf. In a letter to the IRTC chairman, Justice Henchy, he suggested that Century be allowed to 'grow into' its obligation to provide a specified minimum of news and Irish-language programming. The effect of this would be to ease the financial strain on the company in the crucial start-up period. However, Henchy stood his ground, and insisted that the regulations could not be eased or altered in any way. 'We weren't going to be the first public authority to preside over the demise of the Irish language,' commented IRTC member Kieran Mulvey.

There were no prizes for guessing who opened Century on 4 September 1989. 'We're celebrating the involvement of the private sector in national broadcasting and a new competitive broadcasting environment,' proclaimed Minister for Communications Ray Burke as the country's first national commercial broadcaster went on air for the first time.

Away from the first-day festivities, the alarm bells were already ringing. The chairman, Laurence Crowley, wanted spending cut by

20 per cent. The station's head of finance asked for the launch party to be scaled back because it couldn't afford an elaborate celebration. Stafford promised to do this but the party still turned into a massive affair.

This wasn't the first evidence of profligacy at Century; back in January, Barry, Mulhern and Crowley and their wives, and Stafford, celebrated the award of the licence at company expense with a luxury weekend stay at Claridge's in London. And in spite of its financial difficulties, Century was consistently generous to the political parties. Aside from the Burke donation, it gave £5,000 anonymously to Fianna Fáil — wrongly entered in the books as a business cost — and £2,000 to Fine Gael. Barry also made a personal donation of £5,000 to Charles Haughey.

But these weren't Barry's only acts of generosity. In August 1989, just before Century was due to launch, he made a 'thank you' payment in cash to the RTÉ transmission staff involved in putting the new station's signal on the air. Barry originally said he gave £5,000 to RTÉ executives Peter Branagan and John McGrath in a Dublin pub.

However, the two men disputed this. Branagan said the amount was £1,700, given to fund entertainment for RTÉ staff involved in the project.[28] He gave £1,000 to McGrath and the balance to another executive outside Dublin. Four parties were held with the money given, he understood. McGrath said he wasn't even there, as he was on holidays in Yugoslavia at the time. Barry later accepted that he might have got it wrong about McGrath.

McGrath had already resigned from RTÉ on an unrelated matter by the time this episode became public. In 1996, it was discovered that he had been purchasing televisions and video recorders in RTÉ and taking them for use in a pub he owned. In March 2000, he received a five-year suspended sentence after pleading guilty to defrauding the organisation of £164,000. Branagan was suspended for a time while the Barry payment was investigated by RTÉ but was later reinstated after the station satisfied itself he hadn't spent the money for personal use. He left the station shortly after for a career in the private sector.

Things started to go wrong for Century almost from the moment it went on air. Instead of reaching its target audience of 70 per cent of the population, it could only be picked up by 35 per cent of listeners. Ironically, given Barry's 'thank you' payment to its transmission staff, Stafford blamed these technical difficulties on RTÉ's 'dirty tricks'.[29]

The station's marketing staff had been told there would be 60 per cent coverage from day one, and sold advertising on this basis. They were never shown the agreement with RTÉ which showed that this level of coverage would not be reached until nine months later. The discovery that two-thirds of the country was unable to pick up the new station came as a 'hammer-blow' to its marketing director, Séamus O'Neill. Morale slumped as advertisers cancelled orders and new business became impossible to get.

Within six weeks of its launch, Century was cutting back spending by 40 per cent, and the directors were panicking.[30] Barry and Stafford started querying every expense, from flowers to cleaning costs and mileage.

Burke and Barry continued to meet regularly, and Burke would tell his friend things as a way of 'palming him off or getting him out of my hair,' he told the tribunal a decade later. But Century's access to people in high places was no secret. For the secretary of the IRTC, Seán Connolly, Century was 'too highly politicised'. In September 1989, he noted how Barry and Stafford were effectively sidelining the Commission by going to Burke with their grievances. He complained about 'the almost daily consultation with the minister on matters which should have rightly belonged to discussions and negotiations between Century, the IRTC and RTÉ'.[31]

Then there was the observation by Professor Ray Hills, an English consultant employed by Century to provide technical advice for the licence application. Hills, an expert in 'wideband curtain dipole arrays' and a member of the Worshipful Society of Scientific Instrument-makers, came to Dublin in 1988 for a number of meetings. After one of these, he found himself with Stafford and Barry in the rarefied atmosphere of the Horseshoe Bar in the Shelbourne Hotel. Barry pointed out Ray Burke, who was buying a round of drinks in the bar, and said: 'That's the minister, Ray Burke — he's the one who's going to give us our licence'. Barry denies having made the comment.

Hills, who did not know anything about Irish politics and had no reason to take sides in the Century affair, said it could have been 'a throwaway remark'. But whether it was bravado or the drink talking, or even the truth, the remark is deeply unsettling. 'It was certainly the first time a government minister has ever bought me a drink,' Hills commented.[32]

By the end of 1989, Century was in deep financial trouble. Listenership figures were off the bottom of the scale. Revenues were under half the amount projected, and costs were double the amount expected. The Bank of Ireland, which had loaned the venture £2.3 million, was getting nervous.

Barry pressed his political friend for action and met him, along with Stafford, in December. The previous year, the two men had threatened not to open the station if they didn't get their way on transmission charges. Now they warned they would close Century down unless what they termed RTÉ's abuse of its dominant position was addressed. 'We told the Minister … we would have to close unless we got a guarantee of a level playing pitch,' said Stafford.[33]

Century wanted a cap placed on RTÉ's revenue from advertising, a measure that would effectively divert advertising to commercial broadcasters. Burke agreed to implement the measure. Stafford left the meeting with the understanding that RTÉ's advertising would be reduced by 50 per cent, but Burke told the tribunal he never agreed to such a swingeing cut.

Burke went even further. Just before Christmas, he took the unusual if not unprecedented step of meeting Century's bankers. Barry and Stafford were there again, but no civil servants were present. The Minister, the officials recorded, promised to eliminate RTÉ's 'excesses' by capping its advertising revenue. This was three months before his Cabinet colleagues learned of these proposals.

Then he asked Barry and Stafford to leave for a few minutes. Burke leaned over his desk to the three officials opposite and confirmed his specific 'commitment' to Century. 'He left us in no doubt that his commitment to Century was strong,' one of the officials recalled.[34] The bankers went away with 'a degree of comfort' about the station's prospects. Burke later dismissed the meeting as 'a matter of no importance'. The reason no civil servants were present was because he did not want to 'bring the lads up' from their offices, he explained to the tribunal.

It was the Flood tribunal's investigations into other payments to Ray Burke that led, almost accidentally, to the disclosure of Barry's £35,000 contribution. However, once the tribunal began examining the Century debacle in detail, James Stafford made a series of further allegations every bit as controversial as his colleague's original donation.

Stafford's most astounding claim dates from the period before the licence was awarded. There was a 'price list' for securing the new broadcasting licences, Barry is alleged to have told his business partner, and money would have to be paid to Burke and the Government press secretary, P.J. Mara, in return for a licence. The prices were £90,000 for a television licence, £75,000 for a Dublin radio licence and £25,000 for a local licence. 'If you want to get a broadcasting licence it is going to cost money,' Barry is alleged to have told Stafford. Mara was well known to the wider public through the *Scrap Saturday* satirical show, which regularly lampooned his role as Charles Haughey's adviser and mouthpiece to the media. He was also a long-time friend of Oliver Barry.

Stafford's allegation stood unsupported by any other evidence. In legal terms, it was hearsay of the 'dúirt bean liom' variety. Burke didn't have the power to allocate licences, and Mara certainly didn't. The first draft of the broadcasting bill in November 1987 had assigned this power to the minister, but this caused a political outcry and Burke was forced to set up an independent decision-making body. Burke and Mara emphatically rejected the allegation, and Barry denied making the remark. Mara said it was 'madness' to suggest that he and Burke were going around Dublin like 'head waiters' with a price list for licences.

But Mara did have at least one concrete link to Century. In August 1989, he was one of only two individuals sent a confidential share placement document for the station. This arose out of his 'curiosity,' he later explained, rather than any desire to invest. In addition, he did try to obtain money from Century, though the basis for this claim is disputed. Once again, Stafford's version is at variance with all others. He claims Barry was approached on several occasions by Mara, who said he was 'owed' money by Century.

Barry says the intention was 'to fix him up with a number with Century'. Mara, who wanted to leave his job as government press secretary, was looking for a consultancy, as well as stock options.

The problem with this explanation is that Century was then in the throes of a well-publicised financial crisis. There was no question of taking people on — indeed, the company was shedding staff — so this was hardly the time to engage a media guru looking for £60–70,000 a year, as well as stock options at a favourable price.

Mara says he discussed getting involved in Century with his friend Oliver Barry in late 1989 or early 1990. He was aware of the station's problems but took the view that Barry and Stafford were 'men with deep pockets'. In any case, he thought he could 'bring something to the party'. The matter was discussed at a meeting around May 1990, which was chaired by the financier Dermot Desmond. The others present were Barry, Stafford and Mara. Desmond remembers it as a 'friendly and informal meeting'; Stafford, in contrast, says it was 'not particularly friendly, and very formal'. While their accounts diverge hugely, Desmond and Stafford agree on two things — the meeting did take place, and it was about money. It was also clearly about P.J. Mara.

Stafford's version is this: Desmond said Mara owed him £100,000, and he wanted it repaid, partly though Century coughing up £30,000 — the alleged debt to Mara. Stafford rejected this suggestion, saying there was no contract with, or obligation to, Mara. When he suggested there was something improper about the affair, 'they couldn't get me out of the meeting fast enough'.[35]

The other three men tell a different tale. The meeting was held to resolve the issue of whether Mara would work for Century, they say, and ended quickly when Stafford made clear his opposition. Desmond said he wanted to resolve the matter — 'kill it or fill it' — once and for all.[36]

Desmond had lent Mara money, he acknowledged, but the amount was £46,000, not £100,000, he later explained.[37] 'It was purely Northside chaps helping each other.'[38] Mara said the debt was never mentioned at the 1990 meeting. He later carried out public relations work for Desmond in lieu of repayment.

Stafford also claimed he told the Century chairman, Laurence Crowley, that Desmond had requested £30,000 for Mara, but unfortunately for Stafford's version of events, Crowley has no recollection of being told this. He discussed it with Barry but 'could never get a straight answer'.

Stafford claims Desmond approached him about the alleged debt on one further occasion, at Ciarán Haughey's wedding in Kinsealy in September 1990. The matter was dropped after he threatened to bring it to the attention of the Taoiseach and father of the groom, Charles Haughey, he claims. Yet again on this occasion, the conflict of evidence is total, with Desmond denying the conversation took place. 'If I'd heard such a juvenile comment, I would have retained it,' he remarked.[39]

In the end, Mara stayed put, saying he felt 'obligated' to Charles Haughey during a difficult time in government. In 1992, he moved to the aircraft leasing firm, GPA, and later formed his own public relations firm.

Much later, in November 2001, Stafford lived up to his reputation for unpredictability by appearing to withdraw his allegations of bribery against Mara and Burke. In his final submission to the tribunal, he said the price list allegation was 'a rumour' and he was 'unable to say' what substance there was to it. He also said he left the meeting in Desmond's office 'before any proper explanation could be imparted' to him regarding Mara's employment at Century.

◁≈∘≋▷

1990 brought no relief for the fledgling station. By February, the chief executive had resigned, as had the marketing director. Only forty-five of the original seventy staff remained and ten more were due for redundancy. The station couldn't pay PAYE and PRSI on behalf of its staff. Barry and Stafford were funding the wages out of their own pockets. A *Today Tonight* programme on RTÉ television — described as 'slanderous' by Stafford — claimed Century doubled its annual projected revenues 'at the stroke of a pen' to encourage advertisers.[40]

For Barry, this period was 'the biggest nightmare of my life'. 'Only for me the company would have gone under,' he boasted later. Stafford proposed putting the station into liquidation, but Barry resisted. He cast about for new investors in the station, as well as returning to his friend in Government.

There was always the cap on RTÉ's advertising, which promised to tilt the balance in favour of commercial broadcasters such as

Century. According to the station's bankers, the cap promised by Burke was 'the only window of hope".[41] Barry promised the officials he had the 'political clout' to get 'a level playing-field' and have the cap introduced, they noted. Yet even Stafford would later come to the conclusion that the cap was 'badly thought-out' and 'a right mess'.

Century couldn't get the measure implemented quickly enough, but it was taking time. At the December 1989 meeting with Barry and Stafford, Burke had instructed his officials to have the cap introduced. But after checking with the Attorney General's office, they found this couldn't be done under existing provisions. New legislation was needed, for which Burke got approval from Cabinet in March 1990.

Now Burke had other ideas. Never the most ideological of politicians, he was suddenly possessed by a messianic urge to 'level the playing pitch' even further. When the draft of the Broadcasting Bill was published in May, it contained two new provisions in addition to the cap.

The first would give Burke the power to divert up to 25 per cent of RTÉ's television licence fee income to the IRTC, which could then distribute this to the commercial sector. Just where this proposal, which again would work to Century's benefit, came from is unclear, but it didn't originate within the Department.[42] A month earlier, though, Stafford had written to Burke, in a letter marked 'private and confidential' and copied to Charles Haughey, referring to just such a proposal. The provision caused uproar — Fine Gael had already created a fuss earlier in the year after getting wind of it.

The second proposal was even more controversial. Having started life as a 'sawn-off' version of RTÉ 1 radio, Century finally realised its place on the radio spectrum was as a low-cost music station with broad appeal. RTÉ's version of this, FM2 (now known as 2FM) was prospering in exactly this area of the market. Barry and Stafford set their sights on FM2, accusing RTÉ of cross-subsidising its various services unfairly. They wanted the station closed, or forcibly merged with Century.

The Government never contemplated 'that kind of over-the-top action,' Burke later told the tribunal. However, the proposal he made would have had the effect desired by Barry and Stafford. In May 1990, the Minister told the Dáil it was questionable whether the format of FM2 represented the best use of resources. He suggested it be re-established as an educational and public information service. He listed areas which were 'poorly catered for,' such as Continental languages, Irish and farming. The proposal would have killed FM2 stone-dead as a commercial proposition. 'The proposed legislation could not have been more favourable to Century Radio had they written it themselves,' *The Irish Times* reported the following day.[43]

The same week, Burke made a personal appearance at Century, where he played his favourite music for forty-five minutes. Grateful staff gave him a rapturous reception. But within days he had dropped his controversial proposals for FM2 after widespread opposition. A week later, he also dropped the proposal to divert RTÉ television licence income to the commercial sector. However, the cap on RTÉ's revenue from advertising was rushed through the Dáil and became law before the summer recess in July 1990.

The cap was an unmitigated disaster for Irish broadcasting. Burke's successor as Minister for Communications, Séamus Brennan, laid bare its consequences when he moved to abolish the cap in October 1991. As a direct result of the legislation, independent stations were losing money, TV3 had not been established and RTÉ's advertising costs had increased by 30 per cent. RTÉ claimed later that the cap resulted in a loss of revenue of £18 million and the axing of 200 jobs, and that it 'all but destroyed' the Irish advertising industry. As RTÉ increased its advertising rates to make up for the reduced time available for advertising, agencies took their business across the border. Ulster Television was the main beneficiary of the cap, earning an extra £3 million in the second half of 1990, according to one estimate.[44]

Burke made numerous other interventions in support of Century. In April 1990, the faltering station's bankers were told 'in confidence' that Burke had assured Stafford and Barry they would get approval to reduce their shareholding below 51 per cent.[45] This would allow the station to bring on new investment to stay afloat. It had been one of the conditions of the IRTC's award of the licence to Century that Stafford and Barry would have to retain a 51 per cent stake. Asked to explain the bank officials' note, Stafford said it was incorrect. Such a matter was, after all, for the Commission to decide.

The previous October, Burke had called in a junior official in his department with responsibility for frequency allocation.[46] At the time, the department had allocated Century a particular frequency on the medium-wave band, but the station was seeking a different frequency to suit the equipment it operated. Burke asked about the availability of the frequency Century was seeking, and was told there were 'difficulties'. Other frequencies had been allocated to Century, and there was a lead-in time in any change. The frequency could only be allocated provided it did not cause interference to other stations.

Burke directed his official to allocate the frequency to Century on a non-interference basis. The directive was issued several days later, and the frequency was used by Century until it closed in 1991.

Century continued to flounder. Stafford and Barry blamed everyone but themselves for their problems. The chief villain, of course, was RTÉ. It was abusing its dominant position in the market, they claimed, in a well-rehearsed argument that worked on Burke but for which no evidence was put forward. They claimed RTÉ engaged in below-cost selling of advertising, when the evidence showed that RTÉ's advertising rates went up at the time Century came on air.

Naively, Stafford accused RTÉ of spending £1 million on its radio services, as though any established business wouldn't react to the arrival of a competitor in this way. As Century's marketing manager admitted later: 'If I'd been in RTÉ I'd have done the same thing'. RTÉ also had the temerity to hold on to Gay Byrne by offering him more money. Barry claimed the State broadcaster threatened to take Byrne off *The Late Late Show* if he moved to Century.

Century also claimed that RTÉ's transmission staff failed to get the new station's signal up on time, when the opposite was the case. All the targets for the rollout of Century's signal were met. If anyone misled Century's marketing staff, it was their own bosses.

The IRTC, which had a vested interest in seeing Century succeed, was constantly harried. Even Burke felt the lash when he failed to implement the 50 per cent cap on RTÉ's advertising that Century was looking for. Barry blamed both the Commission and the Minister for failing to force other stations to stick to the 20 per cent news quota condition of the new licences.

Century could have taken its objections to the way RTÉ was funded to the High Court. It could have taken them to the European

Commission. It could have appealed to the Department of Communications. But it didn't, preferring instead to go directly to the Minister.

On the day after the legislation implementing the cap was passed in July 1990, Capital Radio of London agreed to invest in the ailing station. Capital had made its involvement conditional on the introduction of the cap. The IRTC, aware that Century was going to the wall otherwise, agreed to the deal.

Compared to Century, Capital Radio was a giant organisation with deep pockets, but it wasn't stupid. Century would have to be slimmed down and turned into a low-cost, formula-driven pop broadcaster with direct appeal to the young audience popular with advertisers. It was a demonstration of Stafford's and Barry's inadequacies that the station's 'sound' only started to gel after the English investors became involved. However, the road to recovery was longer than Barry and Stafford could afford (Mulhern's involvement was hidden from the new investors). Having invested over £1 million in the operation, Capital wanted control. Barry's and Stafford's days were clearly numbered.

Now that Capital was calling the shots, and their involvement was diminishing, the two founders tried to squeeze as much as they could out of their new partners. For Barry, the main item on his list was a sum of £40,000 he claimed the company owed him.

But what was this money for? There are no invoices for the sum, Capital was told nothing about it before it invested and the station's accounting staff was equally in the dark. The station's head of finance, Noreen Hynes, said she knew nothing about a £40,000 sum. If she had, it would have been entered in the accounts. Barry asserts it was repayment for consultancy work carried out for the station, but the tribunal says his claim is 'a concoction'. It believes the sum relates to the £35,000 paid to Ray Burke, plus £5,000 given to Fianna Fáil.

A bemused Capital asked Barry to substantiate the claim, but it got no information, and the matter dragged on. Barry made what he termed a 'gentleman's agreement' with Stafford, who pleaded on his behalf with Capital. Stafford later acknowledged helping Barry to procure the £40,000 from Capital, claimed for management fees of £1,600 a week for twenty-five weeks.[47] Finally, the board approved the payment to Barry in January 1991 and he was paid a month later.

Capital's understanding was that the payment had been made 'to assist in work being done to change the [capping] legislation'.[48]

Stafford thought Barry would then repay him the £29,000 loan he claimed was outstanding, but he was wrong. He later started legal proceedings against his former business partner in an attempt to recoup the money. It was against this background of a bitter split between the former business partners that Stafford came to make his allegations to the tribunal many years later.

By the end of 1991, events had reached crisis point. Barry and Stafford were fighting with Capital and the sums were going further awry. Barry finally pulled out of the station in October, leaving Stafford and Capital to fight on. Agreement was reached under which Capital would increase its stake above 30 per cent, but when the IRTC vetoed this proposal, the English company pulled out. When Century closed on 19 November 1991, it had achieved a 6 per cent share of the audience. Ironically, its end came just as the station was showing signs of winning more advertising.

Like the Black Plague, Century caused everything it touched to wither. The station lost £8 million in just over two years. It was unable to pay redundancy awards of £15,000 to forty of its former staff. On its closure, the Revenue Commissioners was owed over £150,000. RTÉ was owed £600,000. RTÉ put the cost of its involvement with Century at £20 million. Burke was removed from the Department of Communications in 1991, but it would take a decade before he was to feel the full impact of the curse of Century.

⌘

The tribunal's investigations into Century Radio came about almost by accident. By 1999, it was firmly established that James Gogarty had paid Burke £30,000 at his home a decade earlier. However, despite several years of investigation, the tribunal had failed to find any evidence to support Gogarty's contention that the sum he gave was £40,000, and that this sum was matched by a similar contribution from the developer Michael Bailey.

The lawyers dug deeper into Burke's bank accounts, and came across a lodgement of £39,500, made on 31 May 1989. The date wasn't quite right for any payment related to Gogarty; this was a week *before* he called out to Burke's house. Questioned about the lodgement in July 1999, Burke revealed it consisted of an amalgam of political donations, one of them being a £35,000 cash contribution from a supporter. Later, he told tribunal lawyers in private that Oliver Barry was the largest donor. The revelation directly contradicted Burke's Dáil statement of September 1997, when he claimed that £30,000 was the 'largest contribution' he had received during an election campaign.

But we already knew Burke had been telling lies. More importantly, the lawyers wanted to know, who was Oliver Barry and why was the money given? Was it from Barry personally, or one of his companies? The answers to these questions were to lead the Flood tribunal down a long and winding side-road, where the views were astonishing but the going often difficult. A tribunal set up to examine planning allegations spent a year raking over the process which led to the setting of Ireland's first national commercial station.

Following Burke's revelation, the tribunal went on Barry's trail. Initially at least, it received little cooperation. Barry, whose name was still hidden from the general public, played a waiting game and refused to file a statement. Apart from admitting having made the payment, he provided no other information. Like other people under investigation, he was probably watching with interest the tribunal's various legal battles with reluctant witnesses.

Finally, the tribunal issued a summons against him. The identity of Burke's generous donor was finally disclosed at a public hearing of the tribunal in February 2000. The news caused a sensation. Here was the chairman of the country's first commercial radio station giving the Minister for Communications the price of a new house, just four months after getting the licence.

It was July before the tribunal was ready to begin hearings into 'the Century module'. This time, there was an opening statement from senior counsel Pat Hanratty, in which the main allegations were recounted. Stafford played the role occupied by James Gogarty in an earlier module, by going into the witness box first and restating his allegations, including the claim that Burke and Mara were operating a 'price list' for radio licences.

However, the tribunal's approach to Stafford was much more combative than it had been with Gogarty. Repeatedly, Hanratty cast doubt on the version of events put forward by the witness. Stafford painted himself as the clever, inquiring, upright director somewhat out of the loop in Century's activities. Hanratty frequently questioned this self-view, pointing out areas where Stafford was clearly centrally involved in the making of decisions. For example, Century's account-ant forcefully contradicted Stafford's claim that he only learned about the Burke payment two years after it was made. Stafford also claims he wasn't in the Horseshoe Bar of the Shelbourne Hotel when Barry is alleged to have identified Ray Burke as 'the minister who is going to give us our licence'. However, Ray Hills, the English consultant who remembered the remark, says he was there. Stafford's evidence took much longer than expected, partly due to his circuitous answers and his insistence on ploughing through detailed documentation in a — usually fruitless — search for supporting arguments.

But worse was to come, as the tribunal got lost in the minutiae of transmission charges and legislative proposals. All ten members of the IRTC emphatically denied there was any interference in their decision on the licence. There were occasional flashes of colour, such as Gay Byrne's 18-minute appearance in Dublin Castle. Byrne's evidence in October 2000 coincided with his re-emergence from retirement to present the *Who Wants to Be a Millionaire?* quiz show, so there was a cer-tain piquancy to the tale of his refusal of £1 million a decade earlier.

It was December 2000 before Barry came to give his evidence. The former Century chairman was soon in hot water with the tribunal over six bank accounts he had failed to disclose. It also emerged that his assistant had transferred over £120,000 into his accounts but didn't know what the money was for. As the uncertainty over his accounts deepened, Barry reacted angrily to suggestions that he could have made a second payment to Burke. 'I've only paid the £35,000,' he exclaimed. However, the tribunal's probe of his accounts lasted weeks. Barry declared that his involvement with the tribunal had cost him £400,000.

At the end of his evidence, Barry attacked the 'tribunal inquisitors' for creating an 'adverse innuendo' that he was concealing information. This was all 'grossly unfair'. As for his forgetting to declare bank accounts, this was 'a genuine failure of recollection'.

Ray Burke showed he'd lost none of the ebullient, combative qualities he was known for when he started giving evidence in

February 2001. Occasional flashes of anger showed how he earned the nickname 'Rambo', but the former politician kept his temper reined in and showed little sign of hubris.

His preparation was meticulous. Most of the time, he sat obscured from the press and public gallery in the witness box, hidden behind a row of cardboard boxes containing his notes. Rather than wishing the ordeal over, he took the time to develop an alternative line of thinking to that put forward by the tribunal. Quoting at length from documents he considered favourable, he tried to place his actions in aiding Century in a broader political context.

He explained that commercial radio was introduced in Ireland because that was the trend in other countries. RTÉ's combative attitude was blamed for 'triggering' the decision to set up a national station. One of the reasons he cited for making the directive on transmission charges that was so beneficial to Century was because Fine Gael was pressing him to take action.

As the tribunal worked its way through the various interventions he made in aid of Century, Burke had some detailed explaining to do. He didn't always answer the exact questions asked, leading the tribunal to complain about his 'long rambling answers' which were 'straying off the point'. He denied personal responsibility for introducing the cap, saying the decision was made by Government. But the background to this decision was to remain hidden, as Burke refused to answer questions on the basis of Cabinet confidentiality.

The retired politician was scathing about just about everyone else involved in the Century saga. He accused of RTÉ in engaging in 'black propaganda' about Century's failure to achieve signal coverage. Century made some 'monumental mistakes'. Stafford, he claimed, had 'considerable mental pressures' because of the station's difficulties. As for Oliver Barry, Burke would tell his friend things as a way of 'palming him off or getting him out of my hair'.

The Century hearings ended in August 2001 as they had begun, in a welter of denials and forgetfulness. Former Government press secretary P.J. Mara firmly rejected Stafford's allegations about a 'price list'. However, he endured some uncomfortable moments when it emerged that he had failed to disclose all his bank accounts to the tribunal when first asked. Less than a week before he gave evidence, his lawyers had written to the tribunal disclosing two accounts in the

Isle of Man. Mara apologised for being 'negligent' and 'deficient'. He conceded that the reason he set up an offshore account was because he may have had 'bad thoughts' at the time, but later changed his mind.

⬥

So what, after all this, can we say about the relations between Ray Burke and Century Radio? Was Oliver Barry's £35,000 payment to Burke a simple act of friendship, or something more?

No-one except the two men involved can be sure. What is clear, however, is that the level and number of Burke's interventions in the area in which Century was operating was unprecedented. To summarise, Burke intervened to:

- have the transmission fee payable by Century reduced. This involved a potential saving to Century of £636,000 over seven years.
- have the fee reduced a second time. The saving for Century here was £800,000 in the first year and over £500,000 a year thereafter.
- cap RTÉ's advertising.
- divert part of RTÉ's licence fee to the IRTC for the benefit of the commercial sector. This measure was dropped after a storm of protest.
- change 2FM from a music station with a huge audience to an educational station that no-one would listen to. This was also dropped after widespread protests.
- meet Century's bankers and assure them of the measures he was going to introduce.
- allocate to Century the medium-wave frequency it sought.
- nominate the solicitor, accountant and bank used by the IRTC.
- propose that Century should be allowed to 'grow into' its (expensive) news and Irish language obligations. The IRTC refused to budge on this.
- suggest that Stafford and Barry be allowed to reduce their shareholding below 51 per cent to facilitate a sale of Century (according to a note made by Century's bankers in April 1990. Burke denies making the suggestion).

Several pieces of evidence point to Century's privileged access and status vis-à-vis the Government. There were the numerous meetings Barry and Stafford had with Burke, and Stafford's contact with Haughey. Barry's solicitor and bankers separately recorded their belief that he had the 'political clout' to get what he wanted in broadcasting. Ray Hills, the English consultant to Century, remembered Barry referring to Burke as 'the Minister who is going to give us our licence,' though Hill conceded it would have been a 'throwaway remark'. Seán Connolly, secretary to the IRTC, said the promoters of Century were 'too highly politicised' and its promoters 'could enlist the support of ministers'.

The irony is that all this influence made no difference to Century, which went down like a lead balloon. Most of the other commercial stations born at the same time had no such advantages, but survived and went on to prosper. Century failed, not because of RTÉ, but because it was badly run.

⋐⋙·⋐⋙

Postscript:
The State decides to end one of its monopolies by awarding a communications licence to a private operator for the first time. The Exchequer could make a lot of money from the sale but the minister responsible opts not to auction the licence to the highest bidder. Competition for the potentially lucrative licence is intense and the winning consortium is led by a high-profile Irish businessman. The involvement of others in the consortium only comes to light later. The financier Dermot Desmond plays an important role, though this only emerges later. The name of his friend, the former Government press secretary P.J. Mara, also features. Shortly after the licence is awarded, the winner makes a large political donation to the party in power. This contribution becomes the subject of a dispute between the different parties involved in the winning consortium. The payment comes to light years later. The giver and the recipient insist it is above board and has no strings attached. The matter is referred for investigation by a tribunal, which uncovers a complex set of financial transactions and wildly conflicting versions of what happened.

It sounds like the story of Century Radio. In fact, this description equally fits the award of the second mobile phone licence to Esat Digifone in 1995. A payment of $50,000 to Fine Gael, when the minister responsible for communications, Michael Lowry, was a trustee of the party, has been the subject of a detailed investigation by the Moriarty tribunal. The similarities between the two episodes, divided in time by six years, are striking. In a further coincidence, Denis O'Brien, the businessman behind Esat Digifone, got his first big break during the 1989 round of radio licence awards, when he won the franchise to run a music station in Dublin.

The main difference between the two tales is in the outcome; Century went bankrupt while O'Brien sold his interest in Esat Digifone for a personal profit of over £230 million. Dermot Desmond's attempt to invest in Century was rebuffed — fortunately for him — while he made £100 million from his investment in Esat Digifone.

8

'A Failure of Recollection'

Tribunal lawyer, Pat Hanratty SC: *Mr Burke, it's one thing not to remember something. But I suggest to you, to remember things which didn't actually occur at all is a very odd kind of failure of recollection. Did you dream it up?*

Ray Burke: *No, I didn't dream it up but obviously my mind has played games with me in relation to it, Mr Hanratty.*

— Ray Burke on being reminded he had received £125,000 in
offshore payments from Brennan and McGowan[1]

By spring 2001, Ray Burke's tribunal ordeal was almost over. It was nearly two years since he had breezed through his denials of Gogarty's allegations. He'd suffered an intense grilling over the Century affair, but had come through with his endless self-belief undimmed. He was in the home straight.

Or was he? For the tribunal lawyers tying up loose ends, there was something amiss about the accounts given by Burke and Brennan and McGowan. Back in April 2000, the two builders had told the tribunal of their lavish fundraising efforts for the politician, held at Cheltenham, Ascot and other glittering social occasions. It had been a big breakthrough for the tribunal. Certainly, Brennan and McGowan weren't conceding any wrongdoing, but the amounts involved were enormous, far greater than any known political contribution for the era of the 1970s and 1980s.

Burke had then followed his builder friends into the witness box, where his story tallied with the evidence they gave. He acknowledged getting two payments in 1984, for £35,000 and £60,000, which were paid into an offshore bank account in Jersey. This, he understood, was an aggregate of the money that came from the political fundraising organised by Brennan and McGowan in England.

The strange thing was that these good-time get-togethers in aid of the politician across the Irish Sea left no trace. Where were the financial records for these fundraisers? And where were the witnesses to these events? Joseph McGowan said they were coordinated by Ernest Ottewell, a mysterious English businessman with an even more mysterious *penchant* for Fianna Fáil. But Ottewell was dead, and his records were inaccessible. Why, too, had Burke misled the Dáil in 1997 by denying he had an overseas bank account?

The tribunal decided to dig deeper. It started with Burke's involvement in the Isle of Man and Jersey and four unexplained sums in his accounts — the £35,000 and £60,000 mentioned above, and two further lodgements for £60,000 and £15,000. In December 2000, the tribunal wrote to Burke seeking an account of the various lodgements. Burke's lawyers provided an explanation later that month and Burke himself gave evidence on the matter in February 2001.

One payment in particular attracted the tribunal's attention. In April 1985, £15,000 was lodged to an account linked to Burke in Jersey. The politician explained he had taken this sum in cash from his Jersey account while in London. He then flew with the money in his hand luggage to Dublin and put it in a safe at home. Ten days later, he flew to London with the cash and went on to Jersey. There, he gave it to a local legal firm, Bedell and Cristin, with instructions to relodge it. The reason he went to Jersey was to arrange for his wife to get access to the account 'in the event of my being hit by a mythical bus across the street,' he explained.

This implausible scenario screamed out for more attention. As Mr Justice Flood asked: 'Why didn't you just spend 30p on a postage stamp to bank the money instead of £300 on the airfare?' Why treat an expensive legal firm as a 'messenger boy' to bring the money to the bank? Burke admitted breaking exchange control laws that applied at the time and pleaded that he was 'never the most organised of individuals in looking after my own affairs'. In Burke-speak, he had been 'deficient in carrying out my paperwork'. But he continued to insist the sum under scrutiny was a re-lodgement, and rejected the tribunal's suggestion that the £15,000 he lodged in Jersey could have come from a different source from the £15,000 he had withdrawn ten days earlier.

As for the £50,000 sum, Burke was now saying this was the result of fundraising in the UK and was paid to him in the Isle of Man, where he had opened an account in 1982 with the help of a friendly bank manager in London. The tribunal learned this account was used to receive a payment of £50,000 from Kalabraki Ltd, an offshore company based in the Channel Islands. Asked in February 2001 what the money was for, he repeated the explanation that it was the result of fundraising carried out by Joe McGowan. 'It wasn't a single effort as I understand. It was a series of fundraisers that had been carried out over the years,' he explained. Burke said he had no knowledge of Kalabraki, or the original donors of the money. So what was Kalabraki? Who owned this mysterious company? And why was it paying Burke money in this manner?

Tribunal lawyers were making parallel inquiries of Brennan and McGowan, though they weren't making much headway. In February 2001 they asked the solicitor to the two builders, John Walsh, if his clients knew anything about Kalabraki. The question drew a blank. In a meeting with the two builders, Walsh offered to find out more about Kalabraki by organising a search of the UK companies register. What the solicitor didn't know was that the owner of Kalabraki — Tom Brennan — was sitting mutely in front of him. Walsh, in the words of a tribunal lawyer, went on 'a wild goose chase'.

This web of deception was about to be blown open. Alerted by Burke's reference to the firm, the tribunal approached Bedell and Cristin in Jersey. It discovered that — lo! — this was the same legal firm used by Brennan and McGowan. Burke later said it was 'pure coincidence and nothing else' that the same firm acted for him and the two builders.[2]

At Bedell and Cristin, the partner who dealt with the three Irishmen, Laurence Wheeler, had retired and wanted nothing to do with the tribunal. However, the firm provided what cooperation it could. The lawyers discovered that Tom Brennan was the sole owner of Kalabraki, the Jersey-registered company that had made the offshore payment to Burke in 1982. Bedell and Cristin also set up Caviar Ltd, the company used by Burke to receive payments in Jersey, with the file reference C-992.

Then the tribunal discovered what it had been looking for all along. A mysterious new file reference, C-758, had been entered alongside the two lodgements to Caviar of £60,000 and £15,000. This reference belonged to Canio Ltd, a hitherto unknown company operated by Bedell and Cristin. Canio, named after a character in an Italian opera, was itself owned by three shelf companies. The tribunal dug deeper and discovered the ultimate owners of the company — Brennan, McGowan and another Irish businessman, John Finnegan.

For the tribunal, things began to fall into place. Tom Brennan had paid Burke £50,000 in 1982, equivalent to three times his combined salaries at the time. Brennan and McGowan had paid him £60,000 in November 1984 and £15,000 in March 1985. So, in total, Brennan and McGowan had given Burke at least £125,000 in round-sum payments, effected through secretive offshore trustee companies. None of this had been declared by Burke or by Brennan and McGowan. And then there was the unresolved question of the £35,000 sum in March 1984, which Burke claimed was a re-lodgement.

On 6 March 2001, the tribunal solicitor wrote to Burke, outlining what had been uncovered. This was just a week after Burke had given a precise and detailed account, in evidence sworn under oath, of how he relodged the £15,000 payment. On 12 March, he retracted every word of this story. In a letter hand-delivered directly to Mr Justice Flood in Dublin Castle — and not passed through his solicitors — Burke admitted that the money had after all come from a separate source. It was, he explained, 'a failure of recollection' on his part. 'Obviously my mind has played games with me,' he told the tribunal later. It was more than a memory lapse, though, as Burke had previously described a complicated sequence of events to explain the £15,000 lodgement in his accounts. He hadn't just forgotten something that had happened; he had 'remembered' something which never took place. Burke rejected the suggestion by Pat Hanratty SC, for the tribunal, that he had 'tailored' his evidence 'to the known facts' but was then 'caught out'.

His failure to recollect the payments from Canio also seems strange given the efforts he made to prepare for their arrival. The £60,000 he got in 1984 wasn't just another line on a bank statement; he travelled to Jersey a week before the payment was made, and the purpose of his trip was to arrange for the transfer of the money.[3]

Burke's retraction and the discovery of his links to Jersey put the tribunal back on the trail of Brennan and McGowan. Once again, tribunal lawyers wrote to their solicitor, John Walsh. It was only now, after the tribunal had established the facts independently, that Brennan and McGowan's memories improved. The two builders set out the structure of their offshore holdings, including Kalabraki, the company Brennan had been unable to remember only a month earlier.

Faced with evidence from the tribunal that the money they gave came in the form of 'specific lump-sum contributions' from offshore companies under their control, Brennan and McGowan wrote to Flood accepting their earlier evidence was incorrect. They now said the payments were political donations 'to Fianna Fáil/Ray Burke', unrelated to fundraising. So where did this leave Joe McGowan's florid recollections of lavish fundraising events for Burke in Britain? 'On occasions the drink was flowing like a river' as donors queued up to help the cause, McGowan had told the tribunal a year before. Now the evidence pointed to a series of secretive offshore payments to the politician by Brennan and McGowan and their companies.

Once again, Burke was shown up as a liar. In 1997, he told the Dáil that £30,000 was the largest contribution he had received during an election campaign. Later, it was discovered that he had received not one, but two, payments of £30,000. Then the tribunal uncovered the £35,000 contribution from Oliver Barry of Century Radio. Burke explained that one by saying he remembered Barry's donation as £30,000. On an earlier trip to the witness box in Dublin Castle, Burke had told the tribunal that no sum he got from Brennan and McGowan was larger than the £35,000 Oliver Barry donated. Pressed further on the matter, he hid behind the excuse that these were 'matters for the Revenue'.

Now the tribunal had found evidence of payments of £50,000 and £60,000 from Brennan and McGowan. No wonder people asked whether there were other, bigger sums still waiting to be discovered.

Piece by piece, the tribunal reconstructed the history of Caviar, the offshore company Burke used to receive the payments. In 1984, Burke approached Oliver Conlon, the solicitor with whom he had had frequent dealings in the 1970s, to set up a shelf company in Jersey. Conlon, who was left in no doubt about the 'considerable urgency' of the matter, was instructed to handle the correspondence for the company.[4] Burke originally wanted the name Athenaeum but when this wasn't available he settled for the bizarre but not inappropriate title of Caviar Ltd. Everything about this affair involved conceal-ment or lies. The beneficial owners of the company were registered as 'P.D. Burke' and 'A. Burke', derived from the politician's full name — Raphael Patrick Dermot Burke — and his wife's, Ann. The address used was that of his sister-in-law in Hampshire, England.

Conlon registered Caviar in April 1984, using offshore directors from Jersey and Sark. The stated aim of the company was to 'take investments, probably in the Republic of Ireland'. It was never used for this purpose; instead, Burke used it to receive payments from Brennan and McGowan. The first lodgement into the account set up for Caviar was £35,000 in April 1984. Originally, Burke had said this was money from the fundraising efforts in Britain, but now he insists it represented part of a larger amount he had withdrawn in the Isle of Man and then lodged in an AIB branch in London before moving it to Jersey. Interestingly, Burke visited Jersey at the time of this pay-ment, just as he did later in the year when Brennan and McGowan put £60,000 in his offshore account.

Correspondence was sent to Conlon in sealed envelopes 'for the attention of Mr A. Burke'. Conlon, who denied any knowledge of the matter, later asked Bedell and Cristin to send their letters directly to Burke. The tribunal asked why anyone would go to such trouble, using offshore accounts and different names, if the funds were legiti-mate. Political donations don't attract gift tax, so there should have been no problem in bringing the funds back to Ireland. Burke justified the arrangements on the grounds of 'confidentiality'. It was set up in this way because the funds were raised abroad. 'There was no tax evasion involved.'

Further mystery surrounded Burke's banking activities in London. He claimed to have an account at the Bruton Street branch of AIB, which he used to route many of the payments between his offshore accounts in Jersey and the Isle of Man, including the £15,000 pay-ment in April 1985. By another strange coincidence, this was the same branch used by Brennan and McGowan. For a long time, the tribunal and the bank were unable to find any evidence that he held an account there. It didn't help that the former minister used so many different versions of his name. To resolve matters, the tribunal sought to locate the retired manager of the branch, Timothy McHale.

McHale was one of those minor characters with an interesting past that flew across the tribunal's radar from time to time. This wasn't the first time his retirement from the bank had been interrupted by the legal profession. Five years after he retired in 1989, a number of AIB customers in the UK claimed he had 'interfered with' their accounts. The bank established an 'immediate and thorough' investigation when the story broke in 1997. 'This investigation established that a small number of customers' accounts had been interfered with,' it said.

AIB, which is reported to have paid out £800,000 to put matters right, indicated then it regarded the matter as closed. Contacted in October 1997 by the *Mail on Sunday*, McHale denied the allegation: 'I don't know what you are talking about. I deny these allegations completely'. Customers were said to be satisfied with the measures taken by the bank and no further action was expected from the British police, *The Irish Times* reported at the time. In one of the cases, two brothers received compensation of almost £500,000 after alleging that McHale closed accounts in the Isle of Man without their permission after he had retired.

Later in October 1997, McHale's name figured prominently in a case in which a customer, Gordon Lewis, claimed AIB in London had lost thousands of pounds belonging to him. The Central London County Court cleared AIB of the allegation, and the judge dismissed claims by the customer that McHale had appropriated the cash. The judge said: 'Even allowing that Mr McHale may have been a less reliable official than most in the bank, I cannot support these allegations'. McHale left Britain and retired to live in Lahinch, County Clare.

During the trial, Lewis claimed that McHale advised him to open an offshore account in the Isle of Man. 'Mr McHale said he looked after several people's account and he kept them in his drawer, especially the Isle of Man accounts,' he said. 'Mr McHale had said to me if there were any deposits for him he would like them in cash, because it would be much easier to do that,' Lewis added. 'Mr McHale said it should be in cash because it is very awkward to do anything else in the Isle of Man.' Lewis said that after McHale left the bank, it took AIB four years to find the Isle of Man account.

Called to give evidence to the tribunal in March 2001, McHale said he had no recollection of Burke holding an account in Bruton Street. The two men first met at Cheltenham in the early 1980s, when McHale was in charge of the bank's hospitality box. He had simply routed money through the branch on behalf of Burke. He acknowledged opening Burke's account in the Isle of Man, under the name 'Patrick D. Burke', with an address in England.

Finally, in June 2001, AIB discovered that Burke did have an account at Bruton Street. The account had been in existence for just six days in November/December 1983, and was opened with a lodgement of £15,000. Once again, it was held in the name of 'P.D. Burke' and an English address was given. Burke said the opening lodgement was a transfer from his Isle of Man account.

Before the discovery of Canio and the offshore payments, the tribunal had been on the brink of wrapping up its investigations into Burke's finances. Now it had opened a new can of worms, and further investigation was needed. The tribunal adjourned abruptly in March 2001 to delve further into the mystery.

⋖⊱⋅⋅⊰⋗

The tribunal's investigations put the spotlight firmly on the subject of Ray Burke's finances, which for years had been the subject of curiosity and speculation. Burke denied to the tribunal that he used political contributions for personal spending, though he conceded the money he received all went into 'the same kitty' in an Ulster Bank current account.

Sometimes, it was as hard to see what he spent the money on as to find where it came from. Asked once by the tribunal to list the various expenses incurred by an active politician, Burke spent ten minutes listing the various demands on his pocket.[5] Mostly it came down to drink. There was looking after canvassers (i.e. buying them drink), visiting sports clubs (and buying drink), entertaining the media (more drink, this time in the Dáil bar) and cumann meetings (you guessed it). If Burke spent more money than others, and therefore needed more, it was because he was more successful than other politicians. Burke's success in nine elections was based on organising elaborate and expensive campaigns, he argued.

Asked what he thought he'd received in contributions during his career, he ventured a figure of £275,000. This figure was distinctly underwhelming, given that the tribunal already knew about the £120,000 he got in 1989 and was firmly on the trail of £125,000 in payments from Brennan and McGowan. The evidence unearthed by the tribunal showed that much of the money went on homespun pleasures. There was £18,500 on renovating the kitchen at Briargate, £13,500 on building a tennis court and £23,500 on replacing the ministerial Mercedes with his own car. He also deposited £6,000 in his wife's account to pay for tea, biscuits and the inevitable drinks when supporters called to their home in Swords. Occasionally, politics intruded. Work on the tennis court had to stop in 1989 because of an election. A family holiday was cancelled in 1992 when Burke had to give evidence to the Beef tribunal.

There was something medieval about the picture of Burke travelling about his fiefdom, his pockets bulging with 'walking-around money', dispensing largesse on the grateful citizens of his realm. As for receipts, he painted the following awkward scenario. 'You are in company, you have five or six people with you and you don't want to say to the barman "Could I have a receipt, please" and put it in your wallet and walk away. Some people might be able to do it but not in my life.'

Burke's definition of political expenditure proved too broad for the tribunal, which estimated that 90 per cent of his outgoings went on personal spending. Donations to charities, schools, community games and local sports clubs were all classified by Burke as political expenses. Lunches at the Westbury Hotel, the cost of new suits, drinks at the Dáil bar — all these, too, counted as political expenditure. So were the heating, ESB and phone bills of his home, because this also served as his constituency office.

Burke finally closed his account in Jersey in 1994. He came back to Dublin with £20,000 sterling in cash, which he kept in a safe at his home for six months before lodging it in an Irish account.

⋖⋗⋅⋖⋗

In tribunal-land, one investigation begets another. As we've seen, lawyers had uncovered a web of offshore companies and accounts which were the true source of payments into Burke's offshore accounts. The sums of £60,000 in 1984 and £15,000 in 1985 came not from Burke himself or from fundraising efforts on his behalf in Britain, but from a Channel Islands-registered company, Canio Ltd.

Two facts about Canio now screamed out for further examination. First, the company was part-owned by a prominent auctioneer John Finnegan. A new name to the tribunal, Finnegan was certainly no stranger to unwanted publicity, having featured in earlier controversies over the Telecom site in Ballsbridge and Ansbacher bank. Brennan and McGowan owned the rest of Canio. So why was Finnegan contributing money to Ray Burke?

Second, it emerged that the £60,000 Canio gave to Burke was borrowed money, which came from a mortgage the company took out on lands at Sandyford in south Dublin. For the first time in his four-year involvement with the tribunal, Burke was being presented with evidence directly linking a payment to him to a land deal. The question was no longer simply: 'Why is a leading politician receiving money in such a circuitous and secretive manner?' Now the tribunal wanted to know: 'Why is an offshore company whose only business was the purchase of land for development paying huge sums of money to a leading politician?'

Canio, it was found, was 100 per cent owned by another offshore company called Ardcarn Ltd. This in turned was owned in three equal shares by three further offshore companies, Gasche Investments, Kalabraki and Foxtown Investments. Effectively, these were the personal vehicles for Joe McGowan, Tom Brennan and John Finnegan, respectively.

Canio's only asset was about 100 acres of prime development land in Sandyford, south County Dublin. In 1979, it paid £630,000 for the land, which was once the family farm of former Fianna Fáil minister, Frank Aiken. Unknown to the family, the Aiken lands were bought in trust to preserve secrecy — Brennan said the price would have been higher if it was known that he and McGowan were the buyers — and ownership only passed to Canio when it was incorporated a year later.

There was some irony here. Aiken had brought his distinguished political career to an early end in the 1970s because he couldn't stomach the rise of Charles Haughey in the party. Now, long after his death, his name was being dragged into a distinctly unpatriotic tale of secrecy and offshore tax avoidance through the involvement of a leading figure in the party he helped to found.

To buy the lands, Canio borrowed, and to secure these borrowings it took out a mortgage on the lands. The £60,000 paid to Burke came from these borrowed funds. The bank was told that planning permission was expected for 600 houses and 250 houses would be built immediately. According to the tribunal, the lands were sold on for £1.3 million, and their value was expected to rise to £4 million with planning permission.

Two days before Burke visited Bedell and Cristin in Jersey in November 1984, Joe McGowan also called in on the firm. And six days after Burke's visit, Lombard and Ulster advanced a loan of £525,000 to Canio on the Sandyford lands. The loan was taken out to repay the company's shareholders for their investment. However, along with the money paid to Brennan, McGowan and Finnegan in Jersey, £60,000 was remitted to Burke, even though he had invested nothing in the company. Brennan and McGowan's lawyers proposed that the money be deducted equally from the shares due to the three owners, ostensibly to pay for 'architect's fees' and other costs.

However, Finnegan balked at the retention of £20,000 and, ultimately, £10,000 of his money went to pay Burke. Brennan and McGowan each increased their share to £25,000 to make up the shortfall. This raised the question of why the amount paid to Burke had to be £60,000. Was it a pre-agreed sum, rather than the 'unsolicited political donation' claimed by Brennan?

Burke responded to the discovery of Canio by saying he had had nothing to do with the Sandyford lands. He knew the money he got came from Brennan and McGowan but didn't concern himself with how it was raised. He pointed out that he was not a member of Dublin County Council between 1978 and 1985 (he was on the council from 1967 to 1978 and was chairman from 1985 to 1987).

However, other evidence showed that Brennan and McGowan had spoken to their friend about the land. Back in 1985, Brennan and McGowan became embroiled in complex and bitter litigation with two banks and their solicitor, George Russell. This blew up after the two banks discovered they had both granted mortgages to the builders using the same security of the Sandyford lands. The financial institutions sued Russell, who held the title deeds as security on behalf of the builders, and Russell in turn sued Brennan and McGowan.

Russell, a small-time solicitor who relied almost entirely on the builders for most of his business, was shattered by the experience. He had virtually no indemnity insurance cover and faced liabilities of up to £3 million. His son Philip Russell, who had just qualified as a solicitor, took up the cudgels on behalf of his father. In July 1985, Philip Russell secretly recorded a conversation involving his father and Brennan and McGowan. In the transcript later provided to the tribunal, McGowan is recorded as saying of Canio's involvement in Sandyford: 'Everybody is behind this sale [to Dún Laoghaire Corporation], Ray Burke, the whole works'. Later, McGowan said: 'Tom [Brennan] has gone out to Ray Burke. ... [word missing] Sandyford and is probably there at the moment'.

Asked at the tribunal about these remarks, Brennan denied that Burke had anything to do with obtaining planning permission on the lands. However, given that Brennan's diary for this period shows that he had seven meetings with Burke, it is hard to see how the topic could not have come up for discussion. McGowan says the builders asked Burke to find out if the county council had any serious interest in buying the lands. The Corporation did make an offer but it was rejected.

Also in July 1985, McGowan swore an affidavit in which he stated he had no interest in Canio or its parent company, Ardcarn. Six months later, he swore a second affidavit in which he admitted he had failed to list Canio as one of his companies. However, this 'brazen lie', as Philip Russell put it, was to come back to haunt McGowan at the tribunal sixteen years later.

The banks ultimately reached a settlement with Brennan and McGowan. As part of this, the two builders paid Russell's legal costs and took out a £900,000 loan through two of their companies to repay the Canio debt.

The role of Binchys, another solicitor's firm that acted for Brennan and McGowan, is also of interest. In 1985, John Caldwell, a partner in the firm, ordered the removal to Liechtenstein of £115,000 of Canio's money. At the time, Brennan and McGowan were involved in litigation with two banks over lands owned by Canio. Caldwell represented the two builders; however, Binchys had also been engaged by Lombard and Ulster to recover money due. So while one solicitor in Binchys was attempting to recover money for the bank, his colleague, Caldwell, was effectively putting it beyond reach.

Lengthy attempts by the tribunal to take evidence from Caldwell took a dramatic turn in September 2001 when he failed to turn up as summonsed. The solicitor, who was also being investigated for his links to Frank Dunlop, Liam Lawlor and Jim Kennedy, disappeared. Shortly before his scheduled appointment with the tribunal, he gave up his solicitor's practising certificate and informed the tribunal that he no longer resided in Ireland or had Irish citizenship. Flood, outraged at this act of defiance by a leading member of his profession, began High Court proceedings to enforce his summons. Caldwell finally relented and turned up in Dublin Castle in October.

Canio was just one of many offshore companies set up by Brennan, McGowan and John Finnegan as vehicles for their elaborate and highly lucrative land speculation schemes. On further investigation, the tribunal discovered that the Sandyford deal was just the last of eight transactions in which the three men secretly collaborated. All the transactions followed the same pattern, starting with the acquisition of land in Dublin by offshore companies. In all cases, Finnegan's involvement with Brennan and McGowan was kept secret. The land was sold to a Brennan and McGowan company in Ireland for a higher price and the proceeds were moved offshore. This money was then shared out between the two builders and Finnegan. There was no evidence that Burke got money from any of the other transactions, but some of the money he received out of the Sandyford deal originated in previous deals. To understand what was going on, the tribunal would have to examine all the transactions.

The investigation that followed was prolonged and painstaking. It didn't seem to have much direct bearing on the tribunal's remit to investigate corruption, but that didn't make the practices uncovered any less shocking. For once, a light was being shone on the secretive tax avoidance industry, where an army of professionals plots to outwit the Revenue Commissioners with ever more ingenious deceptions and devices. This was the twilight end of business, where companies were just names on files and letters of sale and purchase were faked to keep the Revenue Commissioners at bay.

A central question in the tribunal's investigations was the unexplained involvement of John Finnegan. Known in the trade as 'the Dancer', the principal of Finnegan Menton had been striking deals around Dublin for over three decades. A suave, raffish type with an aversion to publicity, Finnegan was an established member of the city's commercial elite. At 68 years of age, he found himself stumbling into the arena of the Flood tribunal almost by accident.

However, he had already had plenty of experience of unwelcome attention. In 1999, his was one of the first names to be linked publicly to the controversial Ansbacher bank, when he was cited in the High Court as being the beneficiary of a £1.88 million loan secured by Ansbacher Cayman bank. Earlier in the 1990s, he had featured prominently in the controversy over the former Johnston Mooney and O'Brien site in Ballsbridge when Telecom Éireann acquired the site for £9.4 million in 1990, more than twice the amount it had been sold for just a year earlier. Finnegan had been asked by his friend Michael Smurfit, who was then chairman of Telecom, to scout around for any sites which could serve as new headquarters for the semi-state. After Telecom bought the Ballsbridge site, Finnegan sought a finder's fee of £150,000 from the semi-state. After the intervention of Smurfit, he settled for £40,000.

Like Brennan and McGowan, Finnegan set up an offshore family trust run by expert lawyers. He availed of the services of Haughey's bagman, the late Des Traynor, for tax advice. Ever the creative adviser, Traynor set up the Amber Trust as a charitable trust, and included the World Wildlife Fund among the beneficiaries. However, the Fund says it has no record of contributions from Finnegan or his trust. In fact, there was nothing charitable about the trust and Finnegan claimed he didn't even know that Traynor had set it up in this way.

When his involvement in Canio was revealed, Finnegan vehemently denied any knowledge of the payment to Burke or the mortgage taken out on the Canio lands. The auctioneer was 'kept in the dark' by his two partners about the Burke payment, his lawyers asserted. The reference in various documents to a reserved fund for 'architect's fees' was 'a charade' and Finnegan was the only person fooled by it.

What is clear is that the reference to 'architect's fees' was a fiction to disguise a political donation. No work of this type had been carried out, nor was it intended to be. In fact, much of the correspondence seems to have been made up to give the impression of normal commercial transactions between companies that were just files in an office in Jersey.

The documents also show that someone went to great lengths to keep secret Finnegan's involvement in Canio. When Lombard and Ulster asked for details of Canio's owners before granting a mortgage on the Sandyford lands, Finnegan is recorded as giving instructions that his name should be replaced as beneficial owner by that of an English businessman, Roger Wreford. 'Wreford's name has been substituted for that of Finnegan because Finnegan wants to remain silent,' noted Brennan and McGowan's accountant Hugh Owens, in a fax in June 1984.

However, Finnegan's lawyers protested that Wreford was not acting for Finnegan in the matter, and never had. Finnegan also denied knowledge of a series of contracts purporting to transfer ownership of the lands from Canio to a number of Brennan and McGowan building companies. He said he became concerned about these contracts in 1982. Their effect was that Brennan and McGowan could control Canio without reference to him. Brennan maintained that Finnegan had full knowledge of the contracts. 'We all knew what was happening,' he said.

Brennan and McGowan ultimately bought out Finnegan's interest in Canio for £700,000. Canio was dissolved in October 1999, a few months after Burke was first called to give evidence at the tribunal. The Sandyford lands were rezoned from agriculture to housing and built upon by a number of companies, including some owned by Brennan and McGowan.

The tribunal's investigations showed that Finnegan had a dual role in the land deals he undertook with Brennan and McGowan. In some deals, he acted in a professional capacity for the vendor. In others, he acted for the purchaser. In yet others, he was a director of the company selling the land. But in all cases, he received a handsome payment offshore from Brennan and McGowan. This happened regardless of whether or not he had invested with the two builders in the purchase of the land. The three men harvested over £660,000 each from the transactions and, since the money was distributed off-shore, it was not subject to the usual Irish taxes.[6]

The arrangement covered deals struck at Monkstown, Donnybrook, Blackrock, Sandyford, Sandymount and Stephen's Green. In each case, Finnegan brought his expertise in land sales, his contacts with the seller or purchaser, or his deal-striking skills to the transaction. He proved adept at overcoming the obstacles which might prevent Brennan and McGowan building on the lands in each transaction. This was achieved by a variety of devices, such as uniting the free-hold and leasehold interests on a property, or removing restrictive covenants which prevented building on the land.

The tax schemes devised by accountant Hugh Owens for Brennan, McGowan and Finnegan were ingenious. Subsidiary companies were set up at the drop of a hat. Most were just names on a file, with no staff, offices or infrastructure. Inter-company transactions, shuttling money back and forward between Ireland and the offshore tax havens, were commonplace. The beneficial owners of companies were nigh impossible to trace, as the only names appearing on offi-cial documents were those of trustee or nominee directors in offshore law firms. Entire series of correspondence were 'orchestrated', in the words of the tribunal, to give the appearance of normal business activities. Contracts were drawn up between different Brennan and McGowan companies that had no reality and were never intended to be executed.

For instance, one letter to the builders' Jersey solicitor, Laurence Wheeler, from the proxy buyer of the Sandyford lands, James Gleeson, signed off with the wish that the two men would meet again at the Ascot races. But, as Wheeler informed the tribunal, he 'didn't know one end of a horse from another' and he didn't know Gleeson 'from Adam'. The real author of the letter, Hugh Owens, later explained that he was 'having a bit of fun' with Wheeler by referring to Ascot.

Take, for example, the first collaboration between Finnegan and Brennan and McGowan, involving land owned by the Sacred Heart nuns in Monkstown. In 1977, the three men set up a shelf company in Jersey, Bouganville Ltd, which bought the freehold of land owned by the nuns for £10,000. Finnegan had already sold the nuns' lease-hold interest for £210,000 to a Brennan and McGowan company a year earlier, and the object now was to merge the freehold and lease-hold titles and thereby greatly increase the value of the land. Normally, the subsequent sale of such lands would attract capital gains tax. However, if a non-Irish company (as in this case) wants to sell the land, there is no requirement to pay this tax provided the company's principal assets are not lands in Ireland.

But this company's only real asset was the land in Monkstown. No problem — Bouganville took out a loan of £20,000 from a Jersey bank. It then obtained an audit which, of course, showed that the freehold interest (which cost £10,000) was not the major asset. Tax was therefore not due. Within a fortnight or so, the bank loan was repaid.

Another loophole exploited by Owens was the distribution *in specie* of a company's assets. In the above case, Bouganville's interest in the land was transferred to a Brennan and McGowan-linked com-pany in Ireland, Greenisle Holdings. Bouganville was then dissolved into the Irish company and its assets distributed by a liquidator. In such a case, no stamp duty or capital gain tax is payable because this distribution is simply the giving back of property by a company to its shareholders in a liquidation. A paper debt of £350,000, allegedly owed by Bouganville to another company owned by the three men for management services that were never actually provided, was discharged. This sum was then shared out in Jersey. The Revenue Commissioners subsequently investigated the Monkstown deal, but their inquiries were severely hampered by the fact that they were not told who owned Bouganville.

Tribunal lawyer Pat Hanratty wanted to know what John Finnegan 'brought to the table' in these deals. In the Monkstown deal, for example, Finnegan earned £105,000 from the two builders arising from a transaction in which he acted for the sellers, the Sacred Heart nuns. 'He got over £100,000 for doing absolutely nothing. He didn't lay out a brass farthing,' Hanratty said. Later, Finnegan said he had in fact invested £33,000 in the deal, a claim that was treated sceptically by the tribunal. Whether or not he put money in, the question remained as to why he received so much in the Channel Islands. The more Brennan and McGowan struggled to answer this question, the more often Hanratty posed it. Brennan suggested Finnegan had 'terrific knowledge' of infill sites in Dublin.

The dupes in all this were the authorities, such as the Revenue Commissioners and the Central Bank. In 1986, for example, Foxtown Investments wanted to move £500,000, representing part of the proceeds from land deals, out of the jurisdiction. Before it could do this, it first had to satisfy the bank that the lands had been bought and sold at a fair price. Confirmation of this came in the form of a certifying letter from Finnegan Menton, which stated that the price of the deal was 'not more than fair value'. Foxtown got its approval.

However, at no time was the bank informed that John Finnegan was the owner of Foxtown. The man whose firm was providing an objective, expert appraisal of the deal was also the person who benefitted from the transfer of the funds overseas. It was, as tribunal lawyer Patricia Dillon SC put it, 'a sham'.

Finnegan and Brennan and McGowan fell out in 1985 over a transaction they were involved in at Herbert Street in Dublin. The builders negotiated to sell the Plantation site after obtaining planning permission for a residential development. However, Finnegan refused to release the title deeds until he was paid £50,000. This sum represented a one-third share of the development, though again he hadn't invested a penny. The row ended when Finnegan agreed to accept a payment of £20,000.

Brennan and McGowan returned to the witness box in early summer 2001. Both were apologetic, but their memories were little better than they had been a year earlier. Brennan's evidence was shambolic, more a sequence of 'I don't know' and 'I can't recollect' than a narrative with any coherence. He denied any knowledge of the detailed tax schemes operated in his name; the accountants set them up, while he only signed the papers and took the profits at the end. An exasperated Pat Hanratty accused the witness of trying to 'hide behind the mask of a fool'.

Flood repeatedly warned him of the dangers of obstructing the tribunal, even as the witness continued to protest his willingness to cooperate. The tribunal also threatened contempt proceedings unless the builder produced financial documents relating to his investments in Liechtenstein and the Isle of Man.

Hanratty then accused Brennan of lying and perjuring himself when he first gave evidence to the tribunal in April 2000. On that occasion, asked if 'you yourself' had made any payments to Burke, Brennan replied that he hadn't. Only later did the tribunal find out about the £50,000 Burke got from Kalabraki in 1982. Then there was the £60,000 and £15,000 that came from Canio, which was part-owned by Brennan. Brennan explained that he 'couldn't remember anything' about these payments when he had given evidence the year before. He claimed that any money Burke got came from his companies, 'not from me personally'. Yet Kalabraki was 100 per cent under Brennan's control.

Brennan explained the £50,000 donation to Burke by saying he knew Fianna Fáil was short of money. There were a lot of elections on at the time and there 'wasn't even money to buy sandwiches or drinks for the workers' in the elections. But how could Fianna Fáil have accessed the money? The payment went from Brennan's off-shore account in Jersey to Burke's offshore account in the Isle of Man. Burke used the name 'P.D. Burke' and gave a false address. It was hardly a transparent transaction.

Brennan, and McGowan after him, now used the mantra of 'Ray Burke/Fianna Fáil' to explain the destination of the payments they made. The £50,000 payment was 'an arm's-length political donation' to Fianna Fáil, paid directly to Burke, for which no favours were asked. But as far as Hanratty was concerned, it was 'a present' to Burke, dressed up 'in the cloak of a political donation to give it a veneer of respectability'.

As the tribunal continued to press for access to records they had now been seeking for over two years, Brennan claimed that he hadn't kept a single item of correspondence with his lawyers in more than twenty-five years in business. He didn't keep files. He knew all about his dealings with advisers in his head. As Hanratty couldn't resist pointing out, it wasn't evident from Brennan's testimony that he carried 'anything' around in his head.

Meanwhile, the exposure of John Finnegan's dual role in the land deals proved too much for the auctioneer to bear and his lawyers brought a High Court challenge against the tribunal. Finnegan wanted to be 'discharged' from the tribunal on the basis that he, on his own word, knew nothing about the payment to Burke. The appeal was doomed from the start. By now, the tribunal's right to inquire into personal financial affairs had been clearly defined by the courts, and Finnegan had nothing new to add to the arguments of Bailey, Redmond, Murphy, Lawlor et al. The main effect of the appeal was to focus yet more attention on the auctioneer's role and to delay the proceedings further. The High Court rejected Finnegan's complaint in July 2001.

Like his business partner, Joe McGowan began his evidence in apologetic mode. In fact, by the end of the first day in the witness box in July 2001, he had apologised over twenty times for the 'errors' in his evidence the previous year. McGowan needed all the humility he could find, as he was in deep trouble. Unlike Brennan, his previous evidence was specific, succinct — and completely inaccurate. 'Did you have any accounts outside the jurisdiction?' he had been asked the previous year. 'Not at any time,' McGowan had answered.

Were monies contributed to Burke outside Ireland, apart from the Ascot and Cheltenham fundraisers? 'I have no idea,' he had replied. 'Did you pay any money to Mr Burke offshore?' 'Certainly not,' McGowan had replied. 'I have never personally contributed to any politician ever at any time in my life.' What was curious, too, was how McGowan and Burke's earlier evidence about specific payments had tallied so perfectly — even when they were both wrong.

McGowan explained his earlier evidence by saying he 'probably didn't do enough research twelve months ago'. Thanks to the tribunal, his mind had been 'jogged' and he had then instructed his solicitors to 'get every document out' about his offshore companies. McGowan said he had an 'absolute blank' about the payment of £60,000 to Burke in 1984. 'If you asked me to go around Punchestown, Badminton or Burleigh, I could name every one of the thirty-two fences.' However, 'the human mind' was another matter.

But if the money Burke got actually came from Brennan and McGowan's offshore accounts, what about their earlier stories about fundraising events? Did these actually happen? McGowan, who could hardly afford to say that his earlier evidence was a lie, insisted

they did. He estimated the total amount of money paid to Burke at
£245,000; this comprised £125,000 in offshore payments, and
£10,000 in fundraising each year between 1972 and 1984.

However, evidence for the fundraising was still non-existent.
Fianna Fáil said it had no records of contributions by McGowan's
friend Ernest Ottewell, who was said to have coordinated the
fundraising efforts. The party said Ottewell 'was not at any time
engaged in fund-raising at national level for Fianna Fáil' and referred
the tribunal's inquiries to 'Mr Raphael Burke'. Burke, too, was denying he got any other monies. McGowan insisted Ottewell was a man
of 'deep personal honour' and couldn't have 'pocketed' the cash.
McGowan's racecourse parties had turned into a big black hole.

The tribunal contacted an accountancy firm in Wales in search
of Ottewell's records, but its phone-call was recorded and a transcript
provided to McGowan. It also contacted Ottewell's son James, who
expressed his disgust at McGowan's evidence of the previous year.

If McGowan could perform verbal gymnastics to explain the contradictions in his tribunal evidence, there was nothing he could do
about the lies he swore in earlier court proceedings.

Tribunal lawyer Patricia Dillon SC produced the affidavit sworn
by McGowan in the High Court case against Brennan and
McGowan's solicitor, George Russell, in 1985. Under a verbal barrage
from Dillon, McGowan conceded that the affidavit contained 'a
tissue of lies'. Dillon accused McGowan of setting out to ruin Russell,
'a decent and honourable man', by deliberately lying in the document. She pointed to numerous statements which were incorrect:
McGowan wrongly swore that he had not moved money out of the
jurisdiction; that he did not have money in the Channel Islands; that
he was not the owner of Canio; and that he had not failed to disclose
his interest in any company.

One paragraph alone contained six untruths. In another paragraph, McGowan denied reading or writing a document that was, it
turned out, in his own handwriting.

'This illustrates a lifetime of lying. When you are cornered, you
lie,' Dillon asserted. 'This is but a written illustration of the way you
conducted your business. When expediency demanded it, you will lie
with impunity. Why should any person accept that anything that
comes out of your mouth is the truth?'

'I can't answer that,' McGowan replied.

Dillon went on to accuse both builders of 'deliberately and wilfully' withholding information about their payments to Burke. 'You made a deliberate attempt to build Chinese walls to hide the fact that your offshore companies made payments to Mr Burke's offshore company.' This information was withheld until March 2001 'when you realised that there was nothing further you could do to conceal it'.

Tribunal lawyers continually asked what John Finnegan 'brought to the table' through his involvement with Brennan and McGowan. In October 2001, Dillon suggested the £100,000 Finnegan got from the Monkstown deal was 'a bribe' for 'delivering' the property to the builders. She described the transaction as 'a dirty little deal'. McGowan rejected this suggestion. He agreed Finnegan had helped to 'sort the whole thing out' by merging the freehold and leasehold titles, but the price paid was 'the market rate'.

Finnegan's lawyers accused the tribunals of being out to 'get' their client 'by hook or by crook' by accusing him of bribery, conflict of interest and the receipt of secret payments. The auctioneer again challenged the tribunal, this time in front of Flood, arguing that questions into his professional activities should not be asked. The challenge was rejected.

While Finnegan's role in the transactions left him open to accusations, the jury was still out on whether he had knowingly contributed money to Ray Burke. From the start, he maintained that Brennan and McGowan left him in the dark about the contribution to Burke; he believed the money held back from the Sandyford deal was for architect's fees.

McGowan insists he told Finnegan about the contribution, but admits he may not have said the money was intended for Burke. He says Finnegan wouldn't agree to a payment of £20,000, but consented to £10,000 being deducted from his share of the Sandyford proceeds.

The other burning question was why Burke had to get £60,000. If Finnegan would only give £10,000, then why didn't Brennan and McGowan stick to giving their original commitment of £20,000 each? Or why didn't they, too, contribute £10,000 each? Instead, as we know, the two builders increased their contributions to £25,000 each, thus making up the total of £60,000.

According to McGowan, Brennan had promised Burke that £60,000 would be forthcoming and they were 'stuck' with this commitment. It was, he said, 'a gentlemen's agreement'.

Meanwhile, Finnegan's lawyers battled to prevent the tribunal gaining access to his trust in the Channel Islands. The auctioneer claimed he didn't have any documentation relating to the trust and said all matters had been handled by the accountant Des Traynor, who set up the trust on his behalf in 1973. However, the auctioneer's assertion that the administrators would not give him access to the accounts of his own trust convinced no-one. Mr Justice Flood described this claim as 'a load of rubbish' and accused Finnegan of doing 'sweet ... nothing' to obtain his accounts. Under pressure from the tribunal, the auctioneer engaged lawyers in Jersey to force the administrators to show him the books. The results of this action were never made public.

In the witness box, Finnegan was asked repeatedly why he received large offshore payments arising from his collaboration with Brennan and McGowan on land deals around Dublin. He was now claiming to have invested money in some of the deals, but this still didn't explain why he recouped two and three times the amounts he put in. In the Monkstown deal, for example, he claimed to have invested £33,000, and was paid over £100,000 in Jersey a month later. This represented an interest rate of 2,400 per cent.

Though he waffled a lot about 'front-loading' anticipated profits on 'around-the-houses' deals he also admitted that he didn't really understand the mechanisms, which were masterminded by accountant Hugh Owens. In truth, the tribunal was never given any meaningful explanation for these payments.

In any case, Owens, who had better reason than anyone else to know about these things, told the tribunal that Finnegan didn't invest any money in the deals. But there was comfort for Finnegan in Owens' assertion that Brennan and McGowan had 'totally deceived' and 'hoodwinked' the auctioneer in relation to the donation to Burke. Finnegan's lawyer punched the air when this remark was made.

The tribunal also tried to shed light on the fourth mysterious payment into Burke's offshore accounts, that of £35,000 in April 1984. The politician had originally told the tribunal that this money represented the proceeds of fundraising for him in the UK. He later said it was a relodgement of monies withdrawn from his Isle of Man account just a short time before. However, this was the kind of story he had given in relation to the £15,000 lodgement and the tribunal had later discovered it actually came from Brennan and McGowan.

The £35,000 lodgement was the first made into an account held by Burke's company, Caviar Ltd, in Jersey. As recounted earlier, Burke instructed his solicitor Oliver Conlon to set up the company 'with considerable urgency' in March 1984. Burke used an unusual form of his name, 'P.D. Burke', and a false address. A fortnight later, £35,000 was deposited in Caviar's account. Just as in the case of the other large lodgements from Brennan and McGowan, Burke visited Jersey at the time of the payment.

March 1984 was also the month of Brennan and McGowan's last business collaboration with John Finnegan. In that month, the two builders received planning permission for an office block on the Plantation site, a tree-filled oasis on Herbert Street. The site was in a designated conservation area opposite one of the finest Georgian terraces in Dublin and was originally a park, although it was later used as a car park.

The Plantation was originally owned by the Pembroke Estate, of which Finnegan was a director. On eight separate occasions from 1965 on, planning permission to develop the site was refused. Then Finnegan introduced Brennan and McGowan to the property. The two builders bought the site through a subsidiary, Criteria Developments, for £40,000 in 1979. Criteria applied for planning permission for office and apartments, but was refused on multiple grounds.

The company appealed to An Bord Pleanála, which overturned the original decision. The tribunal was subsequently told that the board's order granting planning permission to the development was signed by one of Burke's closest associates, Tony Lambert, on 9 March 1984. Criteria sold the site to Green Property for £261,000. McGowan said this represented a profit of £150,000 to be shared between Finnegan and Brennan and McGowan. However, the sale of the property was held up by a dispute between Finnegan and his two partners. Finnegan obtained possession of the title deeds and refused to relinquish them until he was paid £50,000 and fees of some

£12,000. Finnegan advised Brennan and McGowan on the sale, but did not invest any money. He eventually settled for £20,000.

Burke was recalled for his fourth session in the witness box in November 2001. Once again, he plugged the gaping holes in his account with the usual mix of bluster and half-explanation. Once again, there were profuse declarations of his willingness to cooperate with the tribunal. Then there was the tactic of replying to questions that were never asked, and not replying to the questions which were posed. 'Yes' and 'no' were the words the witness found hardest to say.

Mr Burke's explanation for all the payments he received — the £125,000 he got from Brennan and McGowan, the £30,000 from James Gogarty and the £35,000 he got from Oliver Barry — was to say that much of the money resides in a 'political fund' to this day. On scores of occasions, he referred back to the £118,000 in the fund, 'which I cannot touch' until legal and accountancy advice is received.

The tribunal discovered three more accounts held by Burke, two of them offshore, which the former minister had previously failed to disclose. The accounts held funds totalling over £37,000 in the 1970s, at a time when Burke's declared income ranged between £3,500 and £9,500 a year.

Then it emerged that the two builders had paid Burke's auctioneering firm £1,000 a month over seven years, from 1975 to 1982. The total was £85,000, allegedly Burke's commission for selling about 1,700 houses on behalf of the builders. Most of the money ended up in his personal accounts. Yet he was a TD for all this time, a junior minister since 1977 and a full Cabinet minister since 1980. His estate agency employed only one full-time staff member, a secretary, so it was hard to see how he could manage to show so many houses in his down time from the Dáil.

It was also striking the way these round-sum payments, once they ceased in 1982, were followed by the large lump-sum payments through offshore companies which started in the same year and continued until 1985. So the money kept flowing, even if the route grew more circuitous and the stated purpose had changed.

The amounts Burke received thirty years ago still seem large today, but they were colossal then. He earned less than £2,000 a year from his Dáil salary when he first became a TD in the 1970s, yet he was getting £1,000 a month from Brennan and McGowan. In 1974, you could buy a house on Dublin's Waterloo Road for £14,000; today, such a property would cost several million pounds.

The tally for total payments by the builders to Burke now stood at £400,000 — enough to buy an entire Dublin street at the time.

The tribunal's hearings into Burke's finances and his links to Brennan and McGowan ended with a tongue-in-cheek plea by the two builders for Burke's political fund to be donated to charity. They cited Fianna Fáil's reluctance to have any involvement with the money and the fact that Burke had retired from politics as reasons for donating the £118,000 to the St Vincent de Paul, the National Children's Hospital in Crumlin and a third charity that Mr Justice Flood was invited to nominate. Not surprisingly, the tribunal chairman did not take up the builders on their offer.

9

Some Kind
of Homecoming

'The sorriest day in my life was the day I decided to come home again with
a few quid in my pocket and, stupidly, in the belief that things would have
changed in Ireland. They'll never change.'

— Developer Tom Gilmartin on his return to the 'auld sod'[1]

'This man unfortunately had a big dream and lost it all through no fault of
anyone in Dublin except probably his own fault.'

— Liam Lawlor on Gilmartin's disastrous homecoming[2]

'Even if Bertie Ahern survives this week, he won't survive what I have
coming down the line for him.'

— Gilmartin, speaking on FM104 radio, 26 January 1999.
Ahern asked the Dáil to consider whether it condoned or
supported 'this sort of threatening language against a
democratically elected Taoiseach'.

Before there were towns there were villages, and before there
was concrete there was countryside. Travel west from Dublin
past Kilmainham up to a few decades ago and the city petered
out very quickly. The fringe of the county was a large plain bisected
by narrow lanes, lazy rivers and two canals. Country pubs and small
settlements were the focal points of a largely rural existence.

The area between Lucan and Palmerstown had long been home to
a small pit where gravel and stone were extracted from the earth —
hence the name of the townland, Quarryvale. Mostly, though, it was
just fields, divided by the odd brook or hedgerow or canal. Market
gardens supplied food to the slowly-expanding city to the east.

A local woman, Vera Comiskey, has described growing up in the
area in the first half of the twentieth century:

*Businessman Jim Kennedy
finally shows his face to
RTÉ's Charlie Bird … or
does he?*

Liam Lawlor

Justice Feargus Flood, in gunslinger mode.

Tribunal lawyers – and millionaires – John Gallagher and Pat Hanratty.

Colm Allen SC, who represented the Baileys, Frank Dunlop and Oliver Barry, and Garrett Cooney SC, barrister for the Murphys and scourge of James Gogarty.

Garrett Cooney and Justice Flood square up to one another, February 1999.

Tom Gilmartin

Frank Dunlop leaves the tribunal after revealing his payments to politicians, April 2000.

Pádraig Flynn opens the Shankill/Bray bypass in 1991.

Bertie Ahern faces the media on the day of Denis 'Starry' O'Brien's allegations against him, April 2000.

O'Brien fends off the media after losing the libel case brought by Bertie Ahern.

'A winding, wandering pathway makes its way down from the premises to a sun-drenched well-tilled field of vegetables. Scattered amongst the growth are an assortment of flowers, some faded fuchsias and wild pink roses. Looking further on across an old fence of timber which is lined with nettles and furze is a vast quarry that has now grown to be grassland for two cows. Stretching out to the right of the quarry is Godley's wood with tall trees reaching to the sky.'[3]

It couldn't last. With the arrival of the 1960s and an era of industrial expansion, Dublin started to grow faster. The planners took out their maps and looked for somewhere to put the houses people wanted to live in. Mountains hemmed in Dublin to the south and the airport formed an obstacle to the north. But the west stretched out evenly, unimpeded by natural hazard.

Under the plan, the tiny villages of Tallaght, Blanchardstown, Lucan and Clondalkin were to become the foci of massive urban expansion. Later it was decided to fuse Lucan/Clondalkin into one centre. The land in between was to remain as green belt. Each of the three towns would have its own centre, with appropriate facilities, including a shopping centre tailored in size to the needs of the local population.

Slowly, the plan came to be realised. Urban slums were cleared and their populations moved out to newly constructed estates, put up on virgin agricultural soil far from facilities or the bustle of the city. The promised shops and churches and feeder roads took decades to arrive properly. The plans for Lucan/Clondalkin lagged behind. A site in the centre of the area, at Neilstown, was earmarked for a commercial centre to cater for the needs of local people but nothing was built.

Separately, the authorities were planning a C-road to loop around the western perimeter of the city. Dublin's sawn-off version of a ringroad would have links to all the main provincial routes. This meant that any new shopping centre built in the vicinity of the road would be well positioned to attract shoppers from further afield. Of course, the new centres were supposed to be capped in size at 250,000 square feet, but developers started to take an interest anyway.

First into the field was John Corcoran of the Green Property Company.[4] He bought the site for the proposed centre in Blanchardstown in the late 1970s and in 1987 secured the first of three planning permissions for a large shopping centre, which was three times the size of the retail and leisure facilities originally envisaged. However, all attempts to get the Government to bestow urban renewal tax incentives on the site came to naught, in spite of the efforts of lobbyist Frank Dunlop on his behalf. Over in Tallaght, Phil Monahan of Monarch Properties developed The Square, with an area of 450,000 square feet, at least twice as large as the scheme originally mooted. That left Lucan/Clondalkin.

In 1986, an expatriate Irish developer, Tom Gilmartin, came over from Luton to view the proposed town centre at Neilstown. He didn't like what he saw. The site had poor access, and roads and flyovers would be needed. It was located on waste ground in the middle of local authority housing. He rushed back to his car, fearing for its security. Gilmartin hadn't come back from England for this.

Gilmartin was an unknown in Ireland. In Britain, though, he was a roaring Irish success story, a man of modest origins who had built a fortune on hard work and business cunning. From the start, Gilmartin was driven by a desire to prove himself to the folks back home. As a young man in Lislarry, near Grange in County Sligo, he spent his time dreaming of escape from the hardship of rural life. He sat the civil service exams and was told he had done very well, and should prepare to take up a post in Dublin.

But one evening, as he made hay on the family farm, word came that he had not after all been given the post. It had gone to another man, whose father worked in the Government department concerned. Gilmartin downed his pitchfork and declared his intention to get out of Ireland immediately. By the next day he was in England, where he was to remain for over thirty years. He picked up qualifications in agricultural science and engineering. After years working in engineering firms, he moved into property development.

Gilmartin came back to Ireland in 1986 with grandiose ideas to create thousands of jobs in construction and retail. His plans for west Dublin weren't sophisticated, or sensitive. But they were big. The country was on its knees at the time and his message was music to the ears of the politicians.

He began to assemble a site at Bachelors Walk, a stone's throw from O'Connell Bridge. His plan was for a huge shopping centre with almost one million square feet of retail space on three levels, parking for 1,000 cars and a central bus station on the roof. An English company, Arlington Securities, bought into the deal, leaving Gilmartin a 20 per cent stake. Gilmartin discussed his plans with Dublin Corporation. Its officials had reservations about the scheme; the city architect said it was similar to developments which 'wrecked the hearts of English cities like Sheffield and Birmingham'.

The Corporation had played its own part in helping developers wreck the heart of Dublin over previous decades, but by 1986 the thinking that supported this kind of destruction had changed. Gilmartin's crude plans to flatten most of Bachelors Walk to make way for a dreary shopping centre were an anachronism. The officials poured cold water on his plans for the city centre site, but they were enthusiastic about involving the developer in the creation of a town centre in Lucan/Clondalkin. Gilmartin agreed to have a look.

Another developer, Owen O'Callaghan from Cork, held an option on the Corporation's land at Neilstown. O'Callaghan bought the site and sought permission in 1988 for a small shopping centre of 200,000 square feet. He had a money-back guarantee with the Corporation should planning permission be granted to any rival shopping centre larger than 250,000 square feet.

Gilmartin, meanwhile, had found what he was looking for. He began buying up land at Quarryvale, a few miles from Neilstown. Quarryvale was miles away from any housing, but it lay right by the point where planned new motorways would intersect.[5] In England, Gilmartin had mastered the art of siting huge regional shopping centres at key road interchanges, and he wanted to pursue the same strategy in Dublin. He talked about building a £750 million centre with an area of two million square feet — the largest in Ireland and one of the largest in Europe.

His proposals included a leisure complex, a retail warehouse park, 50 acres of sport and recreational grounds and a 72-acre high-tech business park. In addition to this, he talked about building 500 luxury homes, an international conference centre and a 250-bed hotel straddling the Dublin-Galway dual carriageway. The key to success or failure was State support. The 180-acre site at Quarryvale needed rezoning and a change in planning permission to allow the construction of a larger shopping centre than envisaged in the Dublin development plan. Gilmartin also wanted the same kind of favourable tax breaks that Pádraig Flynn had bestowed on The Square in Tallaght a few years previously.

But Gilmartin knew nobody, and he needed to twist a lot of arms in a short time. He got a start from his bank manager, who introduced him to Brendan Fassnidge, a local car dealer. Fassnidge, a good friend of George Redmond, offered to put him in contact with the owners of the lands he had not already bought.[6] Then, in a pub on the Galway Road, he introduced the property developer to the Fianna Fáil TD Liam Lawlor for the first time. Lawlor was living up to his reputation for ubiquity. Wherever there was a deal to be made, but particularly in his home turf of west Dublin, Lawlor was there. With Gilmartin, as with many others, the TD encouraged the belief that he could open doors to the highest levels of power.

Lawlor claims he tried to discourage Gilmartin's plans for Quarryvale. He says Gilmartin 'thought he could ride a coach-and-four through the planning system'. 'This man expected he should be able to build, in his inimitable west of Ireland way, a million and half square feet [shopping centre] and add another half a million.'[7] When the TD explained this was 'totally out of the question,' Gilmartin got 'very upset' and suggested that 'a lot of my senior colleagues [in Fianna Fáil] were very supportive of it'.

Lawlor was more interested in the plans for Bachelors Walk, for which Gilmartin was looking for a cash injection of £54 million. Gilmartin claims he 'gatecrashed' a meeting of Arlington executives in London in May 1988. He says Lawlor introduced himself as an emissary of the Government, sent to London to steer the proposal through, and asked for a substantial share of the proposed development. He demanded payment for his services, and got a consultancy retainer of £3,500 a month. This lasted for ten months, according to Gilmartin; Lawlor said he got three or four such payments, though much later he upped this figure to 'seven or eight'.

They were terminated after Lawlor allegedly went to Gilmartin's bank in Blanchardstown and demanded £10,000 from the developer's account. A bank clerk rang Gilmartin to check, and the developer blocked the payment. Bachelors Walk became 'a dead duck' after that, Gilmartin says. Arlington pulled out, badly burned. Two directors, Ted Dadley and Raymond Mould, were reported as saying they found it extremely difficult to make progress on the development after they refused to make a contribution to Fianna Fáil.[8] Gilmartin says he lost £12 million on Bachelors Walk. Some years later, another company, Zoe Developments, built 300 apartments on the site.

Quarryvale, however, was still on track. Gilmartin says Lawlor introduced him to George Redmond and said the official had to be 'taken care of'. In October 1988, Dublin Corporation decided to sell sixtynine acres of its land in the area. This was three weeks after senior officials, including the city manager Frank Feely and Redmond, were summoned to meet the Taoiseach, Charles Haughey, and three of his ministers. The politicians said they wanted urgent steps taken to boost the construction industry. The Minister for the Environment, Pádraig Flynn, claimed there was a real prospect of private sector investment in Dublin and he was talking to a number of developers with significant projects in mind.

Unusually, the Corporation agreed to sell the land to Gilmartin without going to tender. However, George Redmond, then on the brink of retirement, was watching developments with interest. He tipped off John Corcoran of Green Property, the developer of the town centre at Blanchardstown, about Gilmartin's plans to build a huge rival only a few miles away. The last thing Corcoran wanted was a competitor down the road. Redmond advised him to write to the Corporation expressing an interest in the land. As a result, the Corporation was forced to sell by tender. Redmond says this pushed up the price of the land from £40,000 to £80,000 an acre.[9]

Gilmartin outbid Green Property, but the £5.1 million he paid was almost twice the sum originally agreed with the Corporation. He signed the contract of sale in May 1989 and completed the purchase in February 1990. The deal ended in acrimony, with the Corporation claiming to this day that it is owed an additional £404,000 in interest charges.

Gilmartin embarked on a round of lobbying of senior politicians, all of whom, he says, were anxious to help him. Although virtually unknown in Dublin, he gained access to the corridors of power with ease. The Dáil diary shows that he was 'signed in' to Leinster House five times in 1989, and he met Bertie Ahern at least three times.

Gilmartin says that Lawlor introduced him in February 1989 to the Taoiseach, Charles Haughey, and other Cabinet ministers in the

Fianna Fáil offices in Leinster House.[10] Haughey said 'I know you', but Gilmartin said he had been living in England for the past thirty years. Haughey then told him he knew Gilmartin's home village of Lislarry, because he had a holiday home there. He hoped Lawlor was 'looking after' Gilmartin and offered the developer full support for his plans. Those present at the meeting were Haughey, Ahern, Flynn, Ray Burke, Séamus Brennan and Brian Lenihan, according to Gilmartin. After the meeting, he claims he was approached by a man in the corridor and asked to deposit £5 million in an Isle of Man bank account. He was given the details of the account, but never paid the money. It was after this episode that his projects started to go awry, he says.

Gilmartin later described Lawlor as 'a hustler' and claimed that the politician got over £100,000 in donations and fees for the two projects in which he was involved. When first questioned about the monthly payments in 1998, Lawlor claimed they were consultancy fees. However, the *Sunday Business Post* established that the contributions were not listed on the register of interests of Dublin County Council.[11] Lawlor then explained they were political donations, and he told *The Irish Times* he would be consulting with his accountant to ensure that he had 'fully complied with the tax aspect' of the contributions.[12]

The main obstacle to developing Quarryvale was the zoning issue. Neilstown was the designated town centre. This made sense in planning terms; Quarryvale was at the periphery of local housing estates, while Neilstown lay in the heart of them. O'Callaghan, the Cork-born developer who held the option on the Neilstown site, was in no hurry to build there; rather, he used this interest as a lever to get involved in Quarryvale. Liam Lawlor urged Gilmartin to bring O'Callaghan in on the project, but he resisted this suggestion. In December 1988, O'Callaghan had suggested they jointly develop the site, but Gilmartin rejected his overtures.

Gilmartin says Fianna Fáil ministers were after him 'like lapdogs' during this period because of the investment and jobs potential of his plans. He was introduced to Pádraig Flynn. As Minister for the Environment, Flynn had the power to designate land for urban renewal status. Gilmartin desperately needed this designation for the substantial tax breaks it conferred. He knew Flynn had already extended such a designation to The Square in Tallaght. That was the first time a greenfield, out-of-town site had benefited from a measure originally designed to regenerate decaying inner city neighbourhoods.

Flynn, from Castlebar, County Mayo, was a socially conservative former teacher whose red-hot ambition had taken him to the highest levels within Fianna Fáil. One of Charles Haughey's trusted lieutenants, Flynn entered the Dáil in 1977 and came to prominence as a passionate supporter of the proposal to build an airport at Knock in County Mayo. A tall, flashy character with a weakness for gold watches and wide pin-striped suits, he hid a clever mind behind the image of a buffoon.

In June 1989, Gilmartin met Flynn in his offices in the Custom House. Gilmartin made his usual pitch, describing his plans to help halt the 'human cargo' of emigration by creating thousands of jobs at Quarryvale. But Flynn, who was party treasurer at the time, had other things on his mind, and asked the developer for a contribution to the party. Gilmartin agreed to a contribution of £50,000, to get Fianna Fáil 'off my back'.[13] He wrote out the cheque in front of the Minister, leaving the payee's name blank at Flynn's request. This is Gilmartin's account of their meeting. Flynn has yet to explain what happened, and has said he won't do so until he appears at the tribunal.

Gilmartin believed his donation was going to Fianna Fáil, but the party never got it. 'I was being held to ransom for millions by boys a lot cuter than him [Flynn]. The donation was paid because I was told it would help to curb the activities of these boys,' he told *The Irish Times* in December 1999.[14] He only discovered the money hadn't made its way to the party when he went to see Fianna Fáil's national organiser, Sean Sherwin, about his planning difficulties in October 1989. Gilmartin told the official about the payment he made to Flynn. Sherwin said he knew nothing about any payment but would check it out. Gilmartin claims he told Bertie Ahern about this payment a few weeks later. Ahern cannot recollect being told this.[15]

Gilmartin believed he had Flynn's support, but his problems persisted. Some councillors wanted their cut if they were going to permit the multi-million pound development to go ahead. Gardaí, who at this stage were investigating other allegations of corruption in planning, got in touch with the developer. Gilmartin made allegations about Lawlor and Redmond, but declined to swear a statement, knowing this would sound the death-knell for his project. The investigation petered out.

In May 1991, Dublin County Council voted to rezone Quarryvale for a town centre and business park, effectively supplanting the previously-designated site at Neilstown. In spite of advice from planning officials that the plan was 'seriously detrimental' to existing policies for three 'new towns' to the west of Dublin, councillors voted by 29 votes to 13 to rezone. The motion was supported by Fianna Fáil *en bloc*, as well as a number of Fine Gael councillors.

By now, however, Gilmartin was on the way out. The man who conceived the notion of a giant shopping centre 'where the N4 meets the M50' was bleeding money. Everyone wanted a pound of his flesh. In 1990, he had been forced to borrow £8 million from AIB to buy the Dublin Corporation land, on top of the £7 million he had already invested. As well as having to pay twice the amount he had budgeted for this land, he had failed to secure any tax breaks under the urban renewal scheme. Then there were the payments he says he made to Liam Lawlor and Pádraig Flynn.

Meanwhile, he was facing questions from the Inland Revenue in the UK over one of his developments in Northern Ireland. A tax bill of £700,000 had been assessed, which Gilmartin disputed. Suddenly, stories appeared in the Irish media claiming the Inland Revenue was seeking £7 million from Gilmartin in relation to his investments in Dublin. Interest and penalties would double the final bill, it was reported. The newspaper articles were the first Gilmartin heard of these problems.

The leaks had the desired effect. Institutional investors who were awaiting the result of the rezoning vote ran scared. AIB, worried about its exposure, pressed for action. With the bank's active encouragement, O'Callaghan moved in to take control of the venture. Gilmartin, in his own words, went back to England 'with my tail between my legs'.

For years after, Gilmartin nursed his wounds. From his modest terraced house in Luton, he spent his days looking after a sick wife and watching Irish television. He had all the time in the world to contemplate the disaster; millions lost, an ignominious tussle with the taxman, the chance of a multi-million pound bonanza forgone. Meanwhile, his erstwhile enemies prospered; O'Callaghan pushed forward his plans for the Liffey Valley Centre on the Quarryvale site, while the Fianna Fáil politicians Gilmartin had lobbied continued in positions of power. Pádraig Flynn was made Ireland's EU Commissioner.

Angry and bitter, Gilmartin told anyone who would listen how he had been cheated of millions. Not a man to hold his tongue, he lashed out angrily and unpredictably at his foes. Word got back to the media in Dublin and his allegations started appearing in the Sunday newspapers. Meanwhile, prominent Fianna Fáil figures were coming under closer scrutiny in other matters and the chain of events that led to the setting up of the Flood tribunal was well under way.

In September 1998, the *Sunday Independent* published a story alleging that Gilmartin had paid £50,000 to a prominent Fianna Fáil politician. Fianna Fáil said it never got the money, yet Gilmartin insisted the donation was intended for the party. Flynn, by now in Brussels, professed only vague awareness of the allegation, and of Gilmartin. He refused to confirm or deny receiving the £50,000 cheque, in order not to 'undermine' the tribunal.[16] Bertie Ahern declined to say if Fianna Fáil had received the money. The matter was referred to the Flood tribunal.

Once bitten, twice shy; Gilmartin was still wary of cooperating with any investigation into Quarryvale. After all, he had talked to the gardaí in 1989 and nothing had happened. Later, he would insist he never wanted to talk to the tribunal, which he considered 'futile'.[17] 'I didn't want to get involved. I kept my mouth shut for ten years, until I was forced into talking by the tribunal.'

Mr Justice Flood and his staff travelled to Luton to see Gilmartin in 1998. The developer told them his story and delivered an unsigned statement, which contained the allegation about the £50,000 cheque given to Flynn, but withheld a promise of cooperation. 'Tribunals are about as useful as tits on a bull,' he had concluded.[18] Later, he changed his mind and provided tribunal lawyers with a limited signed statement in October 1998.

Following a decision of an Appeal Commissioner to disregard the findings of the McCracken tribunal and reduce Charles Haughey's tax bill from £2 million to zero, Gilmartin changed his mind again.

'What's the point?' he told the *Sunday Independent* in December 1998. 'If people only knew. If they only knew, like I know, how things really work in that fucking country. I had ten years of being held to ransom, of being blackmailed and threatened. My family was living in fear. My wife fell seriously ill. She still is. I was glad the day we got out and left it all behind, I'd be mad to go back now,' he told journalist Jody Corcoran. The tribunal responded by threatening legal proceedings against him in the British courts to force his cooperation.

Then an extraordinary event happened which caused Gilmartin to change his mind once more. In January 1999, Pádraig Flynn appeared on RTÉ television's *Late Late Show*. Presenter Gay Byrne asked his guest, Ireland's EU Commissioner, if he knew the developer. Flynn replied: 'Yeah, I haven't seen him now for some years. I met him. He's a Sligo man who went to England and made a lot of money. Came back. Wanted to do a lot of business in Ireland. Didn't work out for him. He's not well. His wife isn't well. And he's out of sorts.'

Asked if he had ever taken money from anybody for any reason, Flynn fixed his interviewer with a glassy stare and said: 'I never took money from anyone to do a political favour for anyone as far as planning is concerned.'[19] He went on to bemoan the difficulties of surviving on a salary of £140,000 a year. Running three houses in Dublin, Castlebar and Brussels was 'a very expensive business ... try it some time'.

After he left the studio, a woman saying she was Gilmartin's sister rang the programme and insisted the commissioner's remarks were factually incorrect. There was nothing wrong with Gilmartin's health. Producers made contact with Flynn, who agreed to make a retraction. Gay Byrne told his viewers: 'In the interview it was suggested by Pee Flynn that Tom Gilmartin was sick. As far as Pee is concerned Tom Gilmartin is not sick and has never been seriously sick and we would just like to say sorry and apologise for that'.

But the damage had been done. Gilmartin was watching the show from Luton, along with his wife. He was indignant. 'When I saw that clown on TV I was incensed, the only thing he was missing was the bucket and the red nose,' he told a reporter shortly after.[20] Enraged, he announced his intention to give evidence to the tribunal after all. Furthermore, he revealed that Flynn had repeatedly tried to contact him after the allegation about a £50,000 payment to a (then unnamed) politician surfaced the previous September. As Gilmartin told the *Sunday Independent*: 'Mr Flynn stated that he had not seen me for some considerable time. But it is not for the want of trying on his behalf'.

At the time, James Gogarty was beginning his evidence to the tribunal, but Gilmartin's allegations threatened to put even these dramatic hearings in the shade. Whereas Gogarty was a middle-ranking building industry executive who had little direct contact with politicians, Gilmartin had been feted by a long line of Fianna Fáil bigwigs.

The pressure mounted on Flynn to provide an explanation. However, the EU Commissioner declared it was 'business as usual' and continued to insist that he would deal with the matter at the tribunal, and nowhere else. The Dáil asked Flood whether Flynn had been asked not to discuss the payment and got an ambiguous response. Tribunal interviews were confidential, the chairman said, but it would be 'inappropriate' for the tribunal to appear to advise or counsel Flynn on any response he wished to make to the Dáil. Fine Gael interpreted this as saying 'it's up to you' but Flynn held his silence. Cornered by Irish journalists in the corridors of the European Parliament in Strasbourg, he gave a series of evasive answers and refused to break his silence. Meanwhile, the Government let it be known that he would not be appointed for a third term as Commissioner.

Gilmartin's claims were also making life difficult for the Taoiseach. The developer says he met Ahern four times in connection with his projects, twice in the Department of Labour and twice in a pub on the way to the airport. He also claims that when Ahern asked him during a phone conversation for a donation to the party, Gilmartin told him he had already paid £50,000 through Flynn. 'He made no comment to that,' Gilmartin said.[21] But Ahern could recollect only one meeting with the property developer. His friend, Councillor Joe Burke, went to meet the developer. Ahern had no recollection of any discussion about a contribution or about Flynn.

The discrepancies destabilised the Government, and the PDs pressed Ahern for a fuller explanation. Further checking of diaries showed that Gilmartin's version was closer to the truth, in that Ahern found records of three meetings, not one. However, he still had 'no specific memory' of these meetings, nor of any request for a contribution. 'I am quite certain that I would not have solicited a donation for Fianna Fáil from Mr Gilmartin and I have no recollection of any reference made by him to an alleged £50,000 given to the party treasurer, Mr Pádraig Flynn, in June 1989,' he explained.[22]

In July 1999, the Government appointed the Attorney General, David Byrne, as the new Commissioner to the EU. Pádraig Flynn retired home to Mayo, his political career spent. The Dáil seat passed to his daughter Beverley, who was to become embroiled in a controversy of her own within a few years.

Gilmartin's wait to give evidence to the tribunal turned into a marathon. When he finally got a chance to tell his story publicly in November 2001, it was in a libel trial in the Four Courts rather than Dublin Castle. Fianna Fáil's national organiser Seán Sherwin sued the *Sunday Independent* over an article published in February 1999. Sherwin claimed the article wrongfully claimed he had solicited money from Gilmartin in 1990 for his sister-in-law, who was standing as a candidate in the local elections. Gilmartin, as the source of the information, appeared as a witness for the newspaper.

After a ten-day trial, the jury ruled in Sherwin's favour, but awarded him a derisory £250 in damages. Sherwin was left with six-figure legal costs. But the trial was dominated by Gilmartin's astonishing account of his dealings with various politicians and the pressure he says was brought to bear when he failed to pay bribes. 'You know, you people make the so-and-so Mafia look like monks,' the developer told an unnamed man who tried to shake him down.

Gilmartin's allegations still hang over the political establishment. The snail's pace of the tribunal has delayed the taking of his evidence but this largely doesn't matter now. The information he provided to the tribunal was the crucial lever that helped to open the can of worms that was the rezoning of Quarryale. Like James Gogarty, he wasn't quite the whistle-blower the tribunal envisaged, yet he has undoubtedly done the State some service.

10
Enter Frank Dunlop

'If you are suggesting to me that any monies out of my account were used for illicit or improper purposes, the answer is an emphatic "No".'
— Frank Dunlop evidence to the tribunal, April 2000

'Beart do réir ár mBriathar — Our word is our bond'
— The motto of Dublin County Council

Rezoning turned Dublin County Council into a virtual estate agency for decades. Year by year, the remaining green tracts of county Dublin were gobbled up as councillors voted through a succession of applications by landowners and builders to put agricultural land under concrete. More often than not, there were no facilities, no utilities and no infrastructure available for the new developments. More often than not, the advice of the planners was ignored.

Not all rezoners were in Fianna Fáil. Fine Gael and, to a lesser extent, the Progressive Democrats, Labour and independents have all produced their share of politicians willing to flout common sense and ignore the county development plan.

The pattern was set in the 1970s and 1980s when Ray Burke was the dominant figure in local politics in Dublin. Burke's influence lived on after he resigned his council seat to concentrate on the Dáil in 1978; he returned as chairman of the council from 1985 to 1987. As Frank McDonald noted in *The Irish Times*, Minister Burke complained to his party colleagues about the impact of their land-rezoning activities, but Chairman Burke showed no inclination to curtail the worst excesses while they were happening.

'He did not appear unduly upset by the monthly scenes of a small public gallery packed with property developers, landowners and their agents waiting for rezoning decisions, or the regular hugger-mugger in the hallways — and later in Conway's pub — between them and many of his fellow councillors,' McDonald wrote in October 1997, long before Conway's was catapulted into national prominence by later revelations at the tribunal.

The main argument put forward by the proponents of rezoning motions was that the practice created jobs in the building industry and houses for ordinary people. They conveniently ignored the fact that plenty of rezoned land was already available, and that demand for new houses was low in the 1970s and 1980s. The real beneficiaries from rezoning were the landowners, who saw the value of their holdings increase hugely as a result of councillors' decisions. The fact that many of these landowners were supporters or members of the political parties voting through the changes was just coincidence.

The profit levels in land speculation are as big as in the drug trade. An acre of agricultural lands in County Dublin sells for something between £30,000 and £60,000. With residential zoning and planning permission for housing the same land can go for between £1 million and £1.5 million.

For decades, George Redmond had secretly represented the interests of builders and developers who had problems to overcome. Redmond's knowledge of planning was unmatched, as was the power he wielded from within the heart of the system. But by the 1990s Redmond was gone — he retired in June 1989 — and a new breed of entrepreneur was moving in to fill the vacuum. Working from outside the planning system, such lobbyists used modern public relations techniques to 'love-bomb' councillors, planners, residents' groups, the media — anyone who could sway a decision — and achieve their ends. And when persuasion failed, they could rely on the deep pockets of their clients to try other methods.

Nowhere are the results of this perversion of the planning process more evident than in Quarryvale in west Dublin. To some, the Liffey Valley Centre is the high temple of Irish shopping, a huge, shiny mall offering all the temptations Western society has to offer. But to those who live in the blighted estates around it, the centre is unwanted and unloved. Too far from their homes and too expensive to shop in, it is irrelevant to their lives.

As journalist Susan McKay pointed at the height of the

controversy, there are two shopping centres in Quarryvale. 'One of them is the huge, upmarket Liffey Valley Centre, with its designer shops and massive car parks. The other is hidden away in the middle of the Quarryvale housing estate. This centre was built along with the houses in the mid-1980s. It is a low building made of concrete blocks over which graffiti crawls like ugly weeds. Most of the 12 units are shuttered up and derelict. They've been that way for years.'[1]

In her book *She Moves Through the Boom*, Ann Marie Hourihane describes the Liffey Valley Centre as 'long and low and beige in colour. It could be an airport, it could be a factory, it could be a hospital'. Meanwhile, she writes, in the local authority estate bearing the name of Quarryvale, the streets are littered with burned out cars and broken glass. 'Liffey Valley was a disaster for the Quarryvale housing estate. No-one in Quarryvale shops at Liffey Valley, because they can't afford it. They shop where they used to shop before it was built: at Dunnes Stores at The Mill in Clondalkin, at Crazy Prices in Ballyfermot, or in town.'

By 1990, Tom Gilmartin's dream of creating Ireland's largest shopping centre at Quarryvale was running into serious trouble.The project had stalled, and there was no immediate sign that the required rezoning was forthcoming. Previously open doors were slamming shut all over the place. AIB was getting increasingly restive about its £8 million investment in the beleaguered developer. Gilmartin owned or had options on 85 per cent of what was potentially the best site for a shopping centre in Ireland. However, Owen O'Callaghan's much smaller site at Neilstown had the appropriate town centre zoning, and the chances of transferring this zoning without his agreement were slim. Gilmartin agreed to buy O'Callaghan out of Neilstown for £3 million, six times the price the Cork-born developer had paid for his option on the site in 1988.

By now, however, Gilmartin was finding it virtually impossible to come up with the enormous amounts of money needed to turn land options into firm contracts. He was coming under scrutiny from the Inland Revenue in the UK. His kitty of £4 million was spent and he was borrowing heavily from the banks at a time of high interest rates. AIB, his principal lender, pressurised him to find ways of refinancing the project. The bank started to call the shots. It forced Gilmartin to relinquish sole control of the project by giving Owen O'Callaghan a stake. AIB knew O'Callaghan from a number of modest-sized shopping centres he developed in Cork, but this was their first collaboration on the Dublin scene.

Within months, the project was back on track — and Gilmartin was soon bounced out of the development he had conceived. O'Callaghan at first took a 25 per cent interest in Quarryvale, then upped it in September to 40 per cent. With AIB holding a 20 per cent interest, Gilmartin was now a minority shareholder. At first, Gilmartin fended off AIB's attempts to give O'Callaghan control, but in the end he caved in. With debts of over £8 million, he was in no position to argue.

At this point, he bows out of the story of the development of Quarryvale. His problems with the Inland Revenue mounted. His house in Luton was raided and his assets frozen. He was declared bankrupt in 1992; this was later discharged after a court case. A few years later, with the aid of solicitor Noel Smyth, he recovered some of his investment, a fraction of the total worth of Quarryvale today.

Out went the toothy bluffness of the rags-to-riches-to-rags developer from Sligo via Luton, and in came the unctuous charm of a former Government spindoctor. Frank Dunlop, one-time Fianna Fáil press secretary, now public relations consultant, began his biggest assignment: to persuade seventy-eight Dublin county councillors to disregard all planning advice and local sentiment and rezone Quarryvale to create Ireland's largest shopping centre.

❧•❧

For two decades, Dunlop had been a leading figure on the fringes of Irish politics. As the first Government press secretary, a 'national hand-ler', a public relations guru and a lobbyist, he was never far from the political action. Though seldom directly in the limelight, his face was familiar to the public from television appearances on RTÉ. He was the first to tread a now familiar path leading to a career as a lobbyist. First, get a grounding in media matters as a journalist, then head for Fianna Fáil for the party contacts. Learn about the workings of the civil service while in government and take your knowledge and contacts book to a public relations company for a vastly increased salary.

In his early life, though, Dunlop showed markedly less interest in worldly matters. He grew up in Kilkenny, where his father worked as a carpenter and helped out in Fianna Fáil. After attending the local Christian Brothers, Dunlop studied for the priesthood for four years Then he switched careers dramatically. He studied history and politics at UCD, and played an active role in the Fianna Fáil cumann. RTÉ took him on as a researcher and journalist, and he covered the Troubles in Belfast. After two years, he left RTÉ in 1974, answering Jack Lynch's call to become the Fianna Fáil press secretary. He was just 26.

When Fianna Fáil stormed home in the 1977 election, he became head of the Government Information Services. A year later, the post of Government press secretary was created specially for the 29-year-old. That year, too, he married Sheila Tuite, a party activist from County Meath.

Dunlop became the voice of the Government during a turbulent period within Fianna Fáil. When Charles Haughey succeeded Lynch as party leader in 1979, Dunlop stayed on. Three years later, the Fine Gael-Labour coalition came to power and he moved to the civil service. In 1983, the Fine Gael Minister for Education, Gemma Hussey, removed Dunlop from the post of press officer amid suggestions she was getting a 'bad press'. Dunlop remained in the civil service for a period, then joined Murray Consultants in 1986.

By now, he had an unrivalled knowledge of the workings of power and the public service. He had worked with politicians in all the main parties, including the two factions within Fianna Fáil. A spell in the Department of the Environment must have provided him with an inkling of the millions there was to be made from land speculation. He set up Frank Dunlop and Associates in November 1989, just as Haughey returned to power. The long years of economic hardship were coming to an end and the economy was starting to show signs of a pick-up. George Redmond had just retired. Tom Gilmartin was in town, talking big. It was a good time to be starting your own business.

Suave and voluble, Dunlop threw himself into his business with gusto. The kind of man for whom the mobile phone was invented, he networked energetically with journalists and developers. He was a conduit for information for hungry journalists, a lieutenant and public face for publicity-shy developers, and a winer and diner of politicians with affection deficits.

With his sharp suits and his exaggerated locutions, Dunlop stood out — this was to be his downfall, ultimately. 'I have balls of iron and a spine of steel, if we can't make a shilling here, we'll make it someplace else,' he famously remarked on one occasion in 1993 after losing a heated planning vote over Baldoyle racecourse.

This 'Deep Throat' couldn't resist the lure of publicity — he even co-hosted a political chat-show, *Later with Finlay and Dunlop*, until RTÉ dropped him. With considerable brass neck, he sounded off weekly on television, even as the Flood tribunal was bearing down on him.

Dunlop pushed the boat out further than anyone else in his profession. Not satisfied with the success of his work as a lobbyist, he demanded his own cut of the action. He took a stake in several of the developments he was promoting — the Baldoyle scheme and Citywest, for example. And he didn't just woo councillors for their votes, but paid them large sums and even employed some to work 'hand in glove' with the developers.

Apart from Quarryvale, the most prominent controversy linked to Dunlop in the early 1990s was Baldoyle. Dunlop was a director of Pennine Holdings, which acquired an option on 438 acres of green belt between Baldoyle and Portmarnock and fought an aggressive campaign to have more than one-third of it rezoned for housing. It was a re-run of a previous rezoning battle a decade earlier between the Kerry-born developer and owner of the lands, John Byrne, and local residents. On that occasion Byrne, a friend of Charles Haughey and a veteran of planning controversies, was unsuccessful. This time, Pennine promised locals a park, a golf course, sports facilities and a shopping centre in return for local support. The ownership of the company remained a mystery; no returns had been filed in the Companies Office and the owners hid behind the solicitors who set up the company.

Local residents fiercely opposed the plan. Unlike the Quarryvale situation, they were well organised. Under the intense glare of media publicity, even the most pro-development of councillors wilted. In April 1993, the motion was defeated by 43 votes to three, with 23 abstentions. Dunlop, dressed in his trademark pinstripe suit, tried to hide his disappointment and made the 'balls of iron' quip.

His business continued to flourish. He carried out work for the Construction Industry Federation, the giant Citywest project in West Dublin and many individual developers. He kept his hand in with Fianna Fáil by advising Albert Reynolds on improving the party's public image. Other blue chip clients included Aer Lingus, the Departments of Health and Defence, Woodchester Bank, Tesco Ireland, the National Treasury Management Agency and the Irish League of Credit Unions. In 1998/99, his recorded income was over £530,000, a fourfold increase over the previous year.[2] The real turnover was probably much higher.

Lobbyists as a breed tend to overstate their influence, but Dunlop's access to people in high places was undeniable. As late as 1998, he made a crucial intervention as the Government was formulating plans to limit the size of out-of-town supermarkets. At the time, he counted Tesco and the Cork-born developer Owen O'Callaghan among his clients. When the Minister for the Environment, Noel Dempsey, unveiled his plans before Cabinet in June 1998, someone leaked the information. Dunlop knew about the plans within a day and immediately sent a letter of complaint to Dempsey and the Taoiseach. A week later, the Department of the Environment announced a different limit from the one originally suggested by Dempsey. The Government denied it had been unduly influenced, but it was clear the new limit was more to the liking of big retailers.

⋘°∘°⋙

To adapt a phrase, Owen O'Callaghan is 'a man who rose without trace', which is just how this low-key, unassuming developer would like it. Born in Ballincollig in Cork in 1940, he qualified as a quantity surveyor before turning to building his own developments. Friends say he is a devoted family man, with few interests outside his three children and the GAA.

Yet in spite of all efforts to maintain a low profile, controversy has dogged his career since the mid-1990s. O'Callaghan is one of Fianna Fáil's biggest contributors.[3] In the 1990s, he gave £90,000 to the party, including one payment of £80,000 in the summer of 1994. At the time, the party had debts of over £3 million, which it managed to cut to less than £500,000 in a short space of time. In addition to his handouts to party headquarters, O'Callaghan has also contributed to individual figures in Fianna Fáil; according to his own tally, he gave £60,000 to politicians in Dublin and £26,500 to the party's representatives in Cork. The latter figure includes a £10,000 cheque to Batt O'Keeffe and payments totalling £6,500 to the Minister for Health, Micheál Martin. O'Callaghan says he has also donated money to other parties, but he hasn't specified these amounts publicly.

O'Callaghan came to attention nationally in two rows fanned by the rivalry between Fianna Fáil and Fine Gael. O'Callaghan's company purchased a site at Horgan's Quay in Cork from CIÉ, on which it planned to build a science park. In 1995, after it was learned that CIÉ's property sub-committee had been disbanded without considering the valuer's advice to put the site on the market, the Fine Gael Minister for Transport, Michael Lowry, ordered an investigation. O'Callaghan insisted he acted properly at all times in his negotiations with CIÉ. He responded to the controversy by withdrawing from the deal.

As a Haughey-appointed director of Bord Gáis, he had found himself in another controversy shortly before this, when news leaked out that Hugh Coveney, a Fine Gael minister from Cork, had approached the board chairman about getting the Bord Gáis surveying contract for his company. O'Callaghan was one of two board members who were informed about Coveney's approach. Both he and the other member denied any part in the leak, which led to Coveney's resignation.

O'Callaghan benefited from a number of Government decisions to designate certain areas for urban renewal tax incentives in 1994. One of these sites, at Golden Island in Athlone, was designated in November 1994, on the last morning before the collapse of the Fianna Fail-Labour Government.

His business success is founded on a string of retail and industrial projects built in the 1980s, which established his reputation in the property sector and acted as a springboard for further growth. They included the £60 million Merchant's Quay shopping complex in Cork and the £15 million Arthur's Quay scheme in Limerick, both completed in 1989.

O'Callaghan has been a builder since 1969, when he set up a construction business with his brother, J.J. This company, Omac, built thousands of homes in the Cork area before moving into the shopping centre business. O'Callaghan built shopping centres in Ballincollig and at Paul Street in Cork, as well as buying existing centres. He developed the knack of thriving in periods of economic recession, by buying property cheaply and offloading it when the market rose. Another crucial element has been his success in attracting anchor tenants such as big supermarkets. The Liffey Valley centre, which has no major food retailer apart from the upmarket Marks and Spencer, is the exception.

Not all of O'Callaghan's plans have turned to gold. Low points include his botched attempt to take over the Switzer group, later bought by Brown Thomas, and a disappointing investment in Cork's 96FM. An attempt to take over a rival property group, Green Property, also came to naught.

❖

The date of O'Callaghan's first involvement in Quarryvale is a matter of dispute. In January 1991, he employed Frank Dunlop to lobby for the rezoning, yet O'Callaghan did not become a director of Barkhill, the company set up to develop Quarryvale, until September of that year. Gilmartin and O'Callaghan announced their intention to develop Quarryvale jointly in May 1991.[4] The first motion to rezone Quarryvale was put by Fianna Fáil councillor Colm McGrath in February but it was not considered until May. So why was O'Callaghan employing Dunlop and making contributions to councillors during the election campaign at a time when he had no known commercial interest in the scheme?

O'Callaghan's version is that he signed an agreement with Gilmartin to take a stake in Quarryvale as early as February.[5] According to Dunlop, O'Callaghan hired him 'in circumstances where he informed me that he was hopefully entering into an association with Mr Tom Gilmartin in relation to the Quarryvale lands'.

Gilmartin has made a number of allegations about the conduct of affairs during this final period of his involvement in the project. More than £1 million of his money was taken beyond his reach, he claims, and some was channelled to Dunlop's company, Shefran Ltd. He says he only learned of the existence of Shefran in 1992 when he got a letter from an AIB official querying the payments to the company. When he tried to find out the beneficial owners of Shefran, AIB refused to tell him.

It wasn't surprising that Gilmartin found it difficult to get information on Shefran. The company (an acronym of FRANk Dunlop and his wife SHEila) had no offices, no staff and provided no services. It was a shelf company, with directors in the Channel Islands and a secretary in the Isle of Man. Its sole bank account was at Dunlop's branch of the AIB in College Street, where an official thoughtfully collected any correspondence for the company on behalf of Dunlop. Although he had no ostensible connection to the company and no chequebook, the lobbyist had no difficulty withdrawing cash sums of up to £30,000 from the account.[6]

Whatever about the background financial dealings, Dunlop set about his task energetically. He needed to move fast, as local elections were due in June 1991. The first step was a lengthy round of 'schmoozing' at face-to-face meetings between Dunlop, O'Callaghan and individual councillors. These sessions took place over pints in the local pub, dinner in the Gresham Hotel or, for the lucky ones, lunch in one of Dublin's top restaurants. Dunlop always picked up the tab, but would invoice the client later. He kept no records of these meetings, relying only on his phone as the tool for the job.

A core group of councillors attended regular 'strategy meetings' organised by Dunlop and O'Callaghan. Then there were the election leaflets printed for pro-Quarryvale election candidates — mostly Fianna Fáil, the meetings with community groups and the rebutting of 'campaigns of disinformation' by rival developers.

Dunlop then had to coordinate the votes in the council chamber. It was, as he explained, 'a numbers game'.[7] There was frenetic activity to ensure that a number of people who were not 'onside' would either come 'onside' or absent themselves, which was often as good as a vote. Some councillors had a difficulty being associated with a rezoning in their own area, so efforts were made to assign a more prominent role to councillors living farther away. In return, the politicians talked, in couched terms, about money. Or as Dunlop put it: 'they were clever enough to indicate the necessity to make preparations for elections'.

In May 1991, Dublin County Council voted to rezone Quarryvale by 29 votes to 13. The motion was proposed by Colm McGrath of Fianna Fáil and seconded by Fine Gael's Tom Hand. It was supported by twenty-five Fianna Fáil members and four from Fine Gael. Councillors had earlier listened to the county manager describe the proposal as 'illogical and contrary to proper planning' and one which would 'disrupt the form, balance and nature of the entire area'.[8] During the vote, Dunlop acted as a kind of tick-tack man doing headcounts to ensure that enough of his councillors were present before votes were taken. Asked what he was doing there, listening intently to the 'debate', Dunlop replied: 'I'm here to observe the democratic process in action'.

However, the battle was only beginning. The vote attracted widespread anger and opposition. The council had already received over 16,000 representations on the matter. An Taisce vowed to campaign against the decision. Green Property announced it was 'pulling the plug' on the 750,000 square foot scheme at Blanchardstown because its viability would be 'totally undermined' by the plans for Quarryvale.[9] With Green's John Corcoran squarely blaming the Fianna Fáil councillors, the issue became a political football, and both sets of developers vied for the support of residents' groups in the run-up to the local elections at the end of June.

Fianna Fáil councillors canvassing in Blanchardstown were being 'eaten alive' on the doorsteps, *The Irish Times* reported a few days before polling.[10] Wounded, angry councillors accused Corcoran of conducting 'a disinformation campaign ... against our party'. Corcoran retorted that he 'was not going to lie down and be walked on'. He had spent £8 million preparing the way for the Blanchardstown centre and he wasn't going to see this money go to waste.

On radio, McGrath made a Freudian slip when he said he 'made no apology for the fact that we have picked probably the best site' for a shopping centre. He quickly corrected himself by pointing out that it was the developers who had chosen the site. The election turned into a bloodbath for pro-Quarryvale councillors. Liam Lawlor and eleven other supporters of the rezoning lost their seats.

However, Dunlop and O'Callaghan returned to the task with undimmed energy. The initial vote had to be confirmed by the new council. Having invested millions in the project, O'Callaghan had gone too far to turn back now. The two men spent months lobbying the new councillors, and fended off attempts by opponents to kill off the project. In December 1993, the councillors confirmed their decision to rezone Quarryvale, though they capped its size at 250,000 square feet. The vote was closer this time, with an anti-rezoning motion being defeated by just 37 votes to 32. For Dunlop, it was a magnificent achievement, procured in the teeth of widespread local opposition and heavy media attention. Dunlop continued to lobby on O'Callaghan's behalf and in 1998, South Dublin County Council agreed to lift the cap to provide for future expansion. The Liffey Valley Shopping Centre opened in the same year.

But how had Dunlop achieved this feat? The scale of his victory set tongues wagging. The Quarryvale rezoning was simply too big and too brazen not to capture media attention and incur criticism. The rumours about wrongdoing were widespread but they remained just that — rumours. Dunlop himself, ever garrulous but convinced of his invincibility, may even have helped spread them.

However, the political climate was changing. James Gogarty's allegations had gathered a head of steam, resulting in the setting up of the Flood tribunal to investigate Ray Burke and George Redmond in November 1997. When its remit was widened in the following year to embrace payments to *all* politicians, the alarm bells started ringing. It was just at this time that the tribunal started to suffer enormous difficulties, including a series of damaging media leaks. For many observers, the suspicion was that these leaks had as much to do with Quarryvale as the Gogarty allegations that were then under investigation. If the tribunal were to collapse, that would stymie any possibility of a thorough investigation into the rezoning of Quarryvale.

However, the tribunal didn't collapse. Tom Gilmartin decided to follow the example set by Gogarty. Throughout 1998, he stoked up the political temperature with a series of outbursts to the media. Gilmartin could be erratic and emotional but there was no denying the enormity of his allegations. The tribunal first contacted the lobbyist in September 1998, but made little progress initially. However, after Gilmartin talked to tribunal lawyers in 1999, the lawyers started closing in on Dunlop.

Stories about the financial links between Dunlop and O'Callaghan started appearing in the *Sunday Independent* and other newspapers. It was revealed that Dunlop was paid more than £650,000 to cover the costs of the lobbying campaign for Quarryvale. The money was traced to an account held by Shefran, and Dunlop was identified as the person who controlled that company.[11]

Dunlop responded to the gathering storm in a variety of ways. He fobbed off inquiries by claiming that Shefran was under his 'indirect control'. The reason for the secrecy, he intimated, was to hide his involvement in Quarryvale from Gilmartin, who didn't want anyone else involved in the project. The problem with this explanation was that Dunlop had frequently filed invoices for his work from Frank Dunlop and Associates. His involvement was clear, and his relationship with O'Callaghan was well-known.

Dunlop filed an affidavit of discovery with the tribunal in 1999, saying he had declared all his bank accounts. But this wasn't the case, and a crucial AIB account in Rathfarnham Road, the main source of the payouts to councillors, only came to light the following February. Tribunal lawyers found out about yet another account only when Dunlop was in the witness box.

He also moved to settle his tax affairs. In 1998, he disclosed the money he received through Shefran between 1991 and 1993 to the Revenue Commissioners and made a substantial settlement. The Revenue then began a full audit of his tax affairs.

The lobbyist threatened legal action against journalists writing about his activities. He refused to file a statement with the tribunal, which responded by issuing him with a summons to appear in Dublin Castle in April 2000. He engaged Colm Allen, a senior counsel who was already representing the developer Michael Bailey and the promoter Oliver Barry, as his senior counsel.

⋘∘⋙

Dunlop's first days in the witness box were overshadowed by the verdict delivered in a high-profile murder trial then running in

Dublin. 'Typical of Frank to organise the Catherine Nevin verdict to coincide with his appearance at the tribunal,' quipped one journalist, for once giving the lobbyist perhaps too much credit for news management.[12]

Not that his evidence was all that interesting at first. Dunlop began his evidence in a state of denial, ponderously formulating his repudiations of wrongdoing. There was a dramatic flourish at the end of the week when, to the obliging sound of rolling thunder outside, he wrote the name of a corrupt councillor on a sheet of paper, which was then handed to Flood. For the first time, the tribunal was hearing claims that a politician had actively sought a bribe. This stunt grabbed the headlines, even as it served to divert attention from the witness to the councillors. And to one councillor in particular.

For this was Frank's last spin. The name on the piece of paper was that of a dead councillor. Better still, a dead Fine Gael councillor, Tom Hand. In spite of all the rumours about wrongdoing in the Fianna Fáil group, the one name that Dunlop could come up with at this stage was that of a deceased politician from Fine Gael.

Hand's name was revealed in the following day's *Irish Independent*. Further, the front-page article dragged Fine Gael leader John Bruton into the story. The report by Sam Smyth claimed that another Fine Gael councillor, Olivia Mitchell, had suggested to Dunlop that he should contact Bruton about the allegations concerning Hand. Bruton said he was 'certain' no such allegation was communicated to him. In evidence, Dunlop denied supplying the information to Smyth, though the journalist had rung about the story he was planning to write. Hand was 'the only member [of the council] who ever asked for money for a vote for rezoning' and he had told four other councillors and the Fine Gael leader about the demand, Dunlop explained.[13] He didn't tell the gardaí because Hand would have denied the story.

Whoever planned it, the tactic failed. By trying to smear Bruton — perceived even by his opponents as an upstanding politician — the leaker had bitten off more than he could chew. The focus switched back to Dunlop, who returned from a business trip in the US to give more evidence the following week. Something had changed; the atmosphere was more tense, the questions were harder to answer. Bad turned to worse for the lobbyist as his attempts to clear up the confusion of earlier evidence only left him in even greater difficulty.

The previous February, the tribunal had discovered Dunlop's undeclared account with AIB in Rathfarnham Road. Now it wanted to know about the strange patterns governing the movement of cash in and out of the account. Here was all this money flowing out of his account just at the times Dublin County Council came to debate the rezoning of Quarryvale. Around the time of the first vote, in May 1991, about £170,000 had been withdrawn from AIB Rathfarnham, in amounts ranging between £500 and £35,000. Then the account was dormant until November 1992, when £75,000 was taken out in three lots.

Dunlop agreed it was 'an undeniable coincidence'. He admitted the account was used for 'the concealment of monies'. With the help of an obliging bank official in his normal branch in the city centre, Dunlop never actually had to visit the Rathfarnham Road branch to withdraw funds. But he still wasn't admitting to any wrongdoing — 'If you are suggesting to me that any monies out of my account were used for illicit or improper purposes, the answer is an emphatic "No".'

But his answers were vague and he was clearly on the run. Asked where the money went, he replied: 'Until such time as I am absolutely clear as to the source of the monies and the disposition of the monies, I'd prefer to tell you I cannot answer that question now'. In other words, the tribunal would have to wait until the Revenue Commissioners were finished with him.

He was in even more difficulty explaining the Shefran money. The previous week, he had explained that the £175,000 this company received from Owen O'Callaghan between 1991 and 1993 went on 'house [refurbishment], home and holidays'. Now he gave a radically different explanation, which included £80,000 spent on credit card payments and £30,000 on 'key money' for new business premises. But the amounts didn't add up; now he was accounting for £278,000, far more than the sum he claimed to have received from O'Callaghan. Also, why would he pay 'key money', a legitimate tax-deductible expense, from an account hidden from the Revenue?

Dunlop finally accepted the glaringly obvious about Shefran; that it was used to hide money from the Revenue. The company was kitted out with directors from the Channel Islands and a secretary from the Isle of Man in order to 'disguise' the identity of its true owner. But, as Dunlop conceded, 'Shefran was, to all intents and purposes, me'.

The tribunal chairman invited the witness to 'reflect' on his evidence overnight, and Dunlop took his advice to heart. He arrived in Dublin Castle on 19 April — Spy Wednesday — a different man. Haltingly at first, he revealed the details of payments to fifteen different county councillors ranging in size from £500 to £48,500. The cash was handed over in various locations: homes, offices, Conway's pub on Parnell Street and even the Dáil bar. Crucially, he linked the payments to the councillors' support for the rezoning of Quarryvale. Whereas previously he had insisted there was a distinction between bribes and 'legitimate political donations,' Dunlop now acknowledged for the first time that most of the payments were intimately connected with the councillors' stance on the rezoning.

For the first time, a key 'insider' was 'coming clean' about the dubious details of brown paper bag politics. As the day wore on and Dunlop added yet more names to the list of politicians handed to Mr Justice Flood, the shock waves reverberated around Dublin. While the corridors of Dáil Éireann erupted in panic, the chairman of An Taisce, Michael Smith, brought a bottle of champagne down to Dublin Castle to celebrate with others who had fought to expose corruption in Irish planning. Dunlop was long gone by then. Ashen-faced, the witness had asked the chairman to be excused, saying he was unwell. He walked, stooped, to the quietest corner of the hall and then to a private room. A short time later, the tribunal was adjourned and he was taken away in some distress. Within minutes, two of the politicians he had just named were on the phone to him, trying to find out what he had said. Dunlop refused the calls.[14]

⋙⋘

Many of the county councillors identified (but not publicly named) by Dunlop went to ground in the immediate aftermath of his revelations. The few that could be reached said they had received small amounts of money from the lobbyist to defray election expenses but denied the payments were made in connection with Quarryvale. Liam Lawlor issued a statement saying he wasn't on the council at the time of the vote (in fact, he was on the council in 1991 and supported the first rezoning vote). He denied having any 'hand, act or part' in seeking support for, or voting for 'the Liffey Valley project'. But Lawlor was easily identifiable as the 'Mr Big' to whom Dunlop says he made a payment of £40,000 in cash, followed later by two cheques totalling £8,500.

Dunlop's evidence pointed to the existence of a 'core group' of councillors, both Fianna Fáil and Fine Gael, who received large payments of £20,000, £15,000 and £12,000. These were, by any yardstick, massive payments, far more than any county councillor would need to finance a local election campaign. Further down the pecking order were the bit-players, councillors whose support Dunlop tried to buy with payments of £1,000 or £2,000. As for the £250,000 allegedly demanded by Fine Gael councillor, Tom Hand, the shock here lay not in the fact that Hand was asking for money, but that he was looking for *so much* money.[15]

Fine Gael and Fianna Fáil responded to Dunlop's evidence by announcing separate internal inquiries into the behaviour of their members. Bertie Ahern said any Fianna Fáil member who breached the party's code of standards would be subject to the 'appropriate sanction' though he didn't explain what this was. The Fine Gael leader John Bruton vowed to expel any member who was found to have taken money in return for votes.

A fortnight later, Dunlop returned to the tribunal, and made more astonishing revelations about payments from developers, and to politicians. By now, his allegations extended far beyond Quarryvale. More than twenty-five politicians and fourteen different landowners were implicated in the widespread network of corruption he outlined to the tribunal. Dunlop identified £75,000 he paid to politicians for rezonings on top of the £112,000 he detailed earlier, and another £20,000 after 1993. A further £250,000 in his accounts remained unaccounted for, and may have been paid out later in the 1990s. Landowners paid a total of £185,000 into his 'war-chest' or 'stash of cash' to support rezoning campaigns, Dunlop claimed. He used this fund for personal expenditure as well as payments to politicians.

In all, Dunlop received more than £1.3 million from O'Callaghan for a variety of services during the 1990s. This included about

£900,000 for what he called 'voluminous and monumental' services in relation to Quarryvale. He got £100,000 from O'Callaghan for work on the Horgan's Quay controversy in Cork and £300,000 when the 250,000 square feet cap on Quarryvale was lifted in 1998. He also agreed a fee of £100,000 with O'Callaghan in 1992 for work on promoting the idea of a new national stadium on the developer's site in Neilstown.[16] Dunlop was paid £95,000 of the amount agreed.

O'Callaghan let it be known that he knew nothing about the Rathfarnham account and never authorised any payments to politicians. 'I never instructed or authorised anyone on my behalf to pay monies to any politician for his or her vote. Neither did I instruct or authorise anyone to make political contributions in connection with elections to Dublin County Council,' he said in a statement at the time of Dunlop's first evidence to the tribunal.[17]

In all, Dunlop gave the tribunal the names of about twenty-five politicians to whom he made payments in 1992 and 1993. Some, such as Fianna Fáil's Pat Dunne and Fine Gael's Tom Hand (both deceased), were easy to identify. Others, such as 'Mr Big' and 'Mr Insatiable', were 'outed' quickly as Liam Lawlor and Colm McGrath, respectively.

Reporters passed their quieter moments guessing the identity of the remainder, but were slow to name names for legal reasons. Gradually, though, the names of many of the councillors and landowners came to light.

Inevitably, the spotlight fell on Colm McGrath, proposer of the original motion to rezone Quarryvale in 1991, whom Dunlop described as 'fairly insatiable'. McGrath was first elected as a Fianna Fáil councillor in Clondalkin in 1985, and managed to hold on to his seat when many other pro-Quarryvale candidates were dumped in the 1991 local elections. As the only Fianna Fáil councillor in the Clondalkin area, his support was crucial to the rezoning of Quarryvale. He assumed an even greater role after Liam Lawlor lost his council seat in 1991, and played an important part in winning over sceptical councillors to Owen O'Callaghan's plans in the 1991-93 period.

McGrath received two substantial political contributions from O'Callaghan, the *Sunday Independent* reported in February 1999. As the centre was being built, his company, Essential Services, which employed over 20 people, provided security services on the site. McGrath told the Fianna Fáil inquiry he received £30,000 for this contract.

Politically, McGrath was minor league material. He was an unsuccessful candidate in the 1997 general election, in spite of a determined effort to play up anti-immigrant sentiment in the Dublin South-West constituency. He did serve as chairman of the Dublin Regional Authority in 1998/99, but that was mainly because he had been around for so long. In 1999, he was selected as a candidate in the local elections but was dropped by party headquarters when it emerged that he was under investigation by the Flood tribunal. He ran as an independent, replacing the Fianna Fáil logo on his election literature with the McGrath family crest (with its motto 'This We Hold in Trust'). With over 1,000 votes, he topped the poll in the Clondalkin area.[18]

On the few occasions he could be tracked down for comment, he denied any impropriety. His response when contacted by one newspaper was cryptic: 'I have done absolutely nothing wrong. I am being set up by Mount Street [Fianna Fáil's headquarters]. There is a much bigger story out there involving some people who are now taking the high moral ground'.

Separate from Quarryvale, McGrath was named to the Flood tribunal in December 2000 as having received £30,000 in connection with the rezoning of lands at Lucan in 1993. In conventional tribunal style, Maynooth auctioneer Willy Coonan wrote down McGrath's name on a sheet of paper and handed it to the chairman. The tribunal had asked him to identify the councillor who demanded £50,000 in return for rezoning the land. He says McGrath eventually settled for two cash payments of £15,000, which were paid over in a hotel carpark in Lucan and the square in Maynooth near Coonan's office.

This rezoning caused considerable controversy in the early 1990s. In February 1993, when the council was preparing the Draft Development Plan, McGrath proposed the rezoning, which was passed by 35 votes to 34. However, that October, after more than 2,500 representations had been received, county councillors abandoned the rezoning after a two-and-a-half-hour debate. Labour councillors claimed the vote was abandoned because the proposers didn't have enough votes to win.

Many of the landowners on Dunlop's list were similarly easy to identify, even from the scant details mentioned in evidence. Tiernan Homes, for example, gave Dunlop £30,000, at the time when the rezoning of the firm's fifty-four acres of land at Finnstown, near Lucan, was under consideration.[19] These were the lands previously owned by an offshore company linked to beef baron Larry Goodman and Fianna Fáil TD Liam Lawlor.

A long-established firm of housebuilders, Tiernan Homes is run by Joe Tiernan, who once ran for a council seat for Fine Gael. In 1990, the council voted through a material contravention of its county plan to enable permission to be granted to Tiernan Homes for 470 houses and a shopping centre on the Finnstown land, which had been zoned for agriculture. The decision was successfully challenged in the High Court and overturned by An Bord Pleanála. However, further votes on the council in 1991 and 1993 had the effect of rezoning the lands for a second time for residential development. Councillors ignored the objections of hundreds of Lucan residents and the advice of their planning officials. The rezoning acted as a Trojan horse that opened up large areas of south Lucan for development. Liam Lawlor estimates his former lands are now worth £20 million.

At the conclusive vote in February 1993, Dunlop came out of the public gallery into the lobby and gave a group of men lists of how councillors had voted, *The Irish Times* reported at the time. Dunlop refused to say on whose behalf he was acting. 'Although the property manager [Dunlop] seemed well acquainted with several Fine Gael and Fianna Fáil councillors, none of the latter when asked to identify him could recall his name,' the newspaper reported.[20] Inside the council chamber, members voted by 39 votes to 22 to adopt a motion to confirm the rezoning. Seven years later, Dunlop told the tribunal he advised this developer that 'some monies' should be made available for 'legitimate' election expenses. He got two cheques for £15,000 each in 1991 and 1992, and the money was distributed to selected councillors around election time.

Another name on Dunlop's list was Ballycullen Farms, whose owners Christopher and Gerry Jones had been trying for years to get their farm rezoned for housing, without success. Gerry Jones was a businessman, and former member of Fianna Fáil's national executive, who had figured peripherally in the Arms Trial controversy. In the 1980s, the two brothers put forward the argument that their seventy-seven-acre holding at Ballycullen in south Dublin was no longer viable because of trespass and vandalism. Then Dunlop came to their assistance, and collected £17,500. He introduced them to a number of councillors 'with whom they had ongoing difficulties'. Somehow, the difficulties were resolved. The strategy must have worked, as the council voted by 42 votes to one to rezone the lands. As Dunlop noted, twice the number of houses promised were built on the site and none of the facilities mooted ever appeared.

The fallout from Dunlop's revelations was massive and unpredictable. Some politicians tried to hide, others came forward to take the flak and get the matter over and done with. One of the first TDs to 'out' himself as a name on the lobbyists' list was Labour's Pat Rabbitte. Payment 23 on Dunlop's list was an unsolicited cash payment of £3,000 to a politician, which was 'very readily accepted' but subsequently reimbursed by cheque.

Within days, Rabbitte responded to rumours circulating around Leinster House by acknowledging that he got £2,000 from Dunlop in November 1992.[21] Dunlop arrived with the money at Rabbitte's house shortly before the election that year. It would have been 'discourteous' to turn him away immediately, said Rabbitte. The money was returned several weeks later because he and Democratic Left, of which he was then a member, believed a conflict might arise. Rabbitte pointed out that he had voted against the rezoning of Quarryvale. And he had, after all, given the money back. People shouldn't be too 'po-faced' about his acceptance of money from wealthy interests, he argued. But, angered by the coverage he received in the press, the Dáil's most-quoted backbencher came to the conclusion that the media were 'piranhas'.

Embarrassingly for Rabbitte, it appeared he had failed to disclose the contribution to the tribunal, having decided it was an election donation and had nothing to do with the terms of reference of the tribunal. Further, he had told a reporter only a week earlier that he had received no money from Dunlop.

While Rabbitte opposed Quarryvale, he voted in favour of another prominent rezoning promoted by Dunlop. This was for the creation of a science and technology park, later known as Citywest, from private lands near Saggart in west Dublin. For ten years a local farmer had been trying to have the lands rezoned, but without success. In July 1990, he sold them to a company controlled by Davy Hickey Properties.

Eight months later, the overwhelming majority of councillors, including Rabbitte, voted to rezone the lands for commercial development, against the advice of officials.[22] This followed an aggressive campaign for a huge business and technology park on the site, led by Dunlop.

In 1994, Rabbitte received a £5,000 cheque as a political dona-tion from Davy Hickey Properties. A year later, as a junior minister, he awarded the contract for the science and technology park to Citywest, which received State support of £2 million. When the con-troversy broke in May 2000, Rabbitte defended his preference for Citywest (located in his constituency) over other choices. 'There were no strings attached to the donation,' he insisted.[23] Later that month, however, The Irish Times broke the news that Dunlop had a beneficial interest in Citywest, which by then was hugely successful. Rabbitte said this was news to him.

Fine Gael's investigation into Dunlop's revelations was carried out at speed, and it showed. Most of the party's councillors were totally cleared of any suspicion, though in some cases the justification for this was not immediately obvious. But whereas the investigation was content to take some party members at their word, without investi-gating their bank accounts, it left serious questions hanging about others. The result was a feeling of rancour and bitterness within the party, particularly regarding the treatment meted out to the Dún Laoghaire TD, Liam Cosgrave.

Cosgrave told the committee he got £2,000 in cash from Dunlop in 1992/93. But because the committee said it was not given a detailed account of the circumstances in which this and other pay-ments was made, it was 'unable to come to a definitive conclusion' in relation to the payments. Cosgrave expressed shock and incredulity at the report. It was 'the worst thing that ever happened to me'.[24]

The committee came to a similar conclusion in the case of councillor Anne Devitt, who had refused to allow investigators trace the identity of people who paid cheques into an account she maintained for contributions. Devitt was also having a hard time with the tribunal; it was reported that she was reduced to tears in one interview she had with tribunal lawyers.

There was also an inconclusive outcome in the case of north Dublin councillor Cathal Boland, who claimed the tribunal had 'injuncted' him from cooperating with the Fine Gael inquiry. This didn't stop the party selecting Boland as its election candidate in Dublin North.

Tom Morrissey, a former Fine Gael councillor from Castleknock who defected to the PDs, attacked the investigation. Morrissey said he was 'appalled' by the report and described his fifteen-minute hearing as a 'charade'. He pointed out he had opposed Quarryvale and voted against it. Morrissey said every effort he made to get Fine Gael to investigate rezoning decisions in his area during the 1990s was 'met with indifference by the party hierarchy'. He confirmed he had received an unsolicited £2,000 donation during the Dublin West by-election in 1996, but said he had informed the tribunal about this. After Morrissey threatened legal action, the committee issued a 'supplemental report' in which they unreservedly apologised to him for making a 'factually incorrect' allegation.

In early June, Fianna Fáil published the 200-page report of its Standards in Public Life Committee. Liam Lawlor resigned from the party immediately after the report accused him of being uncooperative and contradictory in his replies. But the document raised plenty of questions for other members of the party.

Twelve out of forty-four councillors interviewed acknowledged receiving money from Dunlop or O'Callaghan. G.V. Wright, a colourless backbencher from Dublin North who was chief whip of the Fianna Fáil group on the council in the early 1990s, told the inquiry he received £20,000 from property developers and their agents between 1991 and 1994, with half of it coming from Dunlop. He said the payments, which included £5,000 directly from Owen O'Callaghan, were unsolicited. However, this account was immediately contradicted by

O'Callaghan, who said he contributed the cheque following 'a direct request from G.V. Wright'.

The next-biggest recipient was Seán Gilbride, a little-known councillor from Balbriggan. He got £13,500 from O'Callaghan in 1992, as well as £2,000 from Dunlop and £1,000 from the developer Michael Bailey.

❦

In the aftermath of Dunlop's *volte face*, all sorts of allegations were made against various politicians and business figures. Many of them were genuine and justified; others were not. One of the most farcical episodes arose from the claim by an obscure Cork builder, Denis 'Starry' O'Brien, that he had given the Taoiseach, Bertie Ahern, £50,000 in the carpark of the Burlington Hotel in Dublin. O'Brien alleged he paid the money in 1989 on behalf of Owen O'Callaghan. He claimed to have made a second £50,000 payment to a former Fianna Fáil minister at a hotel in Cork.

A year later, the story was exposed as a sham and O'Brien as a forger, but it had the country on tenterhooks when it first emerged in April 1999. O'Brien was a former chairman of Glen Rovers, the Cork hurling club of Jack Lynch and Christy Ring, and knew Owen O'Callaghan, who raised money for the club.

O'Brien tried to get O'Callaghan involved in buying lands for a development at Carrigaline, but O'Callaghan declined to participate. O'Brien's property dealings remained small, and his financial status precarious. With time, his grudge over the Carrigaline deal grew by leaps and bounds. He contacted Frank Connolly, the *Sunday Business Post* reporter who broke the Gogarty allegations, in March 1999 and later swore a statement for the newspaper. O'Brien then informed the tribunal, which started its own investigation. The tribunal served the *Post* with an order preventing it from publishing details of the story. It also served an order preventing the newspaper from disclosing the existence of the order. For some reason, both orders were lifted in October. The newspaper, unconvinced of the amount of evidence it had, held off publishing the allegations.

O'Brien claimed he had documentary proof to show that £100,000 was withdrawn from an account of the Irish Nationwide

Building Society in Cork. However, in spite of repeated entreaties, he failed to produce these records. The tribunal first approached the building society in May 1999, asking for information about accounts in the name of Denis O'Brien. It gave no reason why it was seeking the information. In February 2000, it asked Irish Nationwide about a specific account number. The society responded that it had no record of any such account.

In April 2000, as Dunlop was giving evidence, it emerged for the first time that tribunal lawyers were seeking information from the chairman of the society, Michael Fingleton.[25] Tribunal lawyers described Fingleton's attitude as 'cavalier in the extreme' after the society failed to produce the documents sought.[26]

The exchange meant nothing to most people. However, Dunlop's revelations over the succeeding days changed everything. Suddenly, even the thinnest allegation took on the ring of truth. The *Post*, afraid it would lose its exclusive to a revelation on the floor of the tribunal, took up the story again. Later that month, it ran a front-page article claiming that two payments of £50,000, separate from any payment known of up to now, were made to (unnamed) Fianna Fáil politicians in 1989. The money was paid by an (unnamed) property developer in return for assistance with the development of a major retail project in Dublin, the report claimed.

The story caused pandemonium. Although neither the developer nor the politicians were named, there was little doubt in political circles as to who was being written about. The political system was already in convulsions after Dunlop's revelations, and now this?

That day, Bertie Ahern attended a football match. 'I took more stick that day from the ordinary public than I did in my twenty-five years of politics,' he told the subsequent libel trial. On Easter Monday, in Arbour Hill for Fianna Fáil's annual commemoration of the Easter Rising, he was forced to deal with the allegation head-on. Exactly eighty-four years to the day after the rebels marched down Sackville Street for Irish freedom, their spiritual successor had to fend off allegations of involvement in squalid corruption.

He did so in the most forceful terms possible. 'I can say I never received one penny from Owen O'Callaghan, for myself, for the party, or for anyone else. I never got it in the Burlington or anywhere else. I never got money anywhere else either from anything to do with Owen O'Callaghan,' Ahern told reporters. He'd never even met O'Callaghan until 1993, and he'd never met O'Brien.

As O'Callaghan blamed the allegation on 'a serious personal, business or political vendetta' against him, a Green party councillor in Cork called for a stay to be put on the developer's plans for a new shopping centre in the city. O'Brien said he was standing over his allegations. He boasted about having the passbook from the building society which he said would prove that he withdrew two sums of £50,000 by cheque. However, once the society got its hands on the passbook, it was quickly unmasked as a forgery. O'Brien had an account in 1989, but it contained just 39p.

It was only after the story broke that details of O'Brien's chequered past started to emerge. A small-time builder from Glanmire, he had been embroiled for decades in litigation with the banks over his house and business interests.[27] In 1989, a High Court judge accused him of forging a letter and said he would have considered having O'Brien charged with perjury but for the absence of a written transcript in the case. In February 1999, one month before he went to the *Sunday Business Post*, Anglo-Irish Bank Corporation took High Court proceedings against O'Brien and his wife Maeve, claiming it was owed £145,000 with interest. The couple said the bank had incorrectly calculated the interest.

After he was publicly identified as the person making the allegations about Ahern, O'Brien played cat and mouse with the media. When reporters called to the house, he denied being Denis O'Brien. Contacted by *The Irish Times*, he said: 'I think you're probably a nice man. I think I'm a fairly decent man. Have a nice day'. Later in the week, he told me: 'You're on to the wrong house, talking to the wrong man. I'm only an ordinary guy'. He refused to confirm or deny he was the person making the allegations.

After some hesitation, Ahern decided to sue. Up to then he had made something of a virtue out of not involving himself in libel cases, but this was one allegation too far. Ahern opted to sue O'Brien alone, but O'Callaghan issued writs against O'Brien and the *Post*.

O'Brien was ripped to shreds when the case was heard in the Dublin Circuit Civil Court in July 2001. The passbook was shown to be a forgery, he was fishing in Waterford on the day he claimed to have bribed Ahern in the carpark of the Burlington Hotel, and a host of witnesses contradicted his claims. Judge John O'Hagan found the allegation 'utterly, completely and absolutely false and untrue' and awarded the maximum £30,000 damages to the Taoiseach. Ahern said he would give the money to charity, but O'Brien declared his inability to pay. With that, one of the most bizarre episodes in the life of the tribunal was laid to rest.

⋙⋘

There is a remarkable formal photograph of Charles Haughey's last Cabinet in 1989. The Taoiseach sits at the centre, his expression inscrutable as ever, his eyes hooded and his hands resting on the table. Standing square behind him are his three prized lieutenants, Pádraig Flynn, Ray Burke and Bertie Ahern.

Viewed from today's perspective, the group portrait prompts thoughts of skittles in a bowling alley. One by one, starting with the man in the centre, the balls have come rolling down, threatening to knock the smiles off the figures in the photograph. Haughey's controversial lifestyle spawned two tribunals and a trail of appalling revelations. Then Burke and Flynn came under scrutiny for the payments they received.

That just leaves Ahern, the man whom Haughey once described as 'the best, the most skilful, the most devious and the most cunning of them all'. The former Fianna Fáil chief whip and Minister for Finance became Taoiseach in 1997, a few months before his Government was prodded into setting up the tribunal. One of the most remarkable aspects of the years following is the ease with which Bertie Ahern has dealt with the various allegations thrown in his direction. He was, after all, familiar with all the main actors in the various dramas. He was the party treasurer for many years. He met Tom Gilmartin on several occasions, and James Gogarty wrote to him personally to outline his gripes. His information-gathering abilities were unrivalled in the political world.

Yet Ahern brushed off the questions that were raised about him with relative ease. Remarkably, he achieved this not by the detail of his answers but, in many cases, by the lack of detail he provided. The snail's pace of the tribunal hearings meant that it never got round to dealing with the matters in which Ahern had an involvement for most of the Coalition Government's lifetime. And yet the questions are still out there.

All the evidence points to Fianna Fáil knowing more than it cares to admit about controversial donations during the period of Ray Burke's downfall. In May 1998, for example, Ahern addressed the Dáil on the issue of the £30,000 Burke got from Rennicks Manufacturing. It was just after Vincent Browne in *Magill* magazine had uncovered the payment. The Taoiseach explained that it wasn't until the previous March that he learned that the £10,000 bank draft sent to Fianna Fáil by Burke came from money donated by Rennicks. 'Up to then, I had been given to understand that the £10,000 received by Fianna Fáil from Ray Burke in 1989 was drawn from a contribution he received from JMSE,' Ahern said. So did the rest of the political establishment.

However, Burke says the £10,000 he contributed to party head-quarters went in with a compliment slip indicating Rennicks as the source. 'I never gave the leader of Fianna Fáil any impression that was otherwise,' he told the tribunal in 1999. Fianna Fáil has con-firmed that the draft was accompanied by a Rennicks compliment slip bearing the names of 'Ray Burke' and 'Robin Rennicks'. Seán Fleming TD, who worked as an accountant with the party in 1989, says he and the general secretary, Pat Farrell verified this fact in July or August 1997. Fleming told the Dáil in July 1998 that the party fundraiser, Des Richardson, was present during some of this meeting.

Fleming said there was 'a long-standing practice and an unwritten rule' that party officials and fundraisers did not discuss the details of individual donations with the party leader or other senior figures. So it seems that no-one told Ahern.

But this became more than a matter of an individual donation after Burke stood up in the Dáil in September 1997 and appeared to indicate that the £10,000 came from JMSE. Burke said the JMSE payment was the largest single contribution he had received. Both statements were false. Fleming sat behind Burke and heard his claims, but did nothing. Pat Farrell didn't hear any alarm bells ringing. If Des Richardson knew about Rennicks, he doesn't appear to have done anything about it. Still no-one told Ahern.

The Taoiseach's ignorance of the situation seems extraordinary, given his mastery of so many other areas of politics. The date of his learning about the Rennicks payment is of no little significance. If it had been revealed in July 1997, or shortly thereafter, Burke would surely have been ejected from the Cabinet. The revelation would probably have brought down the Government, particularly if Burke had been uncovered as a liar after his speech in September 1997. As it was, he resigned in an unrelated controversy in October that year.

The investigation ordered by Ahern in 1997 into the allegations surrounding Burke is also shrouded in mystery. The shallowness of the inquiry and the way he reconciled conflicting pieces of information invite numerous questions.

We know that Ahern had a mosaic of information from different sources. Burke told him that he got a payment in June 1989. Dermot Ahern, the party chief whip who was sent to interview Joseph Murphy junior, told him the money did not come from JMSE. Michael Bailey told him he, Bailey, didn't pay the money. But the Tánaiste, Mary Harney, told him of rumours from within JMSE that the company *had* paid money to Burke.

So who paid Burke the money? Did Bertie Ahern ask Burke who had given him the money and if not, why not? Why didn't he ask Burke about the bizarre fact that the two people who might have given him the money were denying having paid him anything? Why were so many people denying having given money to Burke? Why didn't the Taoiseach talk to the man who was telling the world he had paid money to Burke, James Gogarty? How did this square with the Taoiseach's promise to 'climb every tree in north Dublin' to investigate allegations of planning corruption?

Finally, the circumstances surrounding the money Tom Gilmartin says he gave to Pádraig Flynn beg a number of questions. Gilmartin says he told Bertie Ahern about the £50,000 contribution to Flynn — and which he intended for Fianna Fáil — in a phone call in 1989. Ahern has no recollection of this conversation, but says he 'would not have asked' Gilmartin for a contribution. Here, it appears the Taoiseach is denying something that wasn't alleged; Gilmartin says Ahern asked if he had made a contribution, not whether he *would* make one.[28]

Whatever about this, Gilmartin certainly told the party's national organiser, Seán Sherwin, about the contribution, and stated clearly that it was intended for Fianna Fáil. Many years later, in September 1998, Sherwin had 'a recollection' of this information and told the party's general secretary, Martin Mackin. Ahern was informed. Internal checks revealed that the party did not receive the money Gilmartin claimed to have contributed. The Taoiseach said he was 'shocked that this money could be floating around because it never floated anywhere that I had been over the years'. He referred the matter to the party's lawyers.

At this time, the Taoiseach was in regular contact with Flynn, who was now Ireland's EU Commissioner. However, he never raised the matter of Gilmartin's contribution. In January 1999, Ahern told the Dáil: 'Any of the meetings I had with Commissioner Flynn were on EU business and matters to do with Ireland. I was not in the business of following up … in seeking a reply from Mr Flynn'.

Of the total of £60,000 Burke got from Rennicks and JMSE, only £10,000 made its way to the party. Of the £50,000 Gilmartin says he gave Flynn, nothing was remitted to headquarters. Thus, Fianna Fáil seems to have missed out on £100,000 in contributions it could sorely have done with. Ahern himself knew how badly the party needed money; as treasurer from 1993, he wrestled with its enormous debt and oversaw a major review of the party's finances. That £100,000 would have been invaluable. Yet no-one seems to have told him about the money. Even when the donations by JMSE, Rennicks and Gilmartin became public, Fianna Fáil made no efforts to access these sums.

Ahern's success in reducing the party debt from £3 million to £500,000 in the mid-1990s is extraordinary. Des Richardson coordinated the fundraising from an office in the Berkeley Court Hotel, from where he tapped many of Ireland's leading business figures for money. A series of dinners was held at which wealthy businessmen were given access to Ahern or Albert Reynolds.

Millionaire property developer and Fianna Fáil donor Ken Rohan hosted one of the dinners, according to the *Sunday Tribune*.[29] Rohan was to become the sole beneficiary of one section of the 1994 Finance Act introduced by Ahern. This allowed him to avoid any tax assessment on the value of paintings and furniture at his mansion, Charleville, in Enniskerry, County Dublin. His company, the Rohan Group, owned the furnishings. Remarkably, the section was made retrospective for 12 years. Also that year, Rohan benefited from the inclusion of his site at the edge of the Grand Canal Docks in Dublin in an urban renewal tax incentive zone.

One of the most generous contributors to Fianna Fáil was Owen O'Callaghan, the developer of Quarryvale, who wrote a cheque for £80,000 in 1994. In the same year, on his last day in office as Minister for Finance, Ahern granted urban renewal designation to a site at Golden Island in Athlone, which was partly owned by O'Callaghan.[30] The tribunal has been examining the urban renewal tax incentives granted between 1988 and 1994. It is also investigating an allegation that Department of the Environment files on the scheme went missing after they were requisitioned by another department.

11
What Now?

'I hope you've a happy retirement, like meself.'
> — James Gogarty bids farewell to the tribunal on 5 July 2000
> with some good wishes for the chairman

If the events described in this book were a play, the stage would be filled with a large cast of characters, delivering some of the best lines in Irish political history. The plot would get confusing sometimes, but at the heart of the action would lie a small, very simple prop.

For in the beginning was … the bag. Brown paper, or white plastic. Stuffed with cash. Or sometimes a cheque or bank draft.

Ray Burke's packet was the size of a brick. Frank Dunlop thought too much of his leather briefcase to hand it over with his big donation. George Redmond stashed his cash in a cheap holdall when returning from the Isle of Man.

But every bag must have its bagman (always male). People like Frank Dunlop whose job it was to mind the money for other, richer individuals. Some bagmen, like Dunlop, had the job of dispensing cash, hospitality and favours. Others were more in the business of collecting the dough for favours given.

Next character in the *dramatis personae* of this tale of money and land is the developer. He starts as a rough-hewn builder up from the country, or back from the sites in England. Builds a few houses for someone else, then puts up a few of his own. Next thing, he's buying up land around the periphery of the cities, leasing it back to the farmers, biding his time for the right opportunity.

By the end of our tale, these men are fabulously wealthy. They sit on vast landbanks of priceless building land. They live on stud farms and breed thoroughbred horses and sheep. Helicopters and chauffeur-driven limousines are their preferred modes of transport. Flunkeys attend to their business affairs and their public image.

But agricultural land without zoning, road access or drainage is worth little. Thus, the next character in our tale is the planner, who makes decisions about how cities should grow, what areas should be built upon and what projects should get planning permission. The right zoning or planning permission can increase the value of land ten-fold and more. Planners do a difficult job under difficult circumstances. They have enormous powers but earn a modest wage. Constantly, they rub shoulders with wealthy and powerful developers and landowners.

During the 1980s, the finger of suspicion pointed to a number of planners in Dublin. George Redmond, the most senior figure in the administration of County Dublin until his retirement in 1989, came under investigation. But even a decade later, he was still refusing to accept that the massive payments he received from developers were linked to planning decisions.

Planners only lay the ground rules, and their powers are not unfettered. So the final member of this cast is the politician. Local politicians determine the overall development plan. They can reverse decisions made by the planners. They have exceptional powers to grant planning permissions and rezonings in extraordinary situations. All that is needed is the necessary majority.

Power, money and greed all made their influence felt on the different actors in this cast. Most just got on with their jobs in a system that was already groaning under the strain. Planners tried to create an ordered environment with limited resources, and politicians represented their constituents as best they could.

But somewhere along the way, someone took a wrong turn. Before long, more followed. The money started flowing. Not bribes, mind you, but 'political contributions'. No connection between payments and individual votes or pieces of advice. No strings attached. No favours sought or given. No questions asked. And, certainly, no receipts.

<figure>⋙⋘</figure>

In June 2001, Flood bowed to the inevitable by asking the Government for two extra judges and a substitute to assist him in the tribunal's work. It was a clear sign that the first half of the tribunal's work was nearly done. By then aged 73, Flood could no longer be expected to shoulder the load alone. Acknowledging that the tribunal had yet to begin hearings into rezoning in Dublin — this alone would involve over 200 witnesses — he held out the prospect of further investigations into 'substantive issues not connected with rezoning decisions which also appear to merit public inquiry'. This would take another two years, and probably more.

By the end of 2001, the tribunal had been in existence for over four years. Its investigations into the allegations made by James Gogarty and the Century Radio affair were finally complete. Hearings into the rezoning of Quarryvale, and other controversial decisions taken by politicians in Dublin, were only beginning.

Apart from his intermittent appearances before the tribunal, Ray Burke, once the all-powerful fixer from north Dublin, had completely faded from view. Following his resignation from the Cabinet and the Dáil on 7 October 1997, Burke retreated to Swords.[1] Nursing a deep sense of betrayal, he spent much of his time at home with his wife Ann. A round of golf, a game of cricket and a quiet pint in one of the local pubs were his main pleasures. His henchmen dropped out of regular involvement in local Fianna Fáil politics, and Burke's two daughters ruled themselves out as possible successors.

Though still only in his mid-fifties, Burke showed no inclination to rush out to work. With a healthy bank balance and a ministerial pension, he didn't need to. His financial situation improved further when he sold Briargate and its surrounding grounds for £3 million in 2000. The couple moved to a smaller house near Griffith Avenue.

George Redmond also moved house at this time, a decision forced upon him by an £875,000 settlement with the Revenue Commissioners in February 2000. He sold his five-bedroomed house on the Deerpark Lawn estate in Castleknock and moved to a smaller house nearby.

No such difficulties afflicted the Bailey brothers, for whom the cost of involvement in the tribunal was a mere blip on their balance sheet. In November 2000, Bovale sold 152 acres of housing land at Balgriffin in north Dublin for £45 million. It was easily the biggest land deal that year. Dublin Corporation had rezoned the land in the 1999 development plan.

In 1989, Bovale had paid JMSE just over £2 million for over 700 acres of north Dublin agricultural land. This included 250 acres at Balgriffin. Now 152 of Balgriffin's acres — with zoning — were worth £45 million. In December 2000, the Baileys reached a settlement with the Revenue Commissioners, reported to be for more than £5 million, arising out of the revelations at the tribunal.[2] However, the auditors of Bovale's most recent accounts, for the year 1998, note that proper accounts had not been kept.

Today, the revisionist view of the Baileys is that they are 'more sinned against than sinning'. Journalist Sam Smyth says their 'tormentors' are 'mostly self-styled suburban smart-asses with a third-level education who take on the role of nineteenth-century Englishmen when confronted with a rural-born millionaire builder whose school lunch-box was always bigger than his schoolbag'.[3]

'The Baileys have been treated like suspected war criminals by warriors who seem convinced their mé féin attitude to taxation and planning regulations puts them among Ireland's Most Wanted,' Smyth wrote in the *Sunday Tribune* in August 2000, a few days after newspapers printed photographs of Michael Bailey whooping it up at the Galway Races.

Joseph Murphy senior died in August 2000, less than a year after giving evidence to the tribunal. The following year, JMSE revealed it had experienced 'considerable trading difficulties' arising from its involvement with the tribunal. As a result, it ceased operations in its main area of business — the design, fabrication and erection of steel structures. None of this would have had much impact on the wealth of the Murphy family, which was centred on its interests in Britain.

Wealthy developers and politicians are not the only people to come out of this affair with their finances untouched. The world has once again forgotten the inhabitants of the dismal housing estates that surround Quarryvale shopping centre, whose poverty remains undiminished. Here is how town planner Brendan Bartley described the world of north Clondalkin in his book, *Poor People, Poor Places*, published in 1999:[4]

What one sees if one ventures into north Clondalkin are littered and unkempt approach roads, rundown neighbourhood centres, public buildings which are invariably surrounded by large palisade fencing and shuttering, poorly kept open spaces, a skyline dominated by large electricity pylons and housing estates which face inwards and turn their back on the public areas. The neighbourhood centres which were to be at the heart of each neighbourhood have failed.

In the meantime, the villages of Lucan and Clondalkin, located at the edges of the proposed new town, have become thriving shopping and business centres, while north Clondalkin, which was intended to be at the heart of the new town, is effectively isolated from both villages and is almost devoid of facilities.

Would the money and effort expended on the tribunal not have been better used on tackling these problems? Some have argued that the tribunals are just talking shops, or long-term parking lots for storing allegations until the heat runs out of them. Many people rightly take offence at the enormous cost of such inquiries, which has made millionaires out of the lawyers they employ.

But any assessment of the tribunal has to take into account a secret history which is not reflected in the daily goings-ons at Dublin Castle. For years the tribunal has contended with forces seen and unseen, a concoction of would-be witnesses and their legal, financial and media advisers who have fought tooth-and-nail to prevent or delay the evidence coming out.

Money proved no object for many of the wealthy individuals who have come under scrutiny. Rafts of expensive lawyers and other advisers were drafted in to serve their interests. High Court actions were launched with little concern for the enormous costs involved, even in circumstances when losing seemed certain. Top-dollar public relations consultants were hired, seemingly to sit on their hands all day.

Beyond the arena of the tribunal, Leinster House took a keen but often disguised interest. Politicians kicked to touch when asked awkward questions. The tribunal would deal with the allegations 'in the fullness of time,' they told journalists. In the early days, when Flood and his team were finding their feet, 'sources' in Leinster House pooh-poohed the latest findings from Dublin Castle in off-the-record briefings to political correspondents. Backbenchers were encouraged to scoff at the tribunal or complain about its cost.

On dozens of occasions, the tribunal was forced to traipse through the High Court and the Supreme Court. It won most of the time, but the loss of time and momentum was immense. In a game with no give-and-take, opponents insisted on using every legal route possible to defend their interests.

The response of many parties to requests for information could be described as leisurely at best. Deadlines came and went, correspondence flew back and forth. Information was drip-fed to the tribunal. The documents sought always seemed to arrive at the last minute, just before a witness was due to enter the box. There were endless earnest protestations of how anxious people were to cooperate, but usually the bare minimum was done to avoid being dragged down to the High Court like Liam Lawlor. Records and receipts were frequently non-existent, and memories were blank. On other occasions, vast amounts of documentation were handed in, amounting to tens of thousands of records. Finding a needle in a haystack was judged preferable to having no needle at all.

Following the 'money trail' was crucial to the success of the tribunal; just look for proof of this at the successful investigations into Frank Dunlop's secret bank accounts or Brennan and McGowan's offshore payments to Ray Burke. Yet the cooperation of some accountants and financial institutions was less than whole-hearted. And if the documents weren't shredded or lost there was always the risk of an unfortunate accident, such as the numerous reports of floods and fires.

This was often a dirty war and some individuals have not shied away from using more irregular stratagems. Fear, intimidation, obstruction, time-wasting and spin-doctoring were the weapons of choice of some of those anxious to keep out of the limelight. 'I have heard credible allegations about the intimidation of potential witnesses. Attempts have been made to buy the silence of would-be whistle-blowers. Unsolicited presents have been delivered to people in the hope that they might be persuaded to give evidence critical of others,' I wrote in April 2000.

Media manipulators tried to kill the tribunal before it was born, then strangle it in its infancy. There were anonymous — and false — claims that James Gogarty would not swear a statement, or was too unwell to give evidence. Later, the selective leaking of confidential documents served two purposes: blackening the name of Gogarty and undermining the credibility of the tribunal. Those who grumbled about leaks were often the very ones suspected of releasing the information.

Deflecting the blame and spreading the muck were standard tactics used by so-called 'media managers'. On three separate occasions when leading Fianna Fáil figures were under fire, stories were pre-emptively leaked to the newspapers to divert attention to Fine Gael. Within days of Frank Dunlop's sensational admissions, the lobbyist himself was considered fair game. It was said he only revealed the payments out of a fear of going to jail. He had failed to pass on all of his clients' intended payments to councillors, it was whispered.

Then there are the weasel words or lies used by politicians to buy time in a crisis. Ray Burke's claim to the Dáil, for example, that he had no overseas bank account, or that £30,000 was the largest single contribution he had received. Or Liam Lawlor's denial that he wasn't on Dublin County Council for the rezoning of Quarryvale.

And then, when all else failed, there was the comfort of a poor memory. George Redmond could say where his last £20 went, but he couldn't remember the names of those who paid him tens of thousands of pounds. Tom Brennan kept all his dealings with lawyers in his head, but he couldn't remember a single relevant detail of his land transactions or his dealings with Ray Burke. 'I can't recall' was the tribunal's most common answer.

All of this partly explains why the tribunal is taking so long. Another consideration is the complexity of modern finance, and the elaborate schemes used by wealthy people to salt away their riches. So far, the 'money trail' has led the tribunal to the Channel Islands, the Isle of Man, Liechtenstein, the British Virgin Islands, Switzerland and the Czech Republic, to name but a few destinations of choice for Irish capital. The time, effort and expense involved in getting information from these tax havens has been enormous, and in many cases the tribunal has run into a brick wall of non-cooperation.

But even allowing for these factors, the tribunal has taken an age to conduct its business. An inquiry established to investigate matter of 'urgent public importance' risks becoming a history lesson. Legal challenges, rows, elections and long holidays have led to lengthy delays. Part of the problem lies with an outmoded legal system which is overly focused on the hearing of oral evidence and reacts too slowly to external events. Tribunal investigators lack the element of surprise enjoyed by the gardaí. If people want to hide or destroy crucial evidence, they have plenty of time in which to do it. But equally, the slow pace can be unfair to those under investigation. It can take months and even years for those against whom allegations have been made to get their chance to rebut evidence and give their version of events.

Then there is the question of what happens at the end of it all. The tribunal does not have the power to bring criminal charges; no tribunal chairman can send someone to jail. Tribunal evidence is not admissible in a criminal trial. Flood can refer matters to the Director of Public Prosecutions or the High Court, and charges may result. But such investigations take place *ab initio* — from square one — if they happen at all. It may be years before anyone goes to jail on criminal charges as a result of findings by Flood or any other tribunal.[5]

To secure the cooperation of witnesses, Flood threatened to use the two main weapons in his armoury, namely, the imposition of costs and the threat of High Court proceedings. The latter course resulted in the jailing of Liam Lawlor following contempt proceedings arising from his failure to cooperate with the tribunal. However, Lawlor's case was the exception; many other witnesses escaped with nothing more than a warning from Flood, even when they were caught lying or dragging their feet.

A number of witnesses have been warned that they might have to pay their own legal costs and those of the tribunal's for their appearance at Dublin Castle. Previous tribunals fought shy of imposing costs on witnesses; indeed, the Beef tribunal has turned into something of a cash cow for the legal profession. But unless Flood levies costs on those responsible for delaying the work of the tribunal, the overall bill will be astronomical. Based on the experience of the Beef tribunal, the present tribunal could end up costing more than £40 million.

Even before it has finished, the tribunal can point to a number of successes to offset this cost. A number of prominent figures have made big settlements with the Revenue Commissioners as a result of their entanglement with the tribunal. Before the tribunal came along, many of those under suspicion clearly felt that paying taxes was only for idiots. George Redmond coughed up £780,000 to the taxman after failing to file returns for a decade. Frank Dunlop took seven years to declare much of his income, just before his appearance before the tribunal. As far back as the 1970s, builders Brennan and McGowan were salting away money in offshore accounts, using skilled accountants and tax lawyers to devise ingenious schemes for avoiding tax. The total amount coughed up by Michael Bailey, George Redmond, Frank Dunlop and others as an indirect result of Flood's investigations is already hitting the £10 million mark, and there is more to come.

But if the tribunal is to leave a lasting legacy, it must result in lasting changes in the way we deal with corruption. Time after time, witnesses have repeated the mantra that 'no favours were asked for or given'. Every shilling a politician collects is claimed as being 'for electoral purposes' — even when the money is paid using front companies or assumed names through an offshore bank. Corruption doesn't operate on the basis of 'will we get a receipt?' It is virtually impossible to make direct links between particular payments and specific acts or decisions by politicians.

As Gene Kerrigan and Pat Brennan noted in their book *This Great Little Nation*:

> The evidence suggest that only the stupid or desperate enter into straightforward money-for-favours deals. More often, the money is seen as an entrance fee into a Golden Circle, where people look out for one another. The more clever business interests spread their money around various political parties. Legislation would invariably be kept within the parameters acceptable to the circle. Things undone mattered every bit as much as things done. The beauty of the system was that you could be part of it and quite sincerely believe yourself to have nothing to do with even the slightest whiff of corruption.'

In such a situation, there is a clear duty on politicians and public officials to avoid conflicts of interest, and for legislation to place the onus on them to do so. The corruption laws on the statute book need to be used or, if they are not equal to the task, updated to take account of modern circumstances.

Anti-corruption legislation dates back to Victorian times, and covers the conferring of 'advantage' and the giving and taking of bribes. The Prevention of Corruption Acts passed between 1889 and

1995 are generally considered to be antiquated, though the reason for their failure has more to do with society's refusal to take white-collar crime seriously. From 1974 until the end of 2000, for example, only one case was considered under this legislation — and in that instance, it was a request for extradition from Ireland for someone facing charges under corresponding legislation in the UK.

The Ethics in Public Office Act, 1995 introduced new requirements on politicians to disclose gifts, consultancies and other interests which could affect their conduct as public representatives. But as anyone who looks at the annual registers can testify, these requirements are extremely weak. Most TDs record 'nil' interests and even where information is provided it is so vague as to be useless. For example, a number of deputies record their activity as a 'consultant' but provide no details of the nature or recipients of these services. Even when the information is wrong or incomplete, as in the case of Liam Lawlor, it takes years to correct.

The need for a standing investigative commission on corruption is more apparent than ever. The kind of skill-set needed is a mix of the work currently done by gardaí, journalists, lawyers and accountants. A specialist body would build up a level of expertise to allow for quicker response times when investigations are called. Its staff would be highly qualified and well paid — and even then it would cost less than the tribunals.

Other legislative changes should provide for restrictions on the activities of lobbyists, and reforms to the libel laws to facilitate investigations by journalists in the public interest. This option would also prove a lot cheaper than the tribunals.

So long as windfall profits can be made from the rezoning of land, the incentive to bribe county councillors will remain. As far back as 1974, the Kenny Report on land speculation recommended that owners be forced to sell land at their current (i.e. agricultural) market values. Variants of this proposal have been put forward many times since then, but to no avail. Meanwhile, the cost of housing has spiralled and even a modest house is beyond the means of ordinary couples.

Yet official lethargy and the endless delays of the tribunal are leading to widespread disillusionment. Even Michael Smith, whose reward helped to bring about the tribunal, has succumbed to pessimism. 'I am jaded at the government's continuing failure to expedite appropriate investigations and at the tribunal's own torpor,' he wrote in February 2002.[6]

So far in this tribunal, the middlemen risen from modest circumstances, such as Frank Dunlop and George Redmond, have been the principal 'fall-guys'. Meanwhile, the wealthy businessmen and politicians the tribunal was set up to investigate remained largely untouched.

Only so far, we hope. But until that changes, who can argue with Smith's verdict: 'We were robbed. We're still being robbed.'

Appendix 1

Sizeable, sometimes enormous, sums of money figure regularly in the pages of this book. The amounts seem large today, but at the time they were paid, they were positively staggering. The table below attempts to give some idea of the current value of the main amounts, in punts and Euro.

This isn't easy. The multipliers used by the Central Statistics Office are extremely conservative; for example, they fail to take proper account of the massive increase in land and property prices over the past thirty years. Since many of the characters in this book were active property speculators or developers, it is reasonable to assume that they would have sunk at least some of their gains in land or houses. To take one example: the £15,000 Ray Burke says he paid for his land and house in Swords in the early 1970s is equivalent to about £90,000 in today's terms according to the CSO; yet Burke sold the property in 2000 for £3 million.

For this reason, I have based the calculations in this table on that other staple of deal-making — the pint of plain. Over the period covered by this book, the price of a pint of Guinness has increased from a few shillings to about £2.50 (€3.17). The calculations based on this indicator of inflation are somewhat higher than the CSO equivalents, but a lot less than the windfall profits achievable through land speculation. All figures are approximate.

Year	Donor	Recipient	Amount	Current value (IR£)	Current Value (€)
1972	Dublin Airport Industrial Estates (Brennan and McGowan)	Ray Burke[1]	£15,000	£220,000	€279,000
1972–84	Brennan and McGowan/ UK fundraising	Burke[2]	£150,000	£781,000	€992,000
1975-82	Brennan and McGowan	P.J. Burke (Sales) Ltd	£85,000	£442,000	€561,000
1970s/ 1980s	Tom Brennan	George Redmond[3]	£250,000	about £800,000	€1.01 million

Year	Donor	Recipient	Amount	Current value (IR£)	Current Value (€)
1982	Brennan	Burke	£50,000	£149,000	€189,000
	Canio Ltd (Brennan, McGowan, John Finnegan)	Burke	£60,000	£134,000	€170,000
1985	Canio	Burke	£15,000	£33,000	€42,000
1988/89	Tom Gilmartin	Liam Lawlor	at least £35,000	£65,000	€83,000
1989	JMSE/ James Gogarty	Burke	£30,000	£49,000	€62,000
1988/89	JMSE/Gogarty	Redmond	£25,000	£46,000	€58,000
1989	Tom Gilmartin	Pádraig Flynn/ Fianna Fáil	£50,000	£82,000	€104,000
1989	Rennicks /Fitzwilton	Burke	£30,000	£49,000	€62,000
	Oliver Barry/ Century Radio	Burke	£35,000	£58,000	€74,000
1991	Frank Dunlop	Lawlor	£48,500	£80,000	€102,000
1991	National Toll Roads	Lawlor	£74,000	£122,000	€155,000

Notes:
1. Burke, Brennan and McGowan say the sum was never paid over.
2. Brennan and McGowan say they raised this amount on behalf of Burke in the UK. However, Burke denies having received money from this source.
3. £250,000 is Redmond's estimate of what he received. Brennan says he gave the official about £50,000.

Appendix 2

Definition of Corruption used by the Tribunal
'The destroying, hindering or perverting of the integrity or fidelity of a person in the discharge of his duty, or the abuse of influence or power or duty by any person, or to bribe, or to induce another to act dishonestly or unfaithfully, or an attempt to do the same, or circumstances of control, influence or involvement with such person to the extent that it gives rise to a reasonable inference of unequal access, or favouritism, or a set of circumstances detrimental to his duties.'

Appendix 3

Terms of Reference of Tribunal of Inquiry into Certain Planning Matters and Payments
(Appointed by Instrument of The Minister for the Environment and Local Government dated the 4th day of November 1997 and as amended by Instrument dated the 15th day of July 1998)
That Dáil Éireann resolves
A. That it is expedient that a Tribunal be established under the Tribunals of Inquiry (Evidence) Act, 1921, as adapted by or under subsequent enactments and the Tribunals of Inquiry (Evidence) (Amendment) Act, 1979, to inquire urgently into and report to the Clerk of the Dáil and make such findings and recommendations as it sees fit, in relation to the following definite matters of urgent public importance:
1. The identification of the lands stated to be 726 acres in extent, referred to in the letter dated 8th June, 1989 from Mr. Michael Bailey to Mr. James Gogarty (reproduced in the schedule herewith) and the establishment of the beneficial ownership of the lands at that date and changes in the beneficial ownership of the lands since the 8th June, 1989 prior to their development;

2. The planning history of the lands including:-
   (a) their planning status in the Development Plan of the Dublin local authorities current at the 8th June, 1989;
   (b) the position with regard to the servicing of the lands for development as at the 8th June, 1989;
   (c) changes made or proposed to be made to the 8th June, 1989 planning status of the lands by way of:-
       (i) proposals put forward by Dublin local authority officials pursuant to the review of Development Plans or otherwise;
       (ii) motions by elected members of the Dublin local authorities proposing re-zoning;
       (iii) applications for planning permission (including any involving a material contravention of the Development Plan);

3. Whether the lands referred to in the letter dated 8th June, 1989 were the subject of the following:-
   (a) Re-zoning resolutions;
   (b) Resolutions for material contravention of the relevant Development Plans;
   (c) Applications for special tax designations status pursuant to the Finance Acts;
   (d) Applications for planning permission;
   (e) Changes made or requested to be made with regard to the servicing of the lands for development;
   (f) Applications for the granting of building by-law approval in respect of buildings constructed on the lands;
   (g) Applications for fire safety certificates;
       on or after the 20th day of June 1985.
   And
       (i) to ascertain the identity of any persons or companies (and if companies, the identity of the beneficial owners of such companies) who had a material interest in the said lands or who had a material involvement in the matters aforesaid;
       (ii) to ascertain the identity of any members of the Oireachtas, past or present, and/or members of the relevant local authorities who were involved directly or indirectly in any of the foregoing matters whether by the making of representations to a planning authority or to any person in the authority in a position to make relevant decisions or by the proposing of or by voting in favour or against or by abstaining from any such resolutions or by absenting themselves when such votes were taken or by attempting to influence

in any manner whatsoever the outcome of any such applications, or who received payments from any of the persons
or companies referred to at (i) above;

(iii) to ascertain the identity of all public officials who considered, made recommendations or decisions on any such
matters and to report on such consider-ations, recommendations and/or decisions;

(iv) to ascertain and report on the outcome of all such applications, resolutions and votes in relation to such applications
in the relevant local authority.

4. (a) The identity of all recipients of payments made to political
parties or members of either House of the Oireachtas, past or
present, or members or officials of a Dublin local authority or
other public official by Mr. Gogarty or Mr. Bailey or a connected
person or company within the meaning of the Ethics in Public
Office Act, 1995, from 20th June 1985 to date, and the circumstances, considerations and motives relative to any such payment;

(b) whether any of the persons referred to at sub-paragraphs 3(ii)
and 3(iii) above were influenced directly or indirectly by the
offer or receipt of any such payments or benefits.

5. In the event that the Tribunal in the course of its inquiries is made
aware of any acts associated with the planning process which may in
its opinion amount to corruption, or which involve attempts to
influence by threats or deception or inducement or otherwise to
compromise the disinterested performance of public duties, it shall
report on such acts and should in particular make recommendations
as to the effectiveness and improvement of existing legislation
governing corruption in the light of its inquiries.

6. And the Tribunal be requested to make recommendations in relation
to such amendments to Planning, Local Government, Ethics in
Public Office and any other relevant legislation as the Tribunal con-
siders appropriate having regard to its findings.

"Payment" includes money and any benefit in kind and the payment
to any person includes a payment to a connected person within the
meaning of the Ethics in Public Office Act, 1995.

B. And that the Tribunal be requested to conduct its inquiries in the
following manner, to the extent that it may do so consistent with the
provisions of the Tribunals of Inquiry (Evidence) Acts, 1921 and 1979:

(i) to carry out such preliminary investigations in private as it thinks
fit using all the powers conferred on it under the Acts, in order to
determine whether sufficient evidence exists in relation to any of

the matters referred to above to warrant proceeding to a full public inquiry in relation to such matters,

(ii)   to inquire fully into all matters referred to above in relation to which such evidence may be found to exist, dealing in the first instance with the acknowledged monetary donation debated in Dáil Éireann on the 10th September, 1997 Dáil Debates Columns 616-638 and to report to the Clerk of the Dáil thereupon,

(iii) to seek discovery of all relevant documents, files and papers in the possession, power or procurement of said Mr. Michael Bailey, Mr. James Gogarty and Donnelly Neary and Donnelly Solicitors,

(iv)   in relation to any matters where the Tribunal finds that there is insufficient evidence to warrant proceeding to a full public inquiry, to report that fact to the Clerk of the Dáil and to report in such a manner as the Tribunal thinks appropriate on the steps taken by the Tribunal to determine what evidence, if any, existed and the Clerk of the Dáil shall thereupon communicate the Tribunal's report in full to the Dáil,

(v)   to report on an interim basis not later than one month from the date of establishment of the Tribunal or the tenth day of any oral hearing, whichever shall first occur, to the Clerk of the Dáil on the following matters:

the number of parties then represented before the Tribunal;

the progress which has been made in the hearing and the work of the Tribunal;

the likely duration (so far as that may be capable of being estimated at that time) of the Tribunal proceedings;

any other matters which the Tribunal believes should be drawn to the attention of the Clerk of the Dáil at that stage (including any matter relating to the terms of reference).

C. And that the person or persons selected to conduct the Inquiry should be informed that it is the desire of the House that –

(a)   the Inquiry be completed in as economical a manner as possible and at the earliest date consistent with a fair examination of the matters referred to it, and, in respect to the matters referred to in paragraphs 1 to 4 above, if possible, not later than the 31st December, 1997, and

(b)   all costs incurred by reason of the failure of individuals to co-operate fully and expeditiously with the Inquiry should, so far as is consistent with the interests of justice, be borne by those individuals.

D. And that the Clerk of the Dáil shall on receipt of any Report from the Tribunal arrange to have it laid before both Houses of the Oireachtas immediately on its receipt.

E. The Tribunal shall, in addition to the matters referred to in paragraphs A(1) to A(5) hereof, inquire urgently into and report to the Clerk of the Dáil and make such findings and recommendations as it sees fit, in relation to the following definite matters of urgent public importance:

1. Whether any substantial payments were made or benefits provided, directly or indirectly, to Mr. Raphael Burke which may, in the opinion of the Sole Member of the Tribunal, amount to corruption or involve attempts to influence or compromise the disinterested performance of public duties or were made or provided in circumstances which may give rise to a reasonable inference that the motive for making or receiving such payments was improperly connected with any public office or position held by Mr. Raphael Burke, whether as Minister, Minister of State, or elected representative;

2. Whether, in return for or in connection with such payments or benefits, Mr. Raphael Burke did any act or made any decision while holding any such public office or position which was intended to confer any benefit on any person or entity making a payment or providing a benefit referred to in paragraph 1 above, or any other person or entity, or procured or directed any other person to do such an act or make such a decision.

And that the Tribunal be requested to conduct its Inquiries in the following manner to the extent that it may do so consistent with the provisions of the Tribunals of Inquiry (Evidence) Acts 1921 to 1998:-

(i) To carry out such preliminary investigations in private as it thinks fit (using all the powers conferred on it under the Acts), in order to determine whether sufficient evidence exists in relation to any of the matters referred to in paragraphs E1 and E2 above to warrant proceeding to a full public inquiry in relation to such matters;

(ii) To inquire fully into all matters referred to in paragraphs E1 and E2 in relation to which such evidence may be found to exist;

(iii) In relation to any matters where the Tribunal finds that there is insufficient evidence to warrant proceeding to a full public inquiry, to report that fact to the Clerk of the Dáil and to Report in such a manner as the Tribunal thinks appropriate on the steps taken by the Tribunal to determine what evidence, if any, existed and the Clerk of the Dáil shall thereupon communicate the Tribunal's report in full to the Dáil;

(iv) To report on an interim basis to the Clerk of the Dáil on the following matters:-

the number of parties then represented before the Tribunal;

the progress which has been made in the hearing and the work of the Tribunal;

the likely duration (so far as that may be capable of being estimated at that time) of the Tribunal proceedings;

any other matters which the Tribunal believes should be drawn to the attention of the Clerk of the Dáil at that stage (including any matter relating to the terms of reference);

and to furnish such further interim reports as the Tribunal may consider necessary.

F   And that the Sole Member of the Tribunal should be informed that it is the desire of the House that:-

(a)   The inquiry into the matters referred to in paragraph E hereof be completed in as economical a manner as possible and at the earlier (*sic*) date consistent with a fair examination of the said matters, and

(b)   All costs incurred by reason of the failure of individuals to co-operate fully and expeditiously with the Inquiry should, so far as is consistent with the interests of justice, be borne by those individuals.

G   And that the Clerk of the Dáil shall on receipt of any Report from the Tribunal arrange to have it laid before both Houses of the Oireachtas immediately on its receipt.

SCHEDULE

Kilinamonan House,
The Ward,
Co. Dublin.
8th June, 1989.

Dear Mr. Gogarty,

PROPOSALS FOR DISCUSSION

Re: Your lands at Finglas, Ballymun, Donabate, Balgriffin and Portmarnock, Co. Dublin.

I refer to our many discussions regarding your following six parcels of land:-
   Lot 1: 100 acres (approx) at North Road, Finglas, including "Barrett's Land".

Lot 2: 12 acres (approx) at Jamestown Road, Finglas.

Lot 3: 100 acres (approx) at Poppintree, Ballymun.

Lot 4: 255 acres (approx) at Donabate (Turvey House and Beaverton House).

Lot 5: 250 acres (approx) at Balgriffin.

Lot 6: 9 acres (approx) at Portmarnock.

I submit the following proposals for your consideration:-

PROPOSAL NO. 1 — Purchase Proposal

Lots 1, 2 and 3 Purchase Price £4,000 per acre

10% deposit payable on the signing of the contract

Completion 1 year from date of contract.

Lot 4 Purchase Price IR£1 Million

Deposit 10% on contract

Completion 2 years from date of contract.

Lot 5 Purchase Price IR £750,000

Deposit 10% on contract

Completion 3 years from date of contract.

Lot 6: Option to be granted for nominal consideration (£100.00) for a period of 2 years at a purchase price of £30,000.00 per acre.

PROPOSAL NO. 2 — Participation Proposal

As an alternative to the outright purchase proposal above I am prepared to deal with Lots 1-5 (inclusive) above on the basis that I would be given a 50% share in the ownership of the said lands in exchange for procuring Planning Permission and Building Bye Law Approval. The time span which I would require to be allowed to obtain the Permissions and Approval and my anticipated financial expenditure (apart from my time input) in respect of the different lots would be as follows:-

Lots 1, 2 and 3

A period of 2 years within which to procure a buildable Planning Permission and Building Bye Laws Approval for mixed development including housing, industrial and commercial.

My financial expenditure up to a figure of £150,000 (to include Architect's fees, Consulting Engineer's fees, Planning and Bye Law charges etc.).

Lots 4 and 5

Time requirement — 3 years.

Financial Expenditure — up to £150,000

In considering the above proposals the following points of information should be borne in mind by all parties:-

1. From the point of view of obtaining Planning Permission the entire lands (1-6 inclusive) have the following shortcomings:-
   NO zoning for development purposes
   NO services.
   NO proposal in current draft development plans (City and County) for the zoning of the lands or any part thereof for development purposes.

2. We face a very severe uphill battle to arrange for the availability of services and for the ultimate procurement of Planning Permission.

3. The steps to be taken on the way to procuring a buildable Planning Permission and Building Bye Laws Approval are notoriously difficult, time consuming and expensive. Material Contravention Orders must be obtained and this involves their procurement of a majority vote at 2 full Council Meetings at which 78 Council Members must be present and it also involves satisfactory compliance with extensive requirements and pre-conditions of the Planning Authority and the inevitable dealing with protracted Appeals to An Bord Pleanala.

4. It is essential that the Planning Application should be brought in the name of an active house building company which enjoys good standing and good working relationship with the Planners and the Council Members and in this regard I confirm that in the event of our reaching agreement regarding the within proposals that all Planning Applications would be made by one of my Companies which meets the said requirements.

5. In the case of all of the lands the applications will be highly sensitive and controversial and we can realistically expect strenuous opposition from private, political and planning sectors. One of my active companies will have to take the limelight in such applications and withstand the objections and protests which will inevitably confront it. Apart from the anticipated financial expenditure as outlined above it should be borne in mind that I will personally have to give extensively of my time and efforts over the entire period of the applications including the necessary preliminary negotiations in regard to services and zoning. It must be borne in mind that I will have to abandon other projects which would be open to myself and my companies in order to give proper attention to this project. If I am successful in changing your lands from their present status of agricultural lands with very limited potential even for agricultural use into highly valuable building lands I would have to be rewarded with a minimum 50% stake in the ownership of the lands. Our advisors would have to work out the details as to how this can be effected in the most tax efficient manner.

I look forward to hearing from you in relation to the above proposals. In the case of the first proposal which relates to the outright purchase of the lands (excluding Lot 6) I would not be adverse to a proposal which would involve the vendors retaining a participation stake of up to 20% in the purchasing company if you felt that an ongoing interest in the future development of the lands would be more acceptable to the present owners.

Yours sincerely,

_____

MICHAEL BAILEY,

Mr. Jim Gogarty,
Clontarf,
Dublin 3

References

Epigraph
1. From Trollope's correspondence, quoted in introduction by Frank Kermode to *The Way We Live Now* (Penguin: London, 1994. First published 1875)

Introduction (pages 1–7)
1. Lee, *Ireland 1912-1985: Politics and Society*, p. 161
2. *The Irish Times*, 29 July 1995
3. Lee, *Ireland*, p. 161
4. Lee, *Ireland*, p. 273
5. *Irish Independent*, 12 October 1945
6. Brennan/Kerrigan, *This Great Little Nation*, p. 170

Chapter 1 With a Little Help from My Friends (pages 8–24)
1. Tribunal evidence, 25 May 2001
2. *Sunday Business Post*, September 1997
3. Tribunal evidence, 15 May 2001
4. Tribunal evidence, 4 October 2001
5. Michael O'Hanrahan evidence, 24 May 2001
6. *The Irish Times*, 3 March 1973
7. Tribunal evidence, 10 April 2000
8. Jim Geraghty evidence, 22 February 2001
9. Ray Burke evidence, 22 February 2001

Chapter 2 Grumpy Old Men (pages 25–50)
1. Brian Leonard SC, for Gerry Downes, a former accountant with the Murphy Group, 12 April 1999
2. Frank Reynolds evidence, 25 January 2000
3. Batt O'Shea evidence, 10 November 1999
4. *Sunday Times*, 14 March 1999
5. *The Irish Times*, 19 August 2000
6. Joseph Murphy junior evidence, 29 November 1999
7. Frank Reynolds evidence, 1 February 2000
8. Batt O'Shea evidence, 10 November 1999
9. Batt O'Shea evidence, 10 November 1999
10. James Gogarty evidence, 12 January 1999

11. Ironically, as managing director of JMSE in 1980, Gogarty cancelled a non-contributory pension scheme for employees.
12. Evidence of Brendan Devine, accountant to JMSE, 10 May 1999. Devine's involvement with the company ceased in June 1988, a year before the Burke payment.
13. Joseph Murphy senior evidence, 21 October 1999
14. *The Irish Times*, 28 October 1999
15. Batt O'Shea evidence, 10 November 1999
16. Conroy affidavit, read at tribunal, 23 September 1999
17. Evidence of Marcus Sweeney, former managing director of JMSE, 6 July 1999
18. Evidence of Brendan Devine, accountant to JMSE, 10 May 1999
19. James Gogarty evidence, 14 January 1999
20. Joseph Murphy junior evidence, 29 November 1999
21. *The Irish Times*, 23 April 1999
22. Tribunal evidence, 23 September 1999
23. Joseph Murphy senior evidence, 26 October 1999
24. Tribunal evidence, 5 March 1999
25. *The Irish Times*, 30 July 1999
26. Michael Bailey evidence, 21 July 1999
27. Tribunal evidence, 23 March 1999
28. Tribunal evidence, 20 July 1999
29. Tribunal evidence, 20 July 1999
30. James Gogarty evidence, 19 January 1999
31. James Gogarty evidence, 19 January 1999
32. Michael Bailey evidence, 21 July 1999
33. Tribunal evidence, 15 April 1999
34. *The Irish Times*, 11 May 1999
35. James Gogarty evidence, 26 January 1999
36. Garrett Cooney SC at the tribunal, 3 March 1999
37. Michael Bailey evidence, 21 July 1999
38. James Gogarty evidence, 20 January 1999
39. Michael Bailey evidence, 22 July 1999
40. Michael Bailey evidence, 22 July 1999
41. Evidence of Christopher Oakley, solicitor to Joseph Murphy senior, to tribunal, 20 January 2000
42. Roger Copsey evidence, 17 December 1999
43. *The Irish Times*, 30 June 1999
44. Tribunal evidence, 28 April 1999
45. James Gogarty evidence, 12 April 1999
46. Garrett Cooney SC at the tribunal, 3 March 1999
47. James Gogarty evidence, 2 February 1999

48. According to the notes made by Gogarty's solicitor, Michael Hegarty, at the time and read at the tribunal, 2 February 1999
49. *The Irish Times*, 6 July 2000

Chapter 3 The Life and Times of JR (pages 51–80)
1. Tribunal evidence, 19 July 1999
2. Asked later (*The Irish Times*, 24 February 1999) why he made this claim, Redmond said it was because the account was closed by then.
3. Statement of George Redmond, 18 March 1999
4. 'Everybody knew George as J.R., after J.R. Ewing in *Dallas*,' former Fine Gael county councillor Jim Fay told *The Irish Times* (3 April 1999), 'Southfork and all that.'
5. *Sunday Times*, 21 February 1999
6. Statement of George Redmond
7. Redmond told the tribunal he paid for both the house and the extension.
8. *The Irish Times*, 13 May 2000
9. McDonald, *The Destruction of Dublin*, p. 141
10. Batt O'Shea evidence, 10 November 1999
11. George Redmond evidence, 12 May 2000
12. *The Irish Times*, 11 April 2000
13. *The Irish Times*, 16 March 1999
14. George Redmond evidence, 11 May 2000
15. Batt O'Shea evidence, 10 November 1999
16. George Redmond evidence, 30 October 1999
17. *Irish Examiner*, 27 May 2000
18. *The Irish Times*, 17 May 2000
19. Statement of George Redmond
20. James Gogarty evidence, 4 February 1999
21. Tribunal evidence, 4 February 1999
22. Evidence of Sinéad Collins, Fingal County Council, 19 May 1999
23. *The Irish Times*, 24 February 1999
24. Tribunal evidence, 5 March 1999
25. Tribunal evidence, 19 April 1999
26. George Redmond evidence, 20 September 1999
27. George Redmond evidence, 20 September 1999
28. George Redmond evidence, 23 September 1999
29. *The Irish Times*, 19 November 1999
30. *The Irish Times*, 22 September 1999
31. A further five accounts were later uncovered.
32. Historical details taken from 'The Peninsula of Portrane' by Thomas King Moylan, as read to the Old Dublin Society on 15 December 1947, and contained in the *Dublin Historical Record*.

33. *Sunday Business Post*, 20 February 2000
34. *The Irish Times*, 15 July 1987
35. *Sunday Independent*, 21 February 1999
36. Jim Fay, *The Irish Times*, 3 April 1999
37. *Irish Examiner*, 27 May 2000
38. *Sunday Business Post*, 21 May 2000
39. *Sunday Tribune*, 21 May 2000
40. Pat Rabbitte, Dáil record, 21 February 1990
41. *The Irish Times*, 17 May 2000
42. *Sunday Business Post*, 14 May 2000
43. Paisley Park's nominee directors hailed from the Isle of Man, Panama and the British Virgin Islands.

Chapter 4 Corruption Denied (pages 81–102)

1. The *Sunday Times* identified the pair against their wishes in January 1998.
2. Public statement by John Gallagher SC, for the tribunal, 14 February 2000
3. *The Irish Times*, 8 October 1997
4. *The Irish Times*, 20 April 2000
5. The British parliament passed a further Prevention of Corruption Act in 1916 but this deals solely with bribery in relation to public contracts.
6. *The Irish Times*, 10 May 2000
7. *The Irish Times*, 24 March 1999
8. Tommy Broughan evidence, 11 May 1999
9. James Gogarty evidence, 18 February 1999
10. Ray Burke told the tribunal that the Taoiseach informed him of this in June 1997 (*The Irish Times*, 9 July 1999).
11. John Bruton, in *The Irish Times*, 20 April 2000
12. A year later, in June 1998, Harney was to tell the Dáil: 'If what is now known in relation to Mr Burke was known to me last June, I would not have been willing to participate in Government with him.'
13. Ray Burke evidence, 5 July 2000
14. Tribunal evidence, 7 May 1999
15. Much later, it emerged that this £10,000 came from a contribution by Rennicks Manufacturing, not JMSE.
16. Dáil record, 28 May 1998
17. Joseph Murphy junior evidence, 6 December 1999
18. Roger Copsey evidence, 17 December 1999
19. Ray Burke evidence, 8 July 1999
20. *The Irish Times*, 29 March 1999

21. Tribunal evidence, 6 May 1999
22. Joseph Murphy junior evidence, 30 November 1999
23. Joseph Murphy junior evidence, 6 December 1999
24. *The Irish Times*, 6 May 1999
25. James Gogarty evidence, 14 April 1999
26. Ray Burke evidence, 4 July 2000
27. Joseph Murphy junior evidence, 6 December 1999
28. John Ryan evidence, 4 May 1999

Chapter 5 The Great Unravelling (pages 103–39)

1. *Sunday Independent*, 15 November 1998
2. *The Irish Times*, 5 November 1998
3. Letter from Mr Justice Flood to newspaper editors, 10 December 1998
4. *The Irish Times*, 29 December 1998
5. Gogarty evidence, 14 January 1999
6. Gogarty evidence, 17 February 1999
7. Tribunal evidence, 8 February 1999
8. Tribunal evidence, 27 April 1999
9. Gogarty evidence, 4 February 1999
10. Allen delivered some of the more memorable lines of the tribunal, but not always intentionally. Never a man to use one word where ten would fit, he frequently tied himself up in verbal knots. Take the following exchanges from 4 February 1999:
    Mr Justice Flood: Could we get on with your application at the moment?
    Mr Allen: The point I wanted to make … sir, in fact — you have — I can, I can tell you sir, that you have, that you have so … I am actually struggling for the word … you have made my position so difficult by the manner in which you have treated me that I have lost the point.
    Allen returned to the point later when he had sufficiently regained his composure.
11. Michael Cush SC, for JMSE, at the tribunal, 25 January 1999
12. Tribunal evidence, 2 March 1999
13. Tribunal evidence, 24 February 1999
14. Tribunal evidence, 22 March 1999
15. *The Irish Times*, 24 March 1999
16. Tribunal evidence, 25 March 1999
17. *The Irish Times*, 26 March 1999. Allen apologised for the remark the following day.
18. Tribunal evidence, 23 March 1999
19. *The Irish Times*, 29 April 1999
20. *The Irish Times*, 14 May 1999

21. Gay Grehan evidence, 20 May 1999
22. Gay Grehan evidence, 2 November 1999
23. Gay Grehan evidence, 3 November 1999
24. Gay Grehan evidence, 4 November 1999
25. *The Irish Times*, 15 February 1999
26. Ray Burke evidence, 7 July 1999
27. Ray Burke evidence, 1 March 2001
28. Ray Burke evidence, 8 July 1999
29. Ray Burke evidence, 12 July 1999
30. Colm Allen SC, 24 March 1999
31. Evidence of Máire-Anne Howard, 6 March 2000
32. Tribunal evidence, 6 April 2000
33. Colm Allen SC, 25 March 1999
34. *The Irish Times*, 23 July 1999
35. Caroline Bailey evidence, 22 November 1999
36. *The Irish Times*, 8 February 2000
37. Christopher Doyle evidence, 6 June 2000
38. *The Irish Times*, 30 May 2000
39. *The Irish Times*, 31 May 2000
40. *The Irish Times*, 22 May 1999
41. Tribunal evidence, 24 September 1999
42. *The Irish Times*, 3 June 2000
43. Tribunal evidence, 21 October 1999
44. Tribunal evidence, 22 October 1999
45. Roger Copsey evidence, 13 December 1999
46. Tim O'Keeffe evidence, 20 December 1999
47. Roger Copsey evidence, 15 December 1999
48. *The Irish Times*, 7 December 1999
49. *The Irish Times*, 22 November 1999

Chapter 6 The Art of Hiding in Full View (pp 140–68)

1. Interview, *Village Word*, May 2001
2. *The Irish Times*, 30 September 1982
3. Liam Lawlor affidavit, *Flood v Lawlor*, sworn 17 July 2001, p. 29
4. *The Irish Times*, 11 October 2000
5. *Sunday Tribune*, 14 May 2000
6. *The Irish Times*, 21 April 2000
7. *The Irish Times*, 23 December 2000
8. *The Irish Times*, 22 December 2000
9. *The Irish Times*, 19 December 2000
10. *The Irish Times*, 19 December 2000
11. John Gallagher SC, 10 October 2000

12. *The Irish Times*, 3 July 1999
13. *The Irish Times*, 25 October 2000
14. *The Irish Times*, 6 October 2000
15. Tribunal evidence, 10 October 2000
16. John Gallagher SC, 10 October 2000
17. *The Irish Times*, 12 October, 2000
18. *The Irish Times*, 25 October 2000
19. *The Irish Times*, 8 November 2000
20. Interview, *Village Word*, May 2001

Chapter 7 Radio Fianna Fáil (pp 169–205)

1. Oliver Barry evidence, 10 February 2000
2. The promoting company was Century Communications Ltd, but the venture was commonly known as Century Radio.
3. *The Irish Times*, 2 December 2000
4. John Mulhern evidence, 10 November 2000
5. Stafford claims he introduced Mulhern to the project over dinner one night.
6. John Mulhern evidence, 10 November 2000
7. Evidence of Michael Grant, Department of Communications, 12 October 2000
8. Burke evidence, 6 March 2001
9. Gay Byrne evidence, 6 October 2000
10. Evidence of Séamus Henchy, IRTC chairman, 21 November 2000
11. Donal O'Sullivan evidence, 15 November 2000
12. Burke evidence, 7 March 2001
13. *The Irish Times*, 22 September 2000
14. Paschal Taggart evidence, 22 November 2000
15. Evidence of Seán Connolly, secretary, IRTC, 20 November 2000
16. Dermot Desmond evidence, 18 October 2000
17. Evidence of Fred O'Donovan, IRTC member, 15 November 2000
18. Evidence of Gerry O'Brien, finance director, RTÉ, 31 October 2000
19. *The Irish Times*, 21 July 2000
20. Evidence of Vincent Finn, director general RTÉ, 8 November 2000
21. Burke evidence, 8 March 2001
22. *The Irish Times*, 21 July 2000
23. Apart from the Burke payment, Barry made contributions totalling about £12,000 to other politicians, most of them in Fianna Fáil, during the 1989 election campaign.
24. Burke evidence, 28 February 2001
25. Oliver Barry evidence, 4 December 2000

26. John Mulhern evidence, 10 November 2000
27. James Stafford evidence, 24 January 2001
28. Peter Branagan evidence, 14 November 2000
29. *The Irish Times*, 27 July 2000
30. Evidence of Michael Laffan, chief executive, Century Radio, 24 November 2000
31. *The Irish Times*, 28 September 2000
32. Ray Hills evidence, 3 October 2000
33. *The Irish Times*, 27 July 2000
34. Evidence of Joseph Maguire, Bank of Ireland official, 6 October 2000
35. *The Irish Times*, 26 July 2000
36. Dermot Desmond evidence, 18 October 2000
37. Barry also lent Mara £2,000 when he had financial difficulties in the 1980s.
38. Both Desmond and Mara hail from Dublin's northside but, as commentators pointed out, they now live south of the Liffey.
39. Dermot Desmond evidence, 18 October 2000
40. *The Irish Times*, 8 November 2000
41. Evidence of Éamonn Gallagher, Bank of Ireland official, 12 October 2000
42. Evidence of Bernard McDonagh, secretary general, Department of Communications, 25 October 2000
43. *The Irish Times*, 30 May 1990
44. Horgan, *Irish Media: A Critical History since 1922*, p. 154
45. *The Irish Times*, 28 July 2000
46. Evidence of Tom Kennington, Department of Communications, 26 October 2000
47. *The Irish Times*, 29 September 2000
48. Evidence of Patrick Taylor, finance director, Capital Radio, 1 December 2000

Chapter 8 'A Failure of Recollection' (pages 206–31)
1. Tribunal evidence, 22 March 2001
2. Burke evidence, 28 February 2001
3. Simon Howard evidence, 17 May 2001
4. Oliver Conlon evidence, 21 February 2001
5. Burke evidence, 22 February 2001
6. Tribunal evidence, 22 June 2001

Chapter 9 Some Kind of Homecoming (pages 232–44)
1. *Sunday Independent*, 20 December 1998
2. *The Irish Times*, 25 October 2000

3. Memoir of Vera Comiskey, granddaughter of Walter and Julia Murray, proprietors of The Deadman's Pub, Palmerstown in the first half of the twentieth century. Communicated to the author by Catherine Comiskey, May 2000.

4. *The Irish Times*, 19 November 1992

5. The Liffey Valley Centre, which today stands on the Quarryvale site, advertises itself as being 'where the M50 (C-ring road around Dublin) meets the N4 (to Galway)'.

6. *Sunday Independent*, 23 April 2000

7. *The Irish Times*, 25 October 2000

8. *Sunday Business Post*, 25 April 2000

9. Redmond evidence, 18 May 2000

10. Lawlor told the Dáil on 27 January 1999 that he never arranged this meeting, nor was he in attendance.

11. Section 32 of the 1976 Local Government (Planning and Development) Act requires a councillor to declare any profession, business or occupation in which he is engaged 'which relates to dealing in or developing land'.

12. *The Irish Times*, 5 October 1998

13. *The Sligo Champion*, as reported in *The Irish Times*, 28 January 1999

14. *The Irish Times*, 30 December 1999

15. *The Irish Times*, 25 June 1991

16. *Sunday Business Post*, 1 November 1998

17. *The Irish Times*, 18 January 1999

18. *Sunday Independent*, 20 December 1998

19. Months earlier, 'sources close to the former minister' had used a remarkably similar formulation, telling the *Sunday Business Post* that Flynn 'never asked for nor received money from anyone at any time related to planning'.

20. *Irish Independent*, 23 January 1999

21. *The Irish Times*, 25 January 1999

22. *The Irish Times*, 27 January 1999

Chapter 10 Enter Frank Dunlop (pages 245–75)

1. *Sunday Tribune*, 21 May 2000

2. *Sunday Business Post*, 14 May 2000

3. *The Irish Times*, 25 April 2000

4. *The Irish Times*, 3 May 1991

5. *Business & Finance*, 4 May 2000

6. Frank Dunlop evidence, 18 April 2000

7. *The Irish Times*, 10 May 2000

8. Dublin County Council minutes of special meeting held on 16 May 1991.

9. *The Irish Times*, 31 May 1991
10. *The Irish Times*, 25 June 1991
11. *The Irish Times*, 8 April 2000
12. *The Irish Times*, 15 April 2000
13. Frank Dunlop evidence, 13 April 2000
14. *The Irish Times*, 10 May 2000
15. As far back as 1991, journalist Frank McDonald says he was told Hand was 'a major taker'.
16. *The Irish Times*, 10 May 2000
17. Quoted in *Business & Finance*, 4 May 2000
18. *Sunday Tribune*, 14 May 2000
19. *The Irish Times*, 13 May 2000
20. *The Irish Times*, 12 February 1993
21. *The Irish Times*, 11 May 2000
22. The vote was 51 for, and 1 against.
23. *Sunday Business Post*, 14 May 2000
24. *Sunday Business Post*, 21 May 2000
25. Tribunal evidence, 18 April 2000
26. Tribunal evidence, 19 April 2000
27. *The Irish Times*, 1 May 2000
28. *Sunday Independent*, 31 January 1999
29. *Sunday Tribune*, 14 and 21 February 1999
30. The Department of the Environment dealt with applications under the scheme, but the Minister for Finance made the ultimate decisions.

Chapter 11 What Now? (pages 276–86)
1. *Irish Independent*, 20 February 1999
2. *Sunday Times*, 24 December 2000
3. *Sunday Tribune*, 6 August 2000
4. Quoted in *The Irish Times*, 20 May 2000
5. Liam Lawlor was jailed on a contempt charge.
6. *The Irish Times*, 9 February 2002.

Bibliography

Brennan, Pat and Kerrigan, Gene, *This Great Little Nation: The A-Z of Irish Scandals & Controversies*, Gill & Macmillan, 1999

Collins, Neil and O'Shea, Mary, *Understanding Corruption in Irish Politics*, Cork University Press (Undercurrents series), 2000

Collins, Stephen, *The Power Game: Fianna Fáil since Lemass*, The O'Brien Press, 2000

Fallon, Ivan, *The Player: The Life of Tony O'Reilly*, Hodder and Stoughton, 1994

Horgan, John, *Irish Media: A Critical History since 1922*, Routledge, 2001

Hourihan, Ann Marie, *She Moves Through the Boom*, Sitric Books, 2000

Lee, Joe, *Ireland 1912-1985: Politics and Society*, Cambridge University Press, 1989

McDonald, Frank, *The Destruction of Dublin*, Gill & Macmillan, 1985

McDonald, Frank, *The Construction of Dublin*, Gandon Editions, 2000

Ryan, Tim, *Mara P.J.*, Blackwater Press, 1992

Trollope, Anthony, *The Way We Live Now*, Penguin Books, London, 1994. First published 1875.

Index